R0061516688

01

P9-CLV-546

PALM BEACH COUNTY
LIBRARY SYSTEM
3650 Summit Boulevard
West Palm Beach, FL 33406-4198

Praise for
Overhauling America's Healthcare Machine

"Finally, a healthcare system that works! *Overhauling America's Healthcare Machine* is a superbly written book on what it takes to reduce administrative bloat, simplify the system, slash costs, and give all Americans sustainable medical and financial security."

—William Bernstein, Bestselling author of A *Splendid Exchange* and *The Birth of Plenty*

"This work turns the conventional wisdom and heated rhetoric surrounding the issue of healthcare financing on their heads. It addresses an entire set of corrosive systemic problems that are almost never discussed, and it gets us closer to a realistic view of the problems and of the direction that must be taken for meaningful change to occur."

—Jim Grigsby, Ph.D., Professor, Department of Medicine and Department of Psychology, University of Colorado Denver

"Scholarly both in thinking and writing. A terrific accomplishment."

—Dr. Donald A.B. Lindberg, Director, National Library of Medicine

"Beautifully written; the data is incredibly complete and presented in an easy way to follow. The model for fixing the system is simple and elegant."

—Margaret Lancefield, M.D., Acting Chair, Department of Medicine, University Medical Center of Princeton

"Very enlightening and does a good job explaining the complexity and issues in healthcare. The writing is tight, clear, and done with an underlying sense of humor."

—Will Engle, Executive Director, Association of Telehealth Service Providers

"If our legislators all read this book, our country would be much better off. It is well-reasoned, supported by lots of research, and (best of all) is well-written, clearly presented, and compelling."
—Dr. Rich, Author of *The Covert Rationing Blog*

"This should be recommended to all physicians and medical students as a primer in the realities of medical practice today as well as the development of current health care policies."
—Dr. Richard Armstrong, Chief Operating Officer,
   Docs4PatientCare

"A thoroughly enjoyable read. I especially liked the commonsense, economic approach that shows how we can fix the system without excruciating tradeoffs."
—Kevin Coltin, Arizona State University

*Overhauling America's
Healthcare Machine*

Overhauling America's Healthcare Machine

Stop the Bleeding and Save Trillions

Douglas A. Perednia, M.D.

Vice President, Publisher: Tim Moore
Associate Publisher and Director of Marketing: Amy Neidlinger
Executive Editor: Jeanne Glasser
Editorial Assistant: Pamela Boland
Development Editor: Neil Levine
Operations Manager: Gina Kanouse
Senior Marketing Manager: Julie Phifer
Publicity Manager: Laura Czaja
Assistant Marketing Manager: Megan Colvin
Cover Designer: Chuti Prasertsith
Managing Editor: Kristy Hart
Project Editor: Jovana San Nicolas-Shirley
Copy Editor: Seth Kerney
Proofreader: Linda Seifert
Indexer: Lisa Stumpf
Compositor: Nonie Ratcliff
Manufacturing Buyer: Dan Uhrig

© 2011 by Douglas A. Perednia
Publishing as FT Press
Upper Saddle River, New Jersey 07458

FT Press offers excellent discounts on this book when ordered in quantity for bulk purchases
or special sales. For more information, please contact U.S. Corporate and Government Sales,
1-800-382-3419, corpsales@pearsontechgroup.com. For sales outside the U.S., please contact
International Sales at international@pearson.com.

Company and product names mentioned herein are the trademarks or registered trademarks
of their respective owners.

All rights reserved. No part of this book may be reproduced, in any form or by any means,
without permission in writing from the publisher.

Printed in the United States of America

First Printing February 2011

ISBN-10: 0-13-217325-5
ISBN-13: 978-0-13-217325-4

Pearson Education LTD.
Pearson Education Australia PTY, Limited.
Pearson Education Singapore, Pte. Ltd.
Pearson Education Asia, Ltd.
Pearson Education Canada, Ltd.
Pearson Educación de Mexico, S.A. de C.V.
Pearson Education—Japan
Pearson Education Malaysia, Pte. Ltd.

Library of Congress Cataloging-in-Publication Data

Perednia, Douglas A.
  Overhauling America's healthcare machine : stop the bleeding and save trillions /
Douglas Perednia.
     p. cm.
  Includes bibliographical references.
  ISBN-13: 978-0-13-217325-4 (hardback : alk. paper)
  ISBN-10: 0-13-217325-5
  1. Medical care—Finance. I. Title.
  RA412.3.P47 2011
  338.4'33621—dc22
                          2010040123

For Nancy and Teddy

Contents

Part I: The Nature of the Beast

Chapter 1   Introduction 3

Chapter 2   Are We Getting What We're
             Paying For? 9
             Life Expectancy 10
             Our Chances of Dying 11
             Does Healthcare Even Make a Difference? . . . 12
             But at Least We Don't Have to Wait
             for Care...! 14
             What's Left? 14

Chapter 3   Where Does All Our Money Go? 17
             Exactly What Are We Buying? 19
                 Hospital Care 19
                 Pharmaceuticals 24
                 Outpatient Care 30

Chapter 4   Into Thin Air 39
             How Much Is That Surgery in the Window? . . . 39
             Paying More for Less 43
             Is Change Allowed? 48

Chapter 5   The Healthcare Machine 53
             Millions of Moving Parts 55

Chapter 6   How and Why They Spin: Inside Key
             Wheels 63
             Doctors and Other Healthcare Providers 64
                 Physician Economics and Motivation 67
             Health Insurers 70

Private Insurers 70
    Private Insurance Economics and
    Motivation 74
    Self-Insured Businesses 87
    Public Insurers 88
Government 101
    How Government Works with Respect
    to Healthcare 101
    Regulators and Providers: Friend or Foe? . . . 105
    Government As a Growth Industry
    Within the Healthcare System 107
Patients 108
    Economic Behavior 109
    Patient Economic Behavior As a Way
    to Control Resource Utilization 110

Part II: Why the Machine Is Breaking Down

Chapter 7   **Too Many Parts** **123**
    Why So Many Parts? 123
    Thousands of Insurers 126
    Medical Licensure 127
    Professional Credentialing 129
    Gilding the Lily: The Multi-Billion Dollar
    Certification Industry 130

Chapter 8   **Sand in the Gears** **135**
    Pricing and Billing for Medical Services 135
        How American Clinicians Get Paid 136
        From Theory to Practice—The Failure
        of RBRVS 141
    Regulatory True Grit 153
        Quality Improvement 153
    Medical Malpractice Liability 167
        What Is the Current System Trying to
        Accomplish? 168
        Medical Malpractice Liability—The Existing
        System 168
    Defensive Medicine 175

Chapter 9   **Friction** 183

Unique Patient Identifiers 183

Medical Recordkeeping and Transaction
Processing 186

    Paper-Based Healthcare Information
    Systems 190

    Electronic Healthcare Information
    Systems 191

Paper Versus Computers—The Evidence
to Date 205

Electronic Healthcare Information
Technology: Friction or Grit? 210

Part III: How to Fix It

Chapter 10   **Defining the Desired Outcome** 219

Presumptive Goals: An Efficient, Effective,
Fair, and Sustainable Healthcare System 220

    Structural Requirement #1—Universal
    Healthcare Coverage 220

    Structural Requirement #2—Retention
    of a Private Market for Additional
    Healthcare Services 221

    Structural Requirement #3—Providers
    Must Be Able to Price Their Services
    Freely 222

    Structural Requirement #4—The Price of All
    Healthcare Goods and Services Must Be
    Transparent, Fully Disclosed, and Easily
    Available 223

    Structural Requirement #5—The System
    Must Ration Healthcare Overtly,
    Rather Than Covertly 224

Chapter 11   **Overhauling Payment for Healthcare
Goods and Services** 227

Essential Elements of an Efficient Health
Insurance Plan 230

Using Universal Coverage to Generate
Efficiencies in Financing 238

Too Many Gears 238

Simplifying and Retooling Payment for
Medical Services 241

Simplifying Provider Payment Based Upon
Well-Established Market Principles 243

Minimizing Insurance and Regulatory
Overhead 251

Application of Market Principles to Other
Healthcare Goods and Services 252

Putting It All Together: Streamlined
Healthcare Financing and Payment 257

Chapter 12   **Dumping Redundancy** **263**

Credentialing Made Easy 265

The Financial Benefits of Eliminating
Redundancy 266

Medical Licensure and Credentialing 267

Unique Patient Identifiers 267

Chapter 13   **Blowing Sand Out of the System** **271**

The Role of Government in Healthcare 271

Government Regulation: The Quest
for Quality 275

Quantifying Cost and Benefit 276

Government Regulation: Forestalling
"Fraud and Abuse" 280

Addressing Medical Malpractice and
Defensive Medicine 282

Reducing Errors Versus Reducing Harm
Versus Reducing Claims 283

Reducing Unwarranted Medical
Malpractice Claims 294

Resolving the Malpractice Claims
That Do Occur 294

The Financial Impact of "Grit Reduction" ... 299

Chapter 14   **Lubricating Points of Friction** 301

Understanding the Role of Transactions
and Information in the Healthcare Industry . . 301

Primary Sources of Friction in Healthcare
Transaction Processing 302

Rationally Applying Healthcare Information
Technologies 304

     What Are We Trying to Accomplish? 305

     Paying Attention to What's Important 306

The Financial Impact of Realistic
HIT Deployment 318

Chapter 15   **Where Does the Money Come
From?** 323

Healthcare Providers 324

Private Health Insurers 325

Pharmaceutical Manufacturers 326

Administrative Staff and Intermediaries 328

HIT Vendors 328

Government 329

Chapter 16   **The End of an Era** 331

Appendix A   **"Brief Strategy B" from the Federal
Guidelines Regarding Smokers Who
Report That They Are Unwilling
to Quit** 337

References 341

Index 359

Acknowledgments

This book is a distillation of what we now know about fixing American healthcare. It describes the collective experience and thinking of millions of Americans, channeled through personal accounts and conversations, written reports, statistics, economic data and healthcare research. I wish that there were some way to individually thank each of the patients, clinicians, executives, economists, researchers and others who directly and indirectly contributed their time, insights and expertise, but there are far too many. Nevertheless, this book could never have been written without you.

Distilling healthcare is one thing, but surviving the process of getting into print is another. There are some individuals who need to be singled out for special thanks on this score.

First and foremost is my editor, Jeanne Glasser, who took an interest in this book when many others had written off healthcare reform as too complicated, boring, or passé to tackle. The fact that it became even more relevant after the passage of the 2010 Affordable Care Act speaks volumes about her foresight, persuasiveness, and determination. Thanks, Jeanne, and thanks to Alex Johnson and Dr. Bill Bernstein for referring me to you. Drs. Jim Grigsby and Phoebe Barton provided invaluable support and counsel while I was still looking for publisher brave enough to take the plunge. Many thanks are also due to some very smart, busy people who contributed their valuable time to review and comment on the manuscript. These include Drs. Margaret Lancefield, Donald Lindberg, Richard Fogoros and Richard Armstrong, Randy Kasten, Kevin Coltin, David Perednia, and Will Engle. Jovana San Nicolas-Shirley and her colleagues did an excellent job of shepherding me through the production process. Finally, I owe a special debt of gratitude to my family and especially my remarkable spouse. Without your endless patience, encouragement and support, none of this would have ever happened.

About the Author

Douglas A. Perednia, M.D., graduated from Swarthmore College with a degree in Economics, and obtained his medical degree at Washington University in St. Louis, Missouri. A medical internist and dermatologist, he has spent many years in clinical medicine, in academia as a principal investigator for the National Institutes of Health, with non-profit healthcare organizations, and as a business executive in private industry. A popular speaker and writer, Dr. Perednia periodically works as a consultant to government, business, and non-profit organizations. In his spare time, he writes for *The Road to Hellth* blog (www.roadtohellth.com), which deals with the interactions between doctors, patients, insurers, government, and the business of medicine.

Part I

The Nature of the Beast

"Believe nothing, no matter where you read it or who said it, not even if I have said it, unless it agrees with your own reason and your own common sense."

—*Buddha*

1

Introduction

"Courage is what it takes to stand up and speak; courage is also what it takes to sit down and listen."
—*Winston Churchill*

Have you ever wondered why everyone talks about spiraling healthcare costs and insurance premiums, but no one ever seems to explain or address their root causes?

Do your eyes glaze over when you hear news reports and politicians talking about healthcare because it seems to be so big and complex that no one could ever understand it?

Have you ever wondered how it's possible for the richest country in the world to spend more than $2.5 trillion on healthcare each year, but still not be able to provide coverage to more than 15% (50 million) of its citizens?

Are you concerned that the huge, complex, and open-ended 2010 healthcare reform law signed into law by President Obama didn't really solve anything, and is simply setting the stage for higher costs and more healthcare system upheaval down the road?

If so, this book is for you.

The good news is that while healthcare in America is dysfunctional and complex, its core problems and their solutions can be readily understood by anyone willing to read and make use of a little visual imagery. This is the big difference between the complexity of *practicing medicine* versus the complexity of the *healthcare system*. Understanding the practice of medicine requires a relatively detailed understanding of anatomy, biochemistry, pharmacology, physiology, pathophysiology, and a host of other specialized knowledge. In contrast, the healthcare system in the United States (as in any country) is simply a set of business relationships and regulations. Anyone who has purchased a product online is perfectly capable of understanding the process of ordering a laboratory test or submitting an insurance claim. The trick to understanding the whole thing is to not be intimidated and to resist being snowed by special interests who might want to assert that "their business requires special expertise" before it can become comprehensible.

But why should you or anyone else care about this slow-motion disaster and how to fix it? Two reasons: your money and your life.

America's existing healthcare strategy is financially unsustainable. Left unchecked, it will continue to consume ever larger amounts of government and personal income. But, it is also medically and socially unsustainable. Government policies are increasingly making medical decisions for both you and your doctor, often with little or no science behind them. Unless our healthcare machine is truly reformed and simplified, we can look forward to being poorer, less healthy, and more rigidly regulated in our personal lives than ever before.

As Figure 1.1 shows, we already pay more for our healthcare than the citizens of any other country in the world—both in absolute terms and on a per capita basis.

Providing medical care to just 85% of the population now costs more than $2.4 trillion annually. That's nearly 17% of our gross domestic product, or about $6,402 for every man, woman, and child—whether or not they're covered by health insurance. This is nearly double the amount spent on healthcare per capita in nearly every other developed country, and it's breaking our collective bank. As a nation, we now spend more on healthcare than any other aspect of living: more than defense ($2,901 per person), more than spending on all types of energy ($3,642 per capita in 2006.)[1], more than on education (about $3,218 per capita), more than on housing (about $3,002 per capita), and almost ten times what we spend each year at Christmas (almost $800 per person). Even worse, the inflation rate for healthcare—about 9% in 2010—is rapidly outpacing growth in

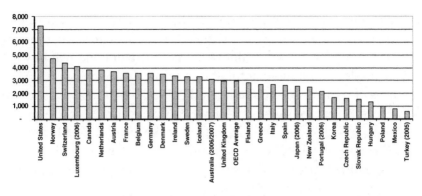

Notes: Health expenditure for insured rather than resident population; current health expenditure for 2007 or latest year available.

Data from: OECD Health Data 2009, OECD (http://www.oecd.org/health/healthdata)

Figure 1.1 Healthcare Spending per Capita in the United States Compared with Other Developed Countries, 2007 (U.S. $ Purchasing Power Parity)

income and is more than twice the overall rate of inflation. The Center for Medicare and Medicaid Services estimates that total U.S. healthcare expenditures will continue to grow to more than $4.1 trillion, or $12,782 per resident, by 2016.

Who pays this tab? You do. Even children aren't immune. It's all a result of the wonderland of U.S. healthcare financing, where cost shifting is the rule rather than the exception.

If you're a typical working person, this escalating cost is making you poorer every year—even if you *think* that your employer is picking up the tab. If you're a businessman, the cost of healthcare is making you less competitive because you're less able to afford high-quality staff. If you're retired and on Medicare, current policies will probably force you to spend more out of pocket or reduce your access to doctors. And if you're a politician, there's a good chance that your political survival will depend heavily upon actions that you take on healthcare over the next few years.

But the greatest sin of the U.S. healthcare system is not that it is expensive, but that it's inefficient. It might not be so bad paying all that money if it meant that everyone was getting excellent access to top-quality care and better health outcomes than those paying less in other countries, but that's hardly the case. Instead, the system that we've created wastes money and resources at an astonishing rate of billions of dollars every day. Between one-third and one-half of what we spend does absolutely nothing to improve health or add value to the lives of patients. Or to put it another way, with the amount we're wasting on a lousy business model, we could pay for the entire annual cost of national defense *and* Christmas. If the current healthcare system was an employee, you would fire it. If it were a vendor, you'd choose another one. And if it were a patient, you'd prescribe immediate surgery to excise the diseased portions.

Unfortunately, the 2010 healthcare reform law does nothing to change any of this.

The Obama/congressional legislation is more than 2,400 pages of complex, special interest–friendly legislation that will implement 168 new federal committees, panels, programs, and Medicare benefit cuts, and cost the American taxpayer an *additional* trillion dollars over the next ten years. It is a top-down approach; one that inevitably creates more rules, complexity, and paperwork, and ultimately pits government regulators against healthcare providers, their patients, and you.

This book describes a different approach—one that it's not too late to take. What we and future generations need is a logical, comprehensive, and apolitical *simplification* of the existing healthcare system; one that could be implemented with roughly 200 pages of legislation instead of 2,000. A system that gives all healthcare providers and their patients more medical and financial security, enhances market-based competition, slashes administrative complexity and overhead costs, reduces the price of healthcare goods and services across the board, and requires no increases in federal funding. An approach that would save about $570 billion annually in national healthcare expenditures, while covering more people than ever before.

The urgency of fixing the healthcare system is best appreciated in the context of a single fact: Resources are finite, while people's wants are infinite. In a world characterized by a growing population, rising commodity prices, expensive energy, and an aging population in developed countries, the luxury of wasting close to a trillion dollars annually has clearly become unsustainable. For all practical purposes, it is an unlegislated tax of nearly $3,000 per American per year.

Improving the efficiency of the system might be the only way to prevent a meltdown of the larger economy and restore growth in the standard of living. And if the opportunity is large, so are the consequences of continuing on our current path.

2

Are We Getting What We're Paying For?

"My mother used to say to me: 'Son, it's better to be rich and healthy than poor and sick.' I think that still makes a heck of a lot of sense, even in these troubled times."

—*Dave Barry*

To justify the status quo, politicians, health insurance companies, and the media say a lot of stupid things. One of these is when they periodically remind us that we in the United States have the "best healthcare in the world." The implication, of course, is that everything is just fine. Being the best means that we're getting what we're paying for, and that the high price we pay is simply the cost of being #1. But is this really true? And what does it even mean to have the "best" healthcare in the world? Most of these pronouncements are consistently (and suspiciously) vague.

There are only a few plausible interpretations of this particular platitude. The first is that the healthcare services that you might be able to get here (should you be fortunate enough to receive them), are better than anywhere else in the world. For example, if you were to suffer a heart attack or be diagnosed with cancer in the United States, presumably the care that you receive here would be "better" than the care you might receive in London, Geneva, or Munich, or a host of other places in the developed world. Of course, the term "better" is in itself vague. Does "better" mean that the care is more sophisticated and advanced (that is, the drugs and machines and surgical techniques are better), or that identical therapies would be better administered in the United States than they would in Europe, Australia, or Japan?

Both of these assertions are virtually certain to be incorrect. The training of physicians in nearly all developed countries has become increasingly uniform, and even in developing countries, many clinicians have received some or all of their training in the United States. Drugs, equipment, and procedures now spread rapidly around the world soon after their development, and nearly all major pharmaceutical manufacturers are now international firms. And there is certainly no evidence that the use of any specific drug, procedure, or piece of medical equipment is significantly different from one developed country to another. The choice of drugs may vary depending upon biases in medical judgment or healthcare payment policies, but the actual administration of a chosen treatment varies little from place to place.

A second way to put American healthcare on top would be if it produced "better" results on average than is the case in other developed countries. That is to say that the usual indicators that might be used to determine whether the health of one country is better than that of another would show a consistent advantage in favor of the United States. Unfortunately, this does not appear to be the case. Let's look at some relatively obvious objective indicators that should help tell us where we stand in the world. None of these seem to indicate that we're getting great value for our money.

Life Expectancy

Does our health system keep us alive longer here than elsewhere? Although it might be hard to compare relatively homogenous populations in other countries to the highly diverse mix of ethnicities in the United States, the answer appears to be "no."

As shown in Figure 2.1, the average life expectancy in the United States is 77½; years, which is a little below the average for 30 other developed countries in the Organization for Economic Cooperation and Development (OECD), and almost 2½; years less than our neighbor to the north, Canada.[1] The life expectancy in Japan is 4½; years longer, at almost 82.

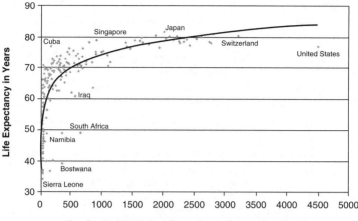

From: UC Atlas of Global Inequality, http://ucatlas.ucsc.edu/spend.php[2]

Figure 2.1   Life Expectancy Versus Spending

If you look at life expectancy at birth, we rank 22nd out of 30, just barely above Portugal and South Korea. This is because being born in the United States is associated with a much higher infant mortality rate than is found in any members of the OECD except Turkey and Mexico.

Our Chances of Dying

Mortality rates are related to, but different from, life expectancy. Life expectancy tells us how long we might expect to be around if we manage to avoid dying early. The mortality rate tells us how many people per unit of population tend to die in any given year. Figure 2.2 graphs the mortality rate in OECD countries for 2007 or the latest year available.

As you can see, the United States stands at around the middle of the pack in terms of performance, despite spending substantially more per capita than most developed countries.

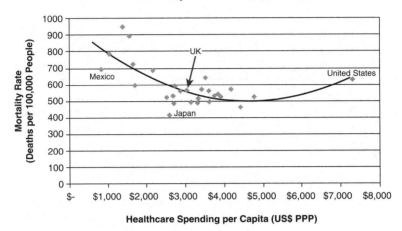

Mortality in OECD Countries

Notes: Spending in U.S.$ purchasing power parity (PPP); data from 2007 or most recent year available.

Data from: OECD Health Data 2009, OECD. http://www.oecd.org/health/healthdata

Figure 2.2   Mortality Rates for OECD Members Versus Healthcare Spending per Capita

Does Healthcare Even Make a Difference?

Like any statistic, mortality rates alone can be deceptive. Whether we die depends to a large extent on whether we're sick with something curable. If Americans get brain cancer or fall from tall buildings at higher rates than the OECD average, the best healthcare in the world might not be able to help the mortality rate much. That's where the concept of *amenable mortality* comes in handy.

Amenable mortality statistics are meant to reflect deaths due to conditions that occurred in the population, but whose clinical course could have been substantially influenced by access to appropriate and timely care. These include a wide variety of conditions, such as curable infectious diseases, high blood pressure, diabetes, and even cancers (such as colon cancer and cervical cancer) that are highly curable if detected early. Deaths due to these conditions are also adjusted for age (because, for example, heart disease in an older population is more likely to prove fatal than heart disease in a younger population), and give a much more interesting view of a healthcare system's overall effectiveness. Amenable mortality reflects a variety of factors that influences outcomes both directly and indirectly, including medical care and public health, education, and screening programs.

The bad news here is that the United States still does not seem to perform nearly as well as we should expect for the amount we're paying.[3]

As shown in Figure 2.3, the United States actually comes in with the highest rate of amenable mortality when compared to a subset of 19 other OECD countries. There appears to be little or no relationship between the amount spent by a given country and effectiveness in reducing unnecessary deaths due to illness.

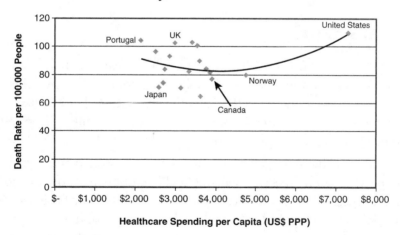

Mortality Amenable to Healthcare

Note: Spending in U.S.$ purchasing power parity (PPP).

Data from: Ellen Nolte and C. Martin McKee, "Measuring the Health of Nations: Updating an Earlier Analysis." *Health Affairs*, 27, no. 1 (2008): 58-71.

Figure 2.3 Mortality Amenable to Healthcare Versus Healthcare Spending per Capita for a Subset of 19 OECD Countries

But at Least We Don't Have to Wait for Care...!

Or do we?

Fortunately, waiting times for elective surgery in the United States and seven other OECD countries are low, whereas 12 other members commonly have waiting times of one to two months for essential procedures such as heart surgery. Waiting times for elective surgeries such as hip and knee replacements in these countries are even longer—around five months. About 25%–35% of patients surveyed in Canada, the United Kingdom, and Australia reported waiting four months for a non-emergency procedure, compared with 5% of Americans.

On the other hand, it's harder to get in to see a doctor quickly in the United States—and often to see a doctor at all, due to financial concerns. When comparing the United States with Canada, Australia, New Zealand, and the U.K., it's not clear that we are seen much sooner than the competition.[4]

What's Left?

A final way to claim that American healthcare is "better" is to claim that the administration and delivery system itself is superior to those used elsewhere. A "better" health care system should make the best possible use of scarce resources, and yet this seems to be exactly the place where our approach seems to fail the most.

None of this is to say that many, or even most, patients in the United States don't receive excellent healthcare services from the doctors, nurses, and others who care for them. Many of our facilities and providers are among the best, if not the best, in the world. However, it's easy to see that claims that the care that we receive is *on the whole* "better" than that received by the populations of other developed countries are clearly overblown. Then why are these claims made so often?

The realistic answer is that being the "best" implies that almost anything that you do differently is likely to make things worse rather than better. It implies that "it's all downhill from here," and helps create an atmosphere in which change is feared. If the healthcare in other developed countries isn't as good and we adopt a policy that makes us more like them, then presumably our own healthcare will suffer. Contending that we're the "best" (even if unsupported by the facts) helps maintain the status quo and induce paralysis with respect to making any sort of substantial changes. Looking at healthcare through a business and political lens, you might say that this approach tends to favor incumbents over challengers, and existing businesses over new ones. It's the sort of result that lobbyists for well-established companies would willingly pay for. After all, if you're already on top, the best competition is the competition that never appears to begin with.

Healthcare as an industry and a major portion of the economy is far more than the sum of its providers, facilities, and medical technology. It is also a mechanism in which the relationships and interactions between patients, families, providers, and facilities are governed by external administrative, financial, and regulatory factors that can improve or destroy the delivery of care services. Most of all, any healthcare system is a set of *financial* incentives and disincentives that governs the actions of, and relationships between, the people involved.

It's not politically correct to say so, but the very best way to get a handle on how and why any healthcare system operates is to see it as a business machine.° The purpose of any business is to make money,

---

° Like the clergy, police and fire departments, and government officials, healthcare providers are supposed to be above worldly considerations in their thinking and conduct of their professional duties. In a 2009 speech to the American Medical Association, President Obama told the audience that the current payment system "...is a model that has taken the pursuit of medicine from a profession—a calling—to a business...." He then added (quite correctly) that: "You did not enter this profession to be bean-counters and paper-pushers." Only those of us who are lucky enough to have worked in healthcare can really appreciate the truth and irony in this. Politicians increasingly control the flow of healthcare dollars without the burden of a Hippocratic Oath to "do no harm." Doctors are therefore naturally suspicious of a political figure telling them "not to worry about" the evils of money. As Kin Hubbard once observed, "When a fellow says, 'It ain't the money but the principle of the thing,' it's the money." Ayn Rand put it even more strongly when she said: "Run for your life from any man who tells you that money is evil. That sentence is the leper's bell of an approaching looter."

and healthcare is no different. When trying to unravel any complex series of relationships in business or politics, it's extremely useful to take the advice Deep Throat provided with respect to unraveling the Watergate scandal: "Follow the money."

3

Where Does All Our Money Go?

"I was walking down Fifth Avenue today and I found a wallet, and I was gonna keep it, rather than return it, but I thought: Well, if I lost a hundred and fifty dollars, how would I feel? And I realized I would want to be taught a lesson."
—*Emo Philips*

Given that we spend more than twice what other developed countries spend on healthcare without achieving substantially better results, what is sucking up all that cash? There are only four possibilities:

1. We're buying far more healthcare goods and services than our friends in other developed countries.
2. The healthcare goods and services that we're buying cost more here than they do elsewhere.
3. Much of the money spent on "healthcare" is actually being spent on things that don't actually improve health, such as administration, overhead, and inefficient business practices—and at a much higher rate than elsewhere.
4. Some combination of the above.

Determining which of these is the case is crucial if we're going to be able to reduce spending and/or improve the type and level of care provided. Identifying the source of excess spending will also show whose monetary ox is likely to be gored by attempts to improve the system. Our ability to eliminate waste in the system and improve the

value received for our healthcare dollar is going to be directly proportional to the wastefulness of the expenditure and its political vulnera-
bility. Of these two, the level of political protection has the bigger
impact on whether the problem will be solved.

When we follow the money, the golden rule that governs healthcare behavior is a simple one:

> In a regulated free-market system, whatever healthcare activ-
> ities and strategies are most profitable and are not prohibited
> or discouraged by laws or regulation are the activities that will
> occur. This will happen regardless of the overall impact of
> these activities on the actual health and welfare of patients
> and their families. Moreover, this rule applies to all partici-
> pants within the healthcare system, including patients, fami-
> lies, and government itself, as well as vendors and providers
> of healthcare goods and services.

In other words, whether you're talking about insurers, the government, drug makers or other vendors, healthcare providers, or even
patients, people are most highly motivated by their own bottom lines.

Ignoring this rule is the most serious mistake that any of us can
possibly make in the course of evaluating and setting healthcare policy. Unfortunately it happens all the time—most frequently to academics, think tanks, public interest groups, and pundits. Because
they are typically unfamiliar with (or even philosophically opposed to)
the business of healthcare, these groups universally attempt to dictate
methods and behaviors instead of creating an environment that
will inherently produce the desired results through economic self-
interest. The usual result is that their efforts are often wasted or even
backfire. (We'll see a number of examples of this in later chapters.)

Perhaps the best gauge of the importance of money in healthcare
is the amount that is spent on political lobbying. In the year 2000,
healthcare officially became the largest lobby in Washington, spending more than any other industry to influence government policy and
legislation. Healthcare lobbyists and contributors spent nearly $400
million in 2010, more than lobbying for traditional powerhouses such
as agriculture, communications, and defense. It's estimated that more
than 7,000 registered Washington lobbyists were actively promoting

various healthcare-related agendas. That's 13 lobbyists for each one of the 535 members of Congress.[1]

That kind of spending means that the stakes are high. Where is all the money going, and how can the efficiency of the system be improved?

Exactly What Are We Buying?

It's not strange that we spend a lot of money on healthcare. To a great extent, healthcare services are a luxury item. (This might seem odd, but humans survived for hundreds of thousands of years without effective hospitals, doctors, or drugs. In fact, many people on Earth still do. Most medical problems will get better over time regardless of whether they're treated.) On the other hand, everyone who can *afford* to buy more healthcare, does. The more you make as a country, the more you spend. In fact, about 90% of healthcare spending can be predicted based upon the level of national income.

Even so, the United States is an outlier. We spend almost twice as much per capita than average for a developed country, and 50% more than the next highest spender. Something that we're doing or buying is setting us apart. What are we spending all that money on? Figure 3.1 shows the "official" view of the way our healthcare dollars are spent, based upon U.S. government statistics. Let's take a closer look at the quantities and prices of each of the larger and more important components.

Hospital Care

Although hospital care accounts for the largest single use of our healthcare dollars, we actually use hospitals considerably less than most other developed countries. Not only do we have fewer admissions, but we're excellent at getting people out of the hospital once they've been admitted. The average length of U.S. hospital stays is the same as the OECD average, although for some conditions such as heart attacks and childbirth, we have some of the shortest stays in the developed world. A hospital stay for a heart attack is just about half as long as in the United States as in the top ten developed countries. We discharge our mothers in less than two hospital days after they give birth, compared with the OECD average of 3.6 days.

TOTAL SPENDING: $2.3 TRILLION

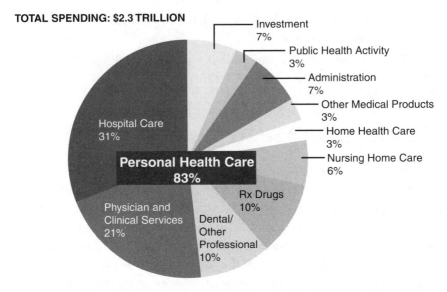

From: California Healthcare Foundation. "Health Care Costs 101." April 2010. (http://www.chcf.org/~/media/Files/PDF/H/HealthCareCosts10.pdf)[2]

Figure 3.1   U.S. Healthcare Spending Distribution by Category, 2008

The bizarre thing about this is that while our hospital utilization is low, our total hospital costs per capita are actually the *fourth highest* in the entire OECD.[3] This suggests that the average U.S. hospital visit is either far more "intense" than is usually the case in other countries, (that is, each hospitalization uses far more goods and services), or that the price we're paying for hospital services is much higher in the United States.

The data regarding intensity seems to be mixed. It's certainly true that the trend in America has been to do everything possible on an outpatient basis—ranging from plastic surgery to removing gallbladders. As a result, most of us need to be pretty sick to make it into the hospital and stay there for any length of time. We're first in the world with respect to performing hospital-based heart surgery, and well above the average for organ transplants and Caesarean section childbirth. But in certain other hospital operations, such as hip replacement, the United States tends to be below the OECD average. And there is at least as much variability in the intensity of hospitalization between different parts of the United States as there is between the United States and the world. At least one study looking at hospitals in the United States and Canada suggests that, at least as of 1987, there did not appear to be much difference in the level of *clinical* services and resources used by Canadian and U.S. hospitals for their respective admissions.[4] A different study from 1993 estimated that resource use in the United States was actually about 24% higher in the United States when compared with Canada.[5]

The circumstances surrounding hospital prices seem to be far clearer. While direct cost comparisons between countries are notoriously tough to make, several studies of selected procedures are pretty consistent. The same hospital visit costs a *lot* more in the United States than in Canada—the only developed country for which direct comparisons are readily available. Let's look at two specific examples: hip surgery and the repair of abdominal aortic aneurysms.

The nice thing about formal comparison studies is that they tend to control for factors such as the procedure, age and physical condition of the patients, complications, outcomes, and so on. This lets us more directly compare costs and prices. Table 3.1 summarizes the results of these two studies.

These differences are quite extraordinary, especially when you consider that each group received essentially the same procedures with the same results. The difference in overhead costs is particularly astonishing. Americans are often paying almost as much for administration costs *alone* as Canadians are paying for *all* their hospital expenses.

But perhaps hospitals are a special case? We've seen that America has fewer hospital beds, acute care bed days, and shorter hospital stays per capita on average than other developed countries. Perhaps our higher hospital costs are part of a strategy that does a great job of delivering more, less expensive services on an outpatient basis? The past 20 years have seen a massive nationwide effort to minimize hospital days in an effort to reduce costs. The average length of stay decreased 24%, from 7.35 days per admission in 1980, to 5.6 days in 2004. Perhaps the savings are realized elsewhere in the system?

TABLE 3.1 Canada Versus U.S. Hospital Procedure Cost Comparison

Total Hip Replacement Surgery (2004)[6]	Canada	United States	% Difference (United States vs. Canada)	Notes
Average Length of Stay	7.2 ± 4.7 days	4.2 ± 2.0 days	−41.7%	There was no significant difference in Canadian versus U.S. post-operative mortality or complications.
Average Hospital "Direct" Costs (in U.S. $)	$4,552	$8,221	+80.6%	Costs derived from departments actually providing goods and services to the patients (does *not* include physician fees).
Average Hospital "Overhead" Costs (in U.S. $)	$2,214	$5,118	+131.2%	Costs incurred by hospital "overhead" departments, such as administration and housekeeping.
Average Total Cost	**$6,766**	**$13,339**	**+97.1%**	

continues

TABLE 3.1 Continued

	Canada	United States	% Difference (United States vs. Canada)	Notes
Repair of Abdominal Aortic Aneurysm (2003)[7]				There was no significant difference in Canadian versus U.S. post-operative mortality.
Average Length of Stay	9.0 days	7.0 days	−22.2%	
Average Hospital "Direct" Costs (in U.S. $)	$11,334	$13,327	+17.6%	Costs derived from departments actually providing goods and services to the patients (does *not* include physician fees).
Average Hospital "Overhead" Costs (in U.S. $)	$4,518	$9,972	+120.7%	Costs incurred by hospital "overhead" departments, such as administration and housekeeping.
Average Total Cost	**$15,852**	**$23,299**	**+47.0%**	More than 90% of Canadian patients were discharged to self-care versus <67% of U.S. patients.

Pharmaceuticals

Making good use of pharmaceuticals is one way of getting people out of hospitals and keeping them out. Medications can relieve pain, increase mobility, shorten the course of infections, improve the control of severe chronic diseases, and even turn certain deadly cancers into chronic outpatient conditions. It's interesting to note that, unlike other forms of healthcare consumption in developed countries, access to medicine actually has a measurable impact on overall life expectancy in later life.° Statistically speaking, doubling pharmaceutical expenditures in developed countries would increase life expectancy at age 40 by about 2 percent, and life expectancy at 60 by roughly 4 percent.[8] And while pharmaceuticals make up only about 10% of U.S. healthcare spending, their ubiquity, importance, and high cost gives them a high profile.

For our purposes, the question is what role demand and/or price of drugs might play in driving U.S. healthcare costs unsustainably higher. First, let's take a look at how much we spend for drugs compared with everyone else. Our first point of reference is Figure 3.2.

By now it should be no surprise that the United States leads the way when it comes to spending. Americans spend more on drugs than anyone else, and about twice the OECD average. But why? Do we use twice as much?

To tell the truth, it's hard to say. It's extremely difficult to compare the true consumption of pharmaceuticals between countries for a

---

° Beyond a certain point, adding more healthcare services such as hospitalization and physician visits produces diminishing returns. In less-developed countries, the greatest determinant of health and well-being is the availability of sanitation and clean water. Only after these needs are met does investment in other healthcare services become economically worthwhile. In most of the OECD countries (and the U.S. in particular), hospitalization and other healthcare services have already had their greatest impact on overall mortality—adding more has relatively little effect. Demographics are one reason: The elderly use far more hospital and physician services, but they have fewer years of life left to save. On average, people older than 65 spend about four times more than those under 65, and much of that is spent right at the end. In 2006, about 25% of Medicare's budget went to patients in their last year of life.

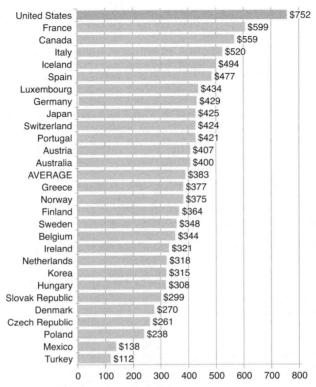

Notes: Amounts are adjusted using U.S. dollar purchasing power parities, and are based on estimates and/or earlier years for 16 countries for Canada, Denmark, France, Iceland, Luxembourg, Portugal, Spain, Sweden, and Switzerland, amounts are 2004 estimates; for Belgium (estimate), Japan (estimate), and the Slovak Republic, the numbers are from 2003; for the Czech Republic, Hungary, and the Netherlands, amounts are from 2002; and for Turkey, amounts are 2000. Recent data are available only for 28 of the 30 OECD countries.

From: Peterson CL, Burton R. "U.S. Healthcare Spending: Comparison with Other OECD Countries." *CRS Report for Congress*, September 17, 2007.

Figure 3.2   Pharmaceutical Spending per Capita, 2004

variety of reasons. For one thing, many of the medications sold world-wide are simply not the same. Different products might share active ingredients, but the dosages, packaging, routes of administration, and combinations can and do vary enormously from country to country. And in addition to prescription medications, there is the over-the-counter market. While it might seem strange to equate Bengay and Ex-Lax with heart medication and cancer drugs, a substantial number of drugs that start out as prescription-only eventually end up being sold over-the-counter. Nonsteroidal anti-inflammatory drugs such as

Advil and Aleve, antihistamines such as Claritin, and antifungals such as Lotrimin have all taken this route. Another important consideration is the high degree of variation in practice patterns and prescribing preferences. Physicians in some countries rely heavily on older drugs that may be less effective, but are more familiar and less expensive.

Despite these limitations, we *can* compare consumption of a limited number of medications that share active ingredients. Figure 3.3 does this for a broad set of drugs used to treat cardiovascular disease and stroke in 12 OECD countries.[9,†] This is a good starting place because cardiovascular disease (especially heart attacks and strokes) happens to be the leading cause of death in most developed countries. In this graph, "DDD" stands for "defined daily dose," which is a way of comparing formulations of the same drug that might not be exactly equivalent. Measuring the DDD per 1,000 people is an indication of what percentage of the population is using a given drug (or in this case, class of drugs). This particular chart classifies all the cardiovascular drugs measured by the study by whether they are "older" drugs that have been around for many years, and thus many have large numbers of generics available, and "newer" drugs—many of which may still be under patent protection.

What we see here is that the United States seems to be an average consumer with respect to older generic medications, but a relatively early adopter with respect to newer drugs. On a per capita basis, we're not the highest user of drugs in either category.

The trendline shows that countries that spend more of their GDP on healthcare seem to consume more new drugs compared to their peers. In contrast, per capita consumption of generic drugs is relatively unaffected by the level of healthcare spending. In economic terms, older drugs are treated like necessities, such as basic food or shelter. Beyond a certain point their consumption by rich people and poor people simply isn't that different. In contrast, new drugs behave

---

† The 12 OECD countries included in the study were Canada, France, Germany, Italy, Japan, The Netherlands, New Zealand, Spain, Sweden, Switzerland, the United Kingdom, and the United States. Study data was available for the years 1989, 1991, 1993, 1995, 1997, and 1999.

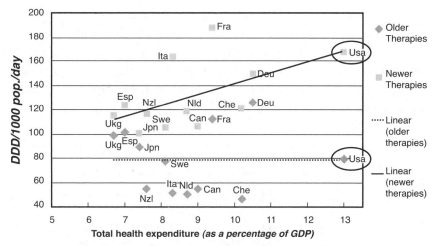

Note: Older therapies, R^2=0.0% Newer therapies R^2=30.7%

From: Dickson M, Jacobzone S. "Pharmaceutical Use and Expenditures for Cardiovascular Disease and Stroke: A Study of 12 OECD Countries." *OECD Health Working Papers* No. 1 (2003).[10]

Figure 3.3 Cardiovascular Drug Consumption As a Function of Total Health Spending, 1997

like luxury goods. Those with higher healthcare budgets tend to buy more of them—presumably to take advantage of the additional benefits they offer.

However, the United States does stand out when you look at very new drugs—those less than two years old. U.S. consumption of recent entrants into the healthcare marketplace (defined as drugs sold for less than two years) is at least double than that of any country except Germany, even if our total per capita consumption of all drugs is not appreciably higher.

The bottom line is that the United States buys more brand-name drugs sooner than other countries, even though its total consumption of medication is not unusually high.

So are we paying more or less for our pharmaceuticals than everyone else?

Logic dictates that if U.S. drug consumption is not excessive and yet we're paying more per capita for drugs than anyone else in the world, our drug prices are higher. As it turns out, that's only partly true. Except for Japan, the United States does indeed pay more for wholesale, single-manufacturer, on-patent drugs than a sample of eight other developed countries. However, the flip side is that we actually pay substantially *less* than most of the other countries for generic and nonprescription drugs, as shown in Figure 3.4.[‡] Patients in all the eight countries listed pay more for OTC medications than the United States, with most paying over twice as much.[11]

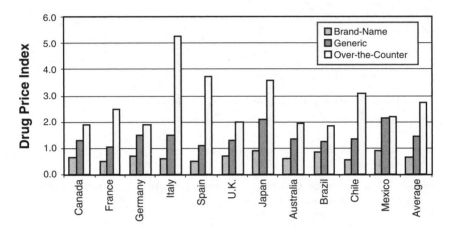

Data from: Danzon PM, Furukawa MF. "International Prices and Availability of Pharmaceuticals in 2005." *Health Affairs* (2008); 27(1): 221-233.[12]

Figure 3.4   Price Indexes: Brand Name, Generic, and Over-The-Counter Drugs. Manufacturer Prices Relative to U.S. Prices, Adjusted for U.S. Market Discounts, 2005 (U.S. Prices Index Equals 1.00)

Given that new medications are expensive and generics are cheap (at least in the United States), the relevant question for healthcare spending then becomes, what do we use most of? If the majority of our medications are generic and over-the-counter, then on average the current healthcare system is producing good value for the money. In fact, the system might be expected to provide better value over time as more and more drugs go off patent. On the other hand, if the

---

[‡] The distinction between wholesale and retail prices here is an important one, because it does not take into account any administrative or overhead costs that could dramatically increase the cost of a drug to consumers before they get they hands on it. In fact, it's perfectly possible that a drug that is inexpensive at the wholesale level could become very costly at the retail level after the costs of distribution, profit, and overhead are taken into account.

majority of our consumption is in brand-name, patented medications, we are paying a high near-term price for our comparative lack of drug price regulation.§ One way to determine where American consumers stand in the balance is to look at the relative proportions of brand-name and generic medications sold versus the relative share of costs that they incur. Newer patented medications make up a little less than half of all the doses taken in the United States, but account for more than 80% of spending on the medications surveyed.[13] In contrast, generics make up nearly 60% of the total volume, but represent less than 20% of the money spent. It's easy to see why insurers try to force the use of generic drugs wherever they can, but the real question is, are we getting good value for our healthcare dollars spent on pharmaceuticals? To a large extent, our abundant use of new drugs is a matter of societal preference rather than a matter of medical "right" or "wrong." Other countries have other preferences and pricing structures. How do we compare apples to apples?

The answer is to try to determine what a typical basket of medicine (based on the U.S. proportions of new and generic drugs) would cost in other developed countries. This is shown in Figure 3.5.

What we see is that, on average, Americans pay about $18 more for a $100 basket of drugs than our OECD counterparts, and about $35 more than the average Canadian. This is quite a bit of money, but to put things in perspective, we should compare this excess to the

---

§ Exactly why new medications are comparatively expensive and generics are cheap in the United States (and vice versa elsewhere) is an interesting question. Danzon et al. point out that this a market response to price regulation. Countries that heavily regulate the price of new medications (such as France, Italy, and Japan) might be successful at keeping the initial price relatively low, but these same low prices discourage others from coming into the market with competing products when patent protection expires. In contrast, the high initial prices in the U.S. market give potential makers of generic substitutes a powerful financial incentive to enter the market. After a number of generics are available, the price of the drug tends to decrease rapidly as a result of competition between multiple manufacturers. The data support this theory. Countries that heavily regulate drug prices do have far fewer makers of generic drugs in their marketplaces for any particular medication, and pay substantially higher prices for the generics that are available. Thus, the initial pain of high prices in the near-term paves the way for lower prices over the long-term.

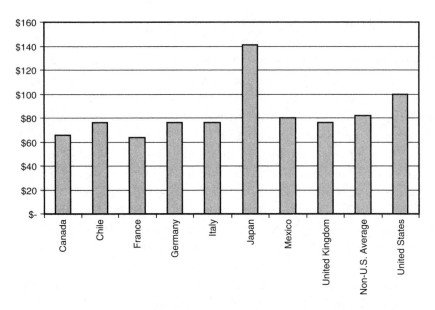

Data from: Danzon PM, Furukawa MF. "Prices and Availability of Pharmaceuticals: Evidence from Nine Countries." *Health Affairs* (2003); Web Exclusive W3, 29 October 2003: 521-536, and Peterson CL, Burton R. "U.S. Healthcare Spending: Comparison with Other OECD Countries." *CRS Report for Congress*, September 17, 2007.[14]

Figure 3.5   Comparative Wholesale Cost of a Proportional Basket of 249 New and Generic Drugs Costing $100 in the United States

total that we spend on healthcare each year. Pharmaceuticals make up about 10% of U.S. healthcare spending, or about $200 billion annually. An 18% reduction in price would save $36 billion per year, or $118 per American per year. This is quite a bit of money in hard economic times, but only 1.8% of the total healthcare budget. To put it in perspective, total U.S. healthcare spending is expected to increase by $146 billion between 2010 and 2011. Bringing drug spending down to the non-U.S. average would reduce that increase by just 25%. While helpful, it's hardly enough to make a huge difference in the big picture. We can certainly work on more efficient pricing for pharmaceuticals, but the real savings will have to be found elsewhere. Perhaps in outpatient care?

Outpatient Care

It's fair to say that the United States does indeed have an outpatient-oriented approach to healthcare. As shown in Figure 3.6, a full

44% of our healthcare dollars are spent on outpatient services, compared with just 27% for inpatient services. Only Sweden does more on an outpatient basis. This is largely a result of moving procedures out of the hospital and into outpatient facilities such as imaging centers, surgery centers, dialysis centers, and even cardiology catheterization labs. Between 1986 and 2006, the percentage of U.S. healthcare spending devoted to hospital care fell from 37% to 31%. The percentage devoted to outpatient care rose slightly, while prescription drug spending rose from 5% to 10% of the total.

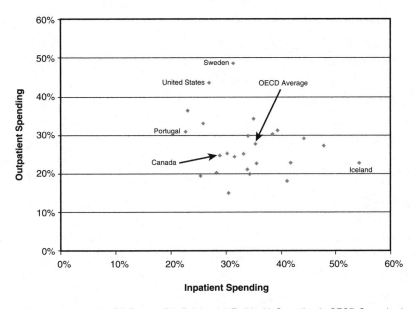

Data from: Anderson GF, Frogner BK, Reinhardt UE. "Health Spending in OECD Countries in 2004: An Update." *Health Affairs* (2007); 26(5): 1481-1489.[15]

Figure 3.6   Inpatient Versus Outpatient Services as a Percentage of Total Healthcare Spending

It's widely assumed that this trend has greatly improved the safety, efficiency, and cost-effectiveness of the healthcare services we receive. In many respects, this makes good sense. Hospitals are full of sick people and drug-resistant bacteria, and they're just about the last place that you'd want to send patients with problems that could be diagnosed and treated elsewhere. And, as we've seen, hospitals also have high fixed overhead expenses. We'd like to see an American outpatient healthcare industry that is lean, efficient, and low-cost, with a high capacity for handling large numbers of patients.

But the actual situation is a bit different than one might expect. Oddly enough, the United States seems to use fewer actual *resources* to manage its outpatients than the average country. We have fewer physicians, and fewer doctor visits per capita than all but 6 of 30 OECD members. In fact, at only 3.9 doctor visits per person per year, the United States actually has one of the *lowest* rates of physician utilization within the developed world.[16] The average number of annual doctor visits per person in Canada, Germany, and Japan are 6.1, 7.3, and 13.8, respectively.

Despite this comparatively low rate of visitation, the United States still managed to spend well over twice as much per capita on outpatient care as its next nearest OECD member (Figure 3.7). How is this possible?

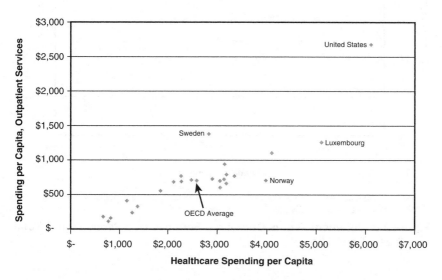

Data from: Anderson GF, Frogner BK, Reinhardt UE. "Health Spending in OECD Countries in 2004: An Update." *Health Affairs* (2007); 26(5): 1481-1489.[17]

Figure 3.7　Annual Per Capita Spending on Healthcare and Outpatient Services in Developed Countries

That's easy. As it happens, we pay higher prices for services in this area of healthcare as well. In 1985, physician fee schedules in the

United States were anywhere from 150% to more than 300% of those charged in Canada (Table 3.2).

TABLE 3.2 U.S. Versus Canada Physicians' Fees, 1985**

Service	Ratio of United States to Canada
Surgery	3.21x
Anesthesiology	3.73x
Radiology	3.59x
Procedures (Weighted Average)	3.34x
Moderate Office Visit	1.56x
Extensive Office Visit	1.55x
Moderate Hospital Visit	4.77x
Extensive Hospital Visit	2.57x
Consultation	1.60x
Evaluation and Management (Weighted Average)	1.82x
All Services	**2.39x**
Actual Average Physician Net Income (As Opposed to Clinic Charges)	**1.35x**

Notes: Values are in 1985 U.S. dollars; value for "All Services" is the weighted average of procedures and evaluation-and-management ratios.

Data from: Fuchs VR and Hahn JS. "How Does Canada Do It? A Comparison of Expenditures for Physicians' Services in the United States and Canada." *New England Journal of Medicine* (1990); 323: 884-890. Tables 3 and 5.

One might expect that this meant that U.S. doctors were making a killing. But the peculiar thing is that the actual net income of U.S. doctors in the study was only 35% higher than that of their Canadian counterparts. The remainder of the money mysteriously "disappeared."

More recent data comparing charges with income across countries is scarce, but show an even more pronounced result. Take a look

°° Along with consultations, evaluation and management (or "E & M" procedures, as they are known in medical jargon) are the bread and butter of what we think of as the average doctor visit. E&M procedures consist of visits in which the patient presents to the clinic and the healthcare provider takes a history, does a physical exam, and then evaluates all the information and formulates an action plan. Consultations are similar in nature, but are usually one-time events requested by another doctor.

at the selective and unweighted list of procedure costs from 1992-93 in Table 3.3. This particular list is flawed by not including the generally lower-paying and more common evaluation and management procedures. Nevertheless, the common procedures that are listed are far more expensive in the United States. In fact, in 1993 the overall ratio of U.S. to Canadian fees in the list is almost *triple* the ratio seen in 1985. Does this mean that American doctors became fabulously rich within that same period of time?

TABLE 3.3   Comparison of Procedure Charges in the United States and Canada—Early 1990s

Specialty	Procedure	Ratio of United States to Canada
Internal Medicine	Electrocardiogram	3.81x
	Flexible sigmoidoscopy	1.45x
	Liver biopsy	5.30x
Pediatrics	Circumcision of newborn	3.91x
General Surgery	Appendectomy	5.14x
	Cholecystectomy	4.61x
	Inguinal hernia	4.79x
	Partial gastrectomy w/o vagotomy	4.61x
	Radical mastectomy	5.31x
	Excision of breast tumor	6.45x
Orthopedic Surgery	Colles' fracture	5.96x
	Hip arthroplasty	8.28x
	Knee arthroplasty	9.21x
Thoracic/Cardiovascular Surgery	Valve replacement	5.26x
	Coronary bypass (multiple)	4.35x
Plastic Surgery	Rhinoplasty	9.58x
	Mammoplasty (unilateral reduction)	9.13x
	Mammoplasty (unilateral augmentation)	22.76x
	Blepharoplasty	10.13x

continues

TABLE 3.3 Continued

Specialty	Procedure	Ratio of United States to Canada
Neurosurgery	Craniotomy for evacuation of hematoma	6.41x
	Laminectomy	7.81x
Obstetrics and Gynecology	Complete care, normal delivery	5.90x
	Complete care, Caesarean delivery	6.11x
	Dilation and currettage	9.11x
	Abdominal hysterectomy	7.10x
Overall	**Ratio Average**	6.90x

Note: Median fees, converted to Canadian dollars.

Data from: Buske L. "MD Fees Much Higher in U.S." *Canadian Medical Association Journal* (1997); 156(6): 960.)[18]

It's a serious question, but to any healthcare provider living through this period, the thought is laughable. The early 1990s marked the end of a golden age in medicine for physicians—financially, politically, socially, and psychologically. It was a time marked by the growth of HMOs, managed care, "capitation," a loss of practice independence, and the perceived loss of financial control over their futures. These years marked the first time that many American doctors began to question their decision to go into medicine. Most doctors and nurses in America are not poor by any means, but their salaries are not unusually high by the standards of developed countries. Adjusted for inflation, the real income of U.S. physicians has actually been declining over the past fifteen years. Table 3.4 describes the trend in real income for U.S. physicians between 1995 and 2003, and compares it with corresponding changes in the income of other professionals and technical workers. As you can see, doctors have done far worse in that interval than their nonmedical counterparts, while the number of hours spent seeing patients actually increased during that same period.

TABLE 3.4   Physicians' Net Income from Practice of Medicine and Percent Change, 1995-2003

	Average Reported Net Income (Dollars)			Average Net Income, Inflation Adjusted(1995 Dollars)			Percent Change in Inflation-Adjusted Income		
	1995	1999	2003	1995	1999	2003	1995-1999	1999-2003	1995-2003
All Patient Care Physicians	180,930	186,768	202,982	180,930	170,850	168,122	-5.6*	-1.6	-7.1*
Primary Care Physicians	135,036	138,018	146,405	135,036	126,255	121,262	-6.5*	-4.0*	-10.2*
Specialists	210,225	218,819	235,820	210,225	200,169	195,320	-4.8*	-2.4	-7.1*
Medical Specialists	178,840	193,161	211,299	178,840	176,698	175,011	-1.2	-1.0	-2.1
Surgical Specialists	245,162	255,011	271,652	245,162	255,276	224,998	-4.9	-3.6	-8.2*
Private Sector Professional, Technical, Specialty Occupations	N/A	N/A	N/A	N/A	N/A	N/A	4.3	2.5	6.9

Notes: The Bureau of Labor Statistics (BLS) Employment Cost Index of wages and salaries for private sector "professional, technical and speciality" workers was used to calculate estimates for these workers. Significance tests are not available for these estimates. All inflation-adjusted estimates were calculated using the BLS online inflation calculator (http://146.142.4.24/cgi-bin/cpicalc.pl). The composition of the physician population changed between 1995-2003—a fact that makes some estimates of percentage changes in real income appear inconsistent (for example, estimates of income changes for all patient care physicians not falling between estimates for primary care physicians and specialists.) These data patterns occur because the proportion of medical specialists steadily increased from 1995 to 2003 (32% to 38%) while proportions of primary care physicians and surgical specialists both declined by about 3 percentage points.

* Rate of change is statistically significant at p < .05.
Source: Community Tracking Study Physician Survey

From: Tu HT, Ginsburg PB. Center for Studying Health System Change Tracking Report. Results from the Community Tracking Study, No. 15. June 2006.[19]

Table 3.5 shows how U.S. professional salaries compared with those in the rest of the world as of 2004. Skilled healthcare professionals often represent some of the most energetic and best educated workers in any country. As a result, they typically command a premium in the overall labor market. Expressing the premium as a multiple of per capita gross domestic product (GDP) provides a way of comparing the value that societies place upon physicians across countries.

As you can see, U.S. physician specialists, general practitioners, and nurses are all in the top tier with respect to GDP ratio. However, with respect to Canada (which was our initial point of net salary compensation for 1985), the physician salary ratio 20 years later is only slightly higher—1.43 for specialists and 1.51 for general practice physicians. But if physician *charges* in the United States were roughly six times higher than the equivalent fees in Canada for the same period, *what happened to the rest of that money?*

This seemingly simple question holds the key to what is wrong with American healthcare today.

TABLE 3.5 Average Compensation of Certain Healthcare Professionals, 2004 (Dollars in U.S. Purchasing Power Parities)[‡‡]

	Specialists		General Practitioners		Nurses	
	in $1,000s	Ratio to per captia GDP	in $1,000s	Ratio to per captia GDP	in $1,000s	Ratio to per captia GDP
Netherlands	$253	6.0	$117	3.6		
Australia	$247	7.6	$91	2.8	$48	1.5
United States	$230	5.7	$161	4.1	$56	1.4
Belgium	$188	6.0	$61	2.0		
Canada	$161	5.1	$107	3.4		
United Kingdom	$150	4.9	$118	3.9	$42	1.4
France	$149	5.0	$92	3.1		
Ireland	$143	4.0			$41	1.1
Switzerland	$130	3.8	$116	3.4		
Denmark	$91	2.9	$109	3.4	$42	1.3
New Zealand	$89	3.6			$34	1.4
Germany	$77	2.7				
Norway	$77	1.9			$35	0.9
Sweden	$76	2.5	$66	2.2		
Finland	$74	2.5	$68	2.3	$29	1.0
Greece	$67	3.1			$33	1.5
Portugal	$64	3.5	$64	3.5	$34	1.9
Czech Republic	$35	1.7	$32	1.7	$14	0.8
Hungary	$27	1.7	$26	1.6	$14	0.9
Mexico	$25	2.4	$21	2.1	$13	1.3
Poland	$20	1.6				
AVERAGE	$113	3.7	$83	2.9	$33	1.3
excluding U.S.	$107	3.6	$78	2.8	$32	1.3
Median	$83	3.3	$80	3.0	$34	1.3

From: Peterson CL and Burton R. "U.S. Health Care Spending: Comparison with Other OECD Countries." *Congressional Research Service Report to Congress*, September 17, 2007. Table 2.[20]

[‡‡] **Notes:** Sorted by specialists' compensation. Amounts are adjusted using U.S. dollar purchasing power parities. Amounts from previous years are trended up to 2004 dollars using the annualized Bureau of Labor Statistics Employment Cost Index for wages and salaries of health services workers in private industry. It is not known whether wage growth in health professions in other countries was similar to that in the United States. Amounts are from previous years for 10 countries: data for Australia, Canada, Denmark (for specialists and nurses), Finland (for nurses), and the Netherlands are from 2003; data for Belgium (for specialists), Denmark (for general practitioners), New Zealand (for nurses), and Sweden are from 2002; data for Switzerland and the United States (for specialists and general practitioners) are from 2001; and data for Belgium (for general practitioners) and the United States (for nurses) are from 2000. Ratios of salaries to GDP per capita reflect the year the data was collected and are not adjusted for inflation. For countries that have both self-employed and salaried professionals in a given field, the amount presented here is the higher of the two salaries. Four countries have both salaried and self-employed specialists: the Czech Republic (where compensation is $29,484 for salaried and $34,852 for self-employed specialists), Greece ($67,119 and $64,782), the Netherlands ($130,911 and $252,727), and the United States ($170,300 and $229,500). One country has both salaried and self-employed general practitioners: in the United States, salaried general practitioners earn $134,600, compared with $154,200 if self-employed. All nurses are salaried among this data. Recent data are available only for 21 of the 30 OECD countries.

4

Into Thin Air

"A child of five would understand this. Send someone to fetch a child of five."

—Groucho Marx

The fact is that about one-quarter of our hard-earned healthcare dollars simply vanish into thin air, and they disappear without providing a single medical good or service. Following these dollars often leads to bizarre and counter-intuitive findings. The common denominator among all of them is an American healthcare system that is unplanned, highly fragmented, and running counter to common sense. It's making us pay more than we should for everything from routine checkups to brain surgery. How charges are set and medical bills are paid are classic examples of how this can happen.

How Much Is That Surgery in the Window?

Prices matter. Neither markets nor businesses work well without efficient and transparent pricing. Rational pricing is the basis of comparison shopping for consumers, sales forecasting for businesses, and financial planning for those funding the purchases. Most importantly, rational pricing allows us to make the best possible use of scarce healthcare resources. If the prices that consumers see are set too low, they will tend to overuse healthcare goods and services. If the price that they see is too high, they'll fail to get enough care early. When prices are set properly, physicians and others are willing and able to maximize the level of services they provide, while patients optimize the amount of care received.

So here's a puzzle. If you ask the average American doctor how much he'll actually be paid for seeing a given patient, the odds are that he'll have no idea. And if you're a patient who is willing and able to pay cash on the barrelhead for services that day, the odds are that you'll pay a far higher price—while generating fewer actual costs— than anyone else in the waiting room. None of this is efficient or makes much sense. Here's how it works.

Pricing for healthcare services begins with "fees." Fees are the prices that hospitals, providers and others officially set for providing their goods and services. Normally these providers would set their prices at a level that covers their expenses plus a reasonable profit. Good business practices would normally have them discount their services for customers paying cash. Cash customers require less paperwork, reduce billing expense, and optimize cash flow—a key requirement for a healthy business. But American providers are not really allowed to do any of these things. Instead, they're forced to respond to a bizarre set of controls and incentives crafted by public and private insurance.

No health insurance company—especially Medicare and Medicaid—ever actually pays the full fee on any bill submitted by a well-run medical practice. Instead, each company will only pay the *lesser* of the amount of the bill submitted, or a pre-set amount that the insurance company has determined in advance that it will pay. These amounts differ with every insurance company. For example, for a given procedure, one company might pay $75, another $55, a third $50, and a fourth $45. As a result, any rational clinic will set its "usual and customary" fees to be higher than the highest amount paid by *any* insurance company. It knows that those prices will be discounted down by *every* insurance company, anyway. Setting their prices lower would only leave money on the table that some insurance company would have gladly paid. Thus, if the true cost of the procedure is $50 including overhead and collection expenses, any rational provider will set his fee to be higher than $75. This will allow him to collect the full amount from insurers #1, #2, and #3, and provide a margin for future discounting by new insurance plans that appear upon the scene. On the other hand, any economically rational provider will decline to see patients covered by insurer #4. To do so would mean losing money and jeopardizing the viability of his practice. No one can stay in business long by consistently losing money.

But what if a patient wants to pay cash, or has to pay cash because they don't have insurance? What will they pay?

Unfortunately, someone paying cash will have to pay the full posted fee and often *cannot* be granted any discounts. This is because insurance companies interpret any discounts given to individuals (which is to say, anyone but another insurance company) as being a reduction in the "usual and customary" charges. This means that the next time insurance companies "negotiate" rates with the discounting doctor; each insurer will reduce their allowed reimbursement still further.° The result will be a "death spiral" of price cutting that will rapidly drive most providers out of business.

Remember insurance company #4—the one that was only willing to pay $45 for the procedure that costs at least $50 to perform? Surely it would make sense for patients that it insures to be allowed to pay the difference between what the provider is willing to accept and what the insurer is willing to pay? Although its insurance coverage would not be complete, at least the charges to the patient would be lower than would otherwise be the case. And the only alternative would be to not allow the patient to receive the services at all.

As it happens, that's not allowed either, at least if the insurance in question is Medicare or Medicaid. Medicare and Medicaid rules specifically forbid providers from charging the patient anything more for procedures than Medicare and Medicaid cover, even if the insurance reimbursement is inadequate to cover the provider's costs. This is hardly a hypothetical scenario. As shown in Figure 4.1, it's actually quite common for both Medicare and Medicaid to pay considerably less than the actual cost of treatment.

The magnitude of these insurance company "discounts" can vary wildly—ranging from just a few percent of what would be a "normal"

° This is because each insurer expects that its own rates will be discounted a certain percentage from the "usual and customary" fee. No insurer ever expects to pay full price, no matter how low the fee.

Community Hospital Payment-to-Cost Ratios, by Source of Revenue, 1980-2006

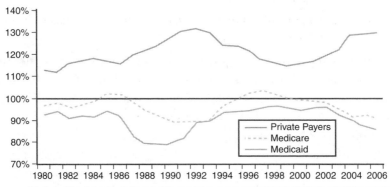

Note: Payment-to-cost ratios show the degree to which payments from each payer cover the costs of treating its patients. They cannot be used to compare payment levels across payers, however, because the service mix and intensity vary. Data are for community hospitals. Medicaid includes Medicaid Disproportionate Share payments.

From: "Community Hospital Payment-to-Cost Ratios, by Source of Revenue, 1980-2007," Kaiser Fast Facts, *The Henry J. Kaiser Family Foundation*, September 2009.[1]

Figure 4.1   Hospital Payment-to-Cost Comparison, 1980-2006

fee determined by a free market, to more than 70%.[†] All this illustrates one reason why charges for U.S. procedures grew so much compared to Canadian charges, as seen in Figure 3.11 in Chapter 3, "Where Does All Our Money Go?" Our system of pricing healthcare goods and services is defective. American doctors can charge anything they want, but in reality their prices are "make believe"—at least for health insurers. In contrast, centrally administered single-payer insurance systems such as Canada's typically pay 100% of a set

---

[†] Obviously, accepting payment that is below your costs is irrational for any business. One inevitable result of underpayment is that doctors simply have to stop accepting new patients with insurance plans that do not provide adequate payment. This is increasingly common for Medicare and Medicaid, who are the current kings of underpayment. In many cases Medicaid's payment for lab tests and other procedures is well below the cost of materials and reagents alone. According to a March 2008 Medical Group Management Association survey of practices, 24% of private medical clinics have already begun to refuse or limit access for Medicare patients. Forty-six percent of practices said that they would begin doing so if Medicare reimbursement rates were cut still further. The situation for Medicaid is far worse because it pays even less than Medicare.

fee, and doctors set their own charges to match. This difference explains much of the "charge ratio inflation" that occurred between 1985 and the early 1990s. As money becomes tighter and insurance companies become more restrictive, the discrepancy between charges and collections grows larger over time. So, artificial pricing accounts for some of the difference in the charge-to-income differential. But there is a second and more important reason: the astonishing growth of nonclinical expenses in American healthcare.

Paying More for Less

In recent years, more and more of the revenue collected by U.S. healthcare facilities ends up paying for costs that have nothing to do with providing actual healthcare goods and services: things such as administration, billing, documentation, and the cost of complying with thousands of rules and regulations. This escalating overhead ends up being built into the fees of doctors and hospitals each year, but doesn't add a penny to their salaries or profits.

Calculating a "true" administrative overhead rate for outpatient practices nationwide is difficult. First, there are well over a million healthcare providers in the United States, including physicians, physician assistants, nurse practitioners, dentists, podiatrists, chiropractors, therapists, and others. Performing valid financial surveys on such a large and diverse population is rarely, if ever, done. Second, practice conditions vary wildly—from solo independent practices to huge medical groups, private HMOs, and government facilities. This makes accounting comparisons extremely difficult. Third, it's often difficult to account for the true cost of "administration and overhead" when providers perform so many different tasks in a given day. Nevertheless, one study did attempt to quantify these costs as of the year 2000. The results are shown in Figure 4.2.

As you can see, between 20–27% of *every* dollar collected by the outpatient clinics surveyed in 2000 went to purely administrative overhead, with much higher rates being prevalent in multi-specialty and primary care practices. Note that these numbers are for administrative expenses only, and specifically do *not* include the other costs that we might normally think of as overhead, such as rent, utilities, clinical staff salaries, transportation, and so on. When these costs are

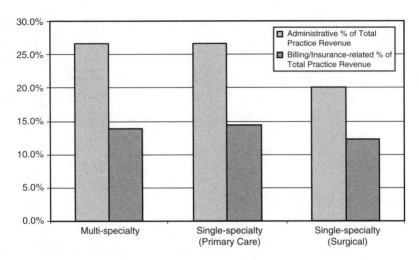

Data from: Kahn JG, Kronick R, Kreger M, and Gans DN. "The Cost of Health Insurance Administration in California: Estimates for Insurers, Physicians, and Hospitals." *Health Affairs* (2005); 24(6): 1629-1639.

Figure 4.2　Estimate of Medical Practice Administrative Costs

included, nonclinical costs as a percentage of revenue can easily climb higher 50%—especially in smaller practices, where overhead costs are not spread across a large number of providers.[†] Billing and insurance-related expenses alone accounted for about 12–15% of gross revenue in 2000.

These numbers are pretty high, but can't be interpreted in isolation. An international point of comparison is needed, and again we'll turn to Canada. Current data comparing nonclinical expense rates between countries is extremely difficult to obtain, but the data that does exist is quite plain. As shown in Figure 4.3, while the number of outpatient medical practitioners in the United States per million of population increased by just 27.4% between 1971 and 1986, the number of healthcare administrators and managers increased by 136%. Over the same period of time, the number of Canadian practitioners increased by 40%, while the number of administrators increased by 67.2%.

[†] The total practice overhead rate for a typical family practitioner (including clinical staff), is about 60%.

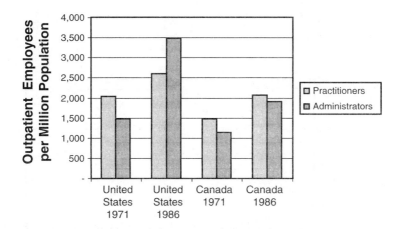

Data from: Himmelstein DU, Lewontin JP, Woolhandler S. "Who Administers? Who Cares? Medical Administrative and Clinical Employment in the United States and Canada." *American Journal of Public Health* (1996); 86: 172-78.[3]

Figure 4.3   Comparative Increase in Administrators and Clinicians in the United States and Canada Between 1971 and 1986

Another way of looking at the same data is to compare the ratio of outpatient administrators to practitioners. In 1971, the United States had about three administrators for every four practitioners. Just 15 years later, there were almost five and a half administrators for every four practitioners. As healthcare researchers Himmelstein, Lewontin, and Woolhandler wrote in 1996:

> Twenty-seven percent of U.S. medical care workers do mostly paperwork. If the United States duplicated Canada's 1986 staffing patterns, the country's hospitals and outpatient facilities would require 1,407,000 fewer clerks and managers.[4]

That was more than fifteen years ago. Today there are far more administrators than ever before, both in absolute numbers and as a proportion of the healthcare workforce. Figure 4.4 goes beyond outpatient care and graphs the growth in total U.S. medical administrative personnel, compared to the growth in physicians between 1968 and 1993. According to the Bureau of Labor Statistics, in 2010 there were more than "4.5 million" Americans employed in healthcare management and administrative support.[5] In contrast, there were only about 820,000 clinically active physicians—more than a 5:1 ratio of administrators to doctors!

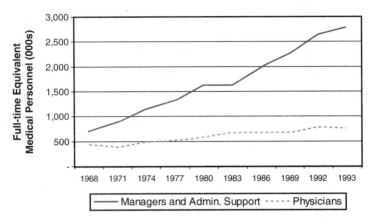

Data from: Himmelstein DU, Lewontin JP, Woolhandler S. "Who Administers? Who Cares? Medical Administrative and Clinical Employment in the United States and Canada." *American Journal of Public Health* (1996); 86: 172-78.[2]

Figure 4.4   Growth in Full-Time Medical Personnel in the United States—1968-1993

Amazingly enough, even these numbers still significantly underestimate the real number of nonclinical jobs in the U.S. healthcare system as a whole. They fail to include the growing ranks of workers dedicated to setting up and maintaining ever more sophisticated computer and information technology (IT) networks. They exclude more than 926,000 additional people in the United States who work for life and health insurance companies, more than 724,000 employees of insurance brokers and consulting firms, and tens of thousands working in corporate health benefits departments and the corporate headquarters of hundreds of supporting companies. Most importantly, these statistics neglect the fact that clinical personnel themselves are being forced to spend more and more time and money on paperwork, computer work, and administrative tasks each year.

The financial impact is best summarized by a comparison of the cost of healthcare administration in the United States and Canada published by Woolhandler et al. in 2003. The results are summarized in Table 4.1.

TABLE 4.1 Comparison of Administrative Cost in the United States and Canada, 1999

	Canada	United States	Ratio: United States versus Canada
Estimated healthcare administration cost per capita	$307	$1,059	3.45x
Administration as a percentage of health expenditures	16.7%	31.0%	1.86x
Overhead among private insurers	11.7%	13.2%	1.13x
Administrative share of health-care labor force	19.1%	27.3%	1.43x
Practice administration cost as a percentage of gross physician income	16.1%	26.9%	1.67x
Fraction of physician time spent in administrative tasks	8.4%	13.5%	1.61x

Data from: Woolhandler S, Campbell T, Himmelstein DU. "Costs of Healthcare Administration in the United States and Canada," *New England Journal of Medicine* (2003); 349: 768-775.[6]

In 1999, healthcare administration costs in the United States were *at least* $294.3 billion. Total per capita healthcare spending has increased by almost 100% since then, while administration-related costs are rising even faster. This means that the total bill for healthcare administrative overhead in 2010 was more than *$600 billion.*

If we were to simply reduce our per capita spending on healthcare administration to the Canadian level, we would save well over $225 billion in healthcare spending every year.§ By now it should be obvious that the major component of disappearing revenue for American healthcare providers is the incredibly high cost of U.S. healthcare overhead and administration. The magnitude of this expense is so

---

§ The careful reader will have noticed that these data regarding administrative costs don't appear to match the percentage of healthcare spending for administration, shown as being 7% of the total in Figure 3.1. This is because the administrative cost in Figure 3.1 includes *only* the direct administrative expenses allocated to the Medicare program, plus the profits of private insurance companies. Why these lower numbers, rather than the actual cost of administration and similar nonclinical expenses, are repeatedly cited in federal government statistics is a mystery.

large that it's almost difficult to appreciate. However, here is just one example: There are currently about 50 million uninsured people in the United States. In 2009, the average annual premium for an employer health plan covering a family of four averaged about $13,375, or $3,344 per person. At this rate, insuring all 50 million uninsured Americans would cost slightly more than $167 billion annually. Reducing per capita healthcare administration costs to Canadian levels would buy coverage for all of them, and still leave almost $60 billion to spare.** As Thomas Sowell put it: "It is amazing that people who think we cannot afford to pay for doctors, hospitals, and medication somehow think that we can afford to pay for doctors, hospitals, medication, *and* a government bureaucracy to administer it."

Is Change Allowed?

In economist jargon, a situation in which one person's gain is another's loss is called a "zero sum" situation, or a "zero sum game." A situation in which both parties to a deal are better off and no one is made worse off is called a "positive sum game." As you can imagine, positive sum games are relatively rare in life and highly sought after. In healthcare, a positive sum result means that no one has to accept a reduction in care to provide benefits to others; access to medications doesn't have to be curtailed to cover the cost of preventive care; benefits for seniors don't have to be pitted against the livelihoods of their doctors; and neither taxes nor insurance premiums have to rise to cover millions of uninsured Americans.

Realizing that huge numbers of healthcare dollars are being wasted on nonclinical expenses presents an unparalleled "positive sum" opportunity. We're already spending plenty of money for healthcare; it's just that we're not spending it on the right things. If we can find a way (or ways) in which to reallocate much of the money that we spend from nonclinical to clinical resources, we really could have the

---

** Of course, there would actually be more to spare than this. If we assume that even 10% of the reduction in administration costs works its way into lower insurance premiums, the cost of coverage would fall to only $150 billion annually, leaving $75 billion unused. This is almost half the amount spent by Americans on prescription drugs each year.

best healthcare system in the world. But are we going to be allowed to? Unfortunately, this is a political rather than a scientific question. Scientific questions can always be answered by the application of logic, observation, and experimentation. Political interests can easily ignore observations, twist logic, and decry even the most rational efforts to make a bad situation better. As we've seen from the dollars spent on lobbying and each election year's political campaigns, healthcare is nothing if not highly politicized.

For the right kind of politician with the right motives, the inefficiency sprinkled through the system could be a godsend. A form of political beatification awaits the men and women who are willing to reallocate resources currently wasted on healthcare transaction processing and current business practices—and do so successfully. They can insure the uninsured without having to raise taxes, help care for children without forcing providers out of business, and fix Medicare and Medicaid without impoverishing future generations or selling out senior citizens. And it's not even necessary to destroy the system that we currently have in order to save it. In theory, these goals can be accomplished without resorting to shopworn calls for a single-payer system, socialized medicine, mandating electronic medical records, or the dozens of other buzzword action items that are topics of campaign stump speeches, think tank white papers, and partisan editorial columns. Exactly what steps can be taken immediately, and how, is the subject of subsequent chapters.

But that hardly means that changing things for the better is a foregone conclusion, or that any improvements will ever be made. Both thinking and changing things are hard work, and changing anything is always a potentially risky course of action. There are clearly vested interests to be considered. This administrative overhead did not appear spontaneously: It was deliberately created by parties who believe that it benefits them in some way. And now there are roughly five million people whose jobs consist of actually doing all of this paperwork rather than providing care. Change will cost some of them their jobs, even though new and far more productive jobs will clearly be created by diverting our resources to improving the health of the population.

Perhaps the only salvation and consolation for the political risk-takers in the healthcare world is that the whole thing is going to implode anyway, and soon, if nothing is done. In early 2008, Geoff Colvin at *Fortune Magazine* laid out the stark financial future of Medicare in an article called "The $34 Trillion Problem." Little has changed since then, despite major elections and the passage of the Patient Protection and Affordable Care Act (PPACA) of 2010:

> Cash flow for Medicare Part A, the part that pays hospitalization expenses for seniors, is already negative. The PPACA increased taxes to help make up for this, but it also greatly expanded Medicaid and legislated many new healthcare subsidies. The new tax receipts can't cover both. According to the Congressional Budget Office, this money "cannot be set aside to pay for future Medicare spending and, at the same time, pay for current spending on other parts of the legislation or on other programs...[8]

An aging population and new benefits created by the PPACA mean that Medicaid and Social Security will eat up ever-larger amounts of GDP. As Colvin explains:

> The federal budget has averaged about 18% of GDP over the past several decades. If that average holds and if the rules of our social insurance programs don't change, then by 2070, when today's kids are retiring, Medicare, Medicaid, and Social Security will consume the entire federal budget, with Medicare taking by far the largest share. No Army, no Navy, no Education Department—just those three programs. [9]

The bipartisan Committee for A Responsible Federal Budget has found that the government's own projections of future Medicare "savings" are highly unrealistic. This means that Medicare's finances will deteriorate much faster than official estimates suggest.[10]

The bottom line is that, "...if Medicare were accounted for like a company pension fund, it would be underfunded by over $34 trillion."[11]

Even the most oblivious presidential administrations will have a hard time sweeping $34 trillion under the rug. (The entire gross domestic product of the United States was $15 trillion in 2010.) And despite the fact that Medicaid programs nationwide are in even worse shape than Medicare, the 2010 healthcare "reform" law will make

16 million more Americans eligible for Medicaid benefits. Drastic reductions in these programs—along with the hopelessly escalating cost of health insurance coverage in the private sector—will produce tens of millions of unhappy voters. There is an excellent chance that the healthcare system as we know it will collapse, with providers dropping Medicare and Medicaid completely, being forced to insist on cash payment for services, and giving up on more restrictive private insurance plans as well. Either that, or they'll simply quit and do something else less stressful and expensive. It will be nearly impossible for Medicare and Medicaid patients to find doctors willing to take them on. Political heads will finally, deservedly and brutally, roll.

The rest of this book is devoted to understanding where the current healthcare system has gone wrong, and to solving the problems. The bad news is that there is a great deal that is fundamentally wrong. The good news is that the problems are consistent, logical, and easily remedied without spending large additional amounts of money or interfering with the doctor-patient relationship. In fact, as we'll see, fixing these problems will leave patients, providers, the U.S. economy, and those politicians who really want to be part of the solution, much better off than they've ever been before.

5

The Healthcare Machine

"Dealing with complexity is an inefficient and unnecessary waste of time, attention, and mental energy. There is never any justification for things being complex when they could be simple."

—*Edward de Bono*

The healthcare system in the United States has become an absurdly complex machine. There is no inherent reason that it has to be, nor did anyone consciously design it to be that way. If American providers worked on a straight cash basis and with far less regulation (as do attorneys, accountants, and other professionals), there is no question that the American healthcare system would be relatively simple and far less expensive.

Let's be clear: Excessive complexity in any important area of human activity is generally a bad thing. Excessive complexity is a corrosive force in society and human interactions. Social and business systems that become too complex are inefficient, difficult and expensive to maintain, and prone to corruption. Examples are easy to find. Complex tax codes rapidly become littered with loopholes and contradictions. The presence of these loopholes supports armies of attorneys and magnifies the cost of compliance and enforcement. This makes taxation far more expensive and less efficient—producing fewer dollars per unit of labor and diverting the resources of businesses and individuals from productive uses to tax avoidance.

Highly complex social codes such as casteism, theocracy, and feudalism tend to limit the mobility and utilization of human resources. Because of their limitations on business and social interaction, rigidly complex social structures have to expend a substantial amount of resources on the maintenance of tradition, superstition, religious beliefs, and fear of punishment to remain intact. And it's no coincidence that economic markets operate best when the transactions are simple, transparent, and easily understandable. Stock and commodity markets may be susceptible to bull and bear markets and the occasional bubble, but large-scale corruption requires introducing the complexity of junk bonds or bundled mortgage instruments.

Another danger of complexity is that it is easily used as a smokescreen by those whose actions may make little or no social, ethical, medical, or economic sense. In this case, complexity becomes a type of camouflage. This approach to hiding things is frequently used when specific areas of interest can't be kept overtly secret. In the natural world, complexity of color or pattern is the basis for the types of camouflage that hide tigers, leopards and military vehicles. In the worlds of law, economics, and bureaucracy, complexity often becomes the basis for discouraging investigation or evading pursuit:

- Money laundering uses a large number of transactions and complex webs of accounts in many different locations to obfuscate both the source and use of illicit funds. Tax cheats use similar mechanisms, in addition to taking advantage of the tax code itself.[1] Hiding money by the use of large numbers of complex transactions was unnecessary when Swiss numbered accounts were confidential and could truly be kept secret.

- A common strategy to forestall legal discovery is to produce so many documents and so much information that the relevant elements are lost in the clutter.

- In bureaucracies, complexity can be intentional or unintentional, but it almost always leads to less efficient and more secretive processes that are prone to abuse. Department of Defense acquisition and purchasing activities are an excellent example.[2]

With this as a background, it is important to separate the complexity of healthcare as a science from the complexity of healthcare as a business. Natural biological systems are inherently complex, and the application of medical science is therefore inherently complex as well. As we'll see later, the very complexity of medical science and clinical medicine makes it particularly difficult to treat patients by using administratively mandated processes.

On the other hand, there is nothing inherently complex about seeing a patient in the office, sending blood to a laboratory for analysis, or billing for an office visit. The business of healthcare could be pretty simple if we allowed it to be. Instead, we've *made* the business of healthcare complicated with our own peculiar implementations of rules, regulations, federalism, and insurance.

Exactly what is it that's so special and so dysfunctional about the healthcare system we've created that it creates vast amounts of overhead for everyone? One useful way of thinking about the American healthcare system and visualizing the dysfunction is to imagine it as a complex machine. Not a particularly modern machine filled with computers and electronic parts, but instead, a complicated mechanical device filled with nothing but cogs, gears, and moving parts.

Millions of Moving Parts

At its core, modern healthcare in the United States is, and always will be, a mechanical process. The wheels of healthcare turn based upon human encounters and their ability to engage other gears in the process of care. To illustrate this, we'll begin with an example of a single patient visiting a doctor for a common problem—in this case, for a routine checkup that results in some common tests and referrals.

One useful way to represent this type of medical encounter is shown in Figure 5.1, in which each of the parties involved in various aspects of the visit are represented by cogwheels or gears that turn based upon their interactions with other elements of the healthcare system.

The events portrayed in Figure 5.1 initially seem fairly simple:

1. A patient schedules an appointment and sees her primary care provider for a routine health checkup.

2. In the course of the visit, her doctor finds that she has a high blood sugar level and symptoms suggesting a diagnosis of diabetes. As a result, he orders lab tests, prescribes a medication, and arranges a referral so that the patient can see a specialist.

However, the referral also has to be approved by the patient's insurance company (this is called a "prior authorization").

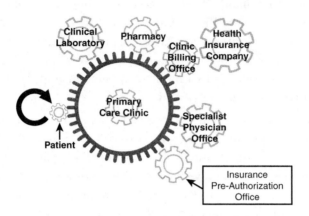

Figure 5.1   Interactions Resulting from a Single Routine Patient Visit

3. In addition to collecting the patient's insurance co-pay, the primary care doctor must also thoroughly document the visit and submit the visit information to his billing office. In turn, the billing office generates a claim that will be submitted to the patient's specific insurer.

Thus, a single visit by this relatively healthy patient generated at least seven different interactions between eight different entities. For the sake of clarity, we will call these interactions "healthcare transactions." A healthcare transaction can be a patient visit, an order to dispense medication in the form of a prescription, an order for a lab test, or the submission of a billing claim to an insurance company. The next step in the process is for the patient to engage in a completely new set of transactions with each of the separate entities to which she has been referred. This is shown in Figure 5.2.

Here we see that, in the course of turning the wheels of healthcare interactions, a single patient visiting a clinical lab, a pharmacy, and a specialist will generate no less than *nine* additional transactions among eight different entities including the patient: one each with the lab, pharmacy and specialist, another between those entities and their billing offices, and one more between each of the three billing offices and the patient's insurer. It's easy to see that these transactions

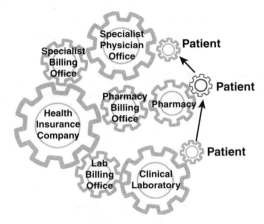

Figure 5.2 Additional Patient Encounters Based on the Initial Visit

will continue to multiply every time our patient requires tests, therapy, x-rays, medical equipment, hospitalization, and anything else required for diagnosis or therapy. We also need to understand that the picture that we've created thus far is, by necessity, simplistic. A more realistic diagram would have to include the possibility of dozens of additional gears representing therapists, hospitals, purveyors of durable medical equipment, nursing homes, government agencies and regulators, medical boards, and a host of others.

The casual observer might think that, although a bit cumbersome, the number and types of healthcare transactions aren't much different from those that take place in many other industries. After all, lots of businesses require the skill and input of a large number of different vendors. Building a house can require the coordination of architects, excavators, concrete and brick masons, carpenters, roofers, painters, and many others. Is healthcare really more complex?

In fact, it is. The problem is one of scale and variability.

Unlike a builder, who can select a few trusted vendors and business partners based upon experience, confidence, and profitability, the average doctor must work with dozens of different insurers, laboratories, pharmacies, imaging centers, and others, in addition to thousands of patients. Although the information required by most of these vendors is generally the same, the forms and paperwork required by each is rarely if ever standardized. Moreover, one insurer might require that all the tests for its patients be sent to one set of labs, pharmacies, and imaging centers, while other insurers specify completely different sets. For all practical purposes each provider faces hundreds or thousands of rigidly customized transactions each day. Economies of scale do not exist. Instead of the machine seen by the patient in Figure 5.2, each provider sees a machine that looks far more like that in Figure 5.3.

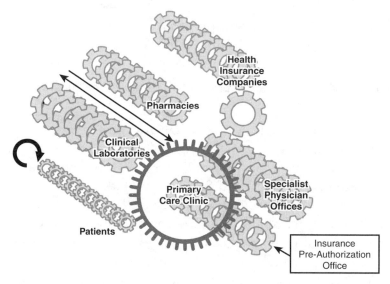

Figure 5.3   A Morning's Worth of Healthcare Transactions as Seen by a Primary Care Provider

The number of wheels that a given provider has to turn grows rapidly as a function of the number of patients, insurers, labs, specialists and other healthcare entities brought into the equation. The speed with which these gears accumulate can be astonishing. If we include not only physicians, but also podiatrists, physician assistants, nurse practitioners, therapists, and others, there are more than one million health care providers in the United States. There are tens of thousands of clinical labs, pharmacies, imaging centers and other vendors. Lording over all of them are 1,300 private health insurance companies, plus Medicare, Medicaid and TRICARE—each with its own different rules and foibles.[3]

It should be obvious that the healthcare business machine we've created has millions of moving parts and tens of millions of possible transaction combinations. Each of these parts is required to mesh with hundreds of other parts each and every day—many of which have different interfaces and expectations. Every encounter and every piece of data collected and distributed among each of the relevant parties represents a separate healthcare business transaction. In aggregate, these transactions number in the tens of billions. In 2006, there were 964 million visits by patients to outpatient physician offices alone, with an additional 102 million visits to hospital outpatient departments. At least one medication was prescribed during seven out of every ten of these visits. The result is that nearly 3.5 billion retail prescriptions were filled at pharmacies in 2007.[4] Each one of these prescriptions involved interactions between patients, clinicians, pharmacies, and insurers, as well as labs, imaging centers, and a host of other cogs in the healthcare machine.

The situation is complicated still further by the way just about all healthcare vendors are paid for their services. Rather than being paid directly by the consumer, almost 88% of healthcare payments come from third parties who have had no direct participation in the healthcare transaction. What this means in practice is that every healthcare encounter is guaranteed to generate a number of "shadow" transactions regarding issues of payment. Because none of the third parties were present in the first place, these take the form of reports describing what happened, when, where, and why. Still more transactions are generated when these same third parties ask for more information, report back what they chose to pay, what the vendor must cover, and what the patient still owes to all the parties involved. It is difficult to imagine a structure that would generate more transactions—and thus more revolutions of the machine—than the current model.

All this work requires energy. In the case of a healthcare provider, energy takes the form of time and money needed to deal with all of these transactions. In machine terms, this time and money is consumed by work, grit, and friction within the system. The work component occurs when things go right, and is what we think of as efficient healthcare delivery. The grit and friction components consist of a range of problems that prevent the work component from being carried out quickly, easily, and efficiently. Characterizing, localizing, and understanding how and where grit and friction occurs in the healthcare marketplace is one of the most important aspects of any effort to reform the U.S. healthcare system.

To continue with the mechanistic analogy, we can identify three specific elements that have a direct effect on our healthcare machine's ability to operate:

1. *The sheer number of wheels that must be turned to deliver and pay for healthcare services.* Requiring health care providers to turn more wheels requires more shifting of gears— a time when energy is lost and no actual care is being transferred into the system—and more energy to turn all those wheels than would otherwise be the case. Dealing with many insurers, pharmacies, and clinical laboratories is inherently more time-consuming and complex than dealing with just a few, especially if none of their paperwork and procedures are standardized.

2. *"Sand" dumped into the gears.* Many parts of our healthcare system are susceptible to jamming from the outside. The introduction of foreign bodies into the moving parts can throw entire parts of the machine out of kilter, dramatically increase the cost of getting things done, and cause many parts of the machine (especially healthcare providers) to fail and leave the system entirely. Examples include the sudden introduction of disruptive, expensive, and time-consuming technologies, such as computerized medical records, elaborate "pay-for-performance" schemes, or having "guidelines of care" mandated by regulators. Oddly enough, one of the most important sources of sand in the parts is the government itself.

3. *Friction in the system.* Friction represents the transfer of scarce time and energy from the provision of healthcare services to a wide variety of miscellaneous tasks. Doctors deal with friction all the time in the form of preauthorization requests, inappropriate denials of tests or treatments, and the need to fill out the same paperwork multiple times.

By now it should be obvious that these elements are metaphorical correlates of inefficiency and administrative overhead within our healthcare system. They're important because we've identified excess overhead as being a primary cause of the high cost and poor performance of U.S. healthcare relative to the resources put into it. Accordingly, most of the rest of this book will be devoted to identifying examples of each element, its causes, and realistic remedies.

But before we can do so, one final task remains. We have to understand the basic internal workings of several key elements of our healthcare system. How these entities function internally dictates what makes them spin and how they interact with the wheels around them.

6

How and Why They Spin: Inside Key Wheels

"God made man to go by motives, and he will not go without them, any more than a boat without steam or a balloon without gas."

—*Henry Ward Beecher*

While there are millions of gears in America's healthcare machine, four types stand out as being the most important politically and economically. Indeed, from the perspective of the cost and efficiency of healthcare, no other wheels even come close. These four entities are *doctors and other healthcare providers, health insurers, government,* and *patients*.

The contents of this chapter help explain why the entire machine behaves in what might seem to be an illogical and irrational fashion. It is often difficult for the average person to understand why different components of the healthcare system might be at odds. After all, we are taught from an early age that doctors are here to cure us, insurance companies are created to protect us, and the government is supposed to look after its citizens. How then is it possible for some or all of these missions to be at odds? The answer lies in the fact that the business model behind an economic entity can sometimes require it to take actions that would otherwise be contrary to its mission statement.

Doctors and Other Healthcare Providers*

Doctors are the most important medical component of any healthcare system. There are about 820,000 active physicians in the United States. About one-third of these are generalists and two-thirds are specialists.† Collectively they influence about 80% of all healthcare spending. Relatively little of that money goes to them, however. In aggregate, physician and clinical services only account for 21% of all healthcare expenditures, or $448 billion in 2006.[1] Instead, physicians account for the vast majority of healthcare spending via the decisions they make and transactions they initiate. Those decisions and transactions account for most everything we experience as patients—from what tests will be ordered, to surgeries or therapies to be performed, whether and what hospitals will be used, which other providers will see patients, what drugs will be used, and how often we'll return for visits. The long, expensive and often arduous education and training that doctors go through makes them better qualified than anyone else to know whether and which transactions should be performed on behalf of a given patient. This does not mean that patients, families, insurers, administrators, or governments necessarily listen to physicians or do what doctors recommend. The situation is far more complex than that. Nevertheless, physicians as a group are terribly important to any healthcare analysis, and they generally behave in rational and predictable ways.

As we saw in Figure 3.11, most doctors in the United States make more money than the average person, but generally less than or equal

---

* We will be using "healthcare providers" as a general term to represent all people within the healthcare system whose primary function is to care for patients. In practice, healthcare providers are numerous and diverse, ranging from highly specialized surgeons to home health providers. From a system perspective, the most important healthcare providers are those whose job requires them to make decisions about resource use. Physicians are the most important providers in this regard.

† "Generalists" are usually considered to be physicians practicing family practice, general medicine, and general pediatrics. Everyone else is considered to be a specialist.

to the money made by the CEO of a small business.‡ Whether U.S. physicians deserve all the money they make is a common question. On one hand, the salary of the prototypical general practitioner is 3.4 times the median household income, and that of the average specialist is 4.8 times higher. On the other hand, training a physician requires a substantial amount of time, money, and dedication—including an undergraduate degree, four years of medical school, and then an additional three to seven years of internship and residency training. The average U.S. physician will be nearly thirty years old before entering the workforce as a fully qualified practitioner. By that time, 86.7% of them will have outstanding educational loans, with an average debt of $129,943.

The combination of a shorter-than-average working life, higher-than-average educational debt, long training times, and declining job satisfaction suggest that high salaries are needed to train and keep good providers around. However, real physician income in the United States has been declining steadily since 1995.[2] From 2004 to 2006 alone, physicians' real income after inflation fell an average of 7.1%, despite seeing more patients.[3] This inflation-adjusted decline is in contrast to dramatic increases in both medical inflation and smaller increases in the wages of nonmedical professionals. Physician income is clearly not the cause of escalating healthcare costs in the United States.

Regardless of salary levels, there is a relative shortage of physicians in the United States; a shortage that is guaranteed to get much worse as a result of the PPACA. One reason for the shortage is that all this training is relatively scarce and expensive. Estimates are that it costs about $250,000 to train a medical student, and then at least $110,000 per year to train a resident physician. This cost, plus the fact that the number of training positions is regulated by government and academia rather than market forces, means that the United States has fewer physicians per capita than the majority of economically developed countries: only 2.4 per 1,000 population, compared to an OECD average of 3.0 per 1,000 population. From 1980 to 2000, the

---

‡ According to Salary.com's 2007 Annual Small Business Executive Compensation Survey, the national median salary for a small-business CEO is $233,500. For a company with 500 to 5,000 employees, the average CEO salary is $500,000. For companies with more than 5,000 employees, the number increased to $849,375.

yearly number of American medical school graduates remained unchanged at about 16,000, while the population as a whole increased by 71 million. As is the case with much of the U.S. economy, imports—in this case, of doctors—made up much of the difference. In 2005, "international medical graduates" (that is, foreign-trained doctors) made up 25.3% of practicing physicians in the United States.

The shortage is particularly severe—and getting worse each year—with respect to primary care physicians. These include family practitioners, internal medicine physicians, general pediatricians, and obstetricians, who serve as the primary care providers for pregnant women. Although the Government Accountability Office (GAO) reported that the supply of primary care physicians actually grew at a rate of about 1% per year between 1995 and 2006, this figure is deceptive.[4] The GAO counted the total number of providers training in specific residency programs required for primary care—internal medicine, family medicine, and pediatrics—but did not take the additional step of determining whether these providers actually intended to enter general practice. In fact, the number of U.S. medical school graduates going into family practice declined by more than half from 1997 to 2005. In 2006, only 13% of first-year internal medicine residents said that they intended to pursue general practice.[5]

While the shortage of primary care physicians in the United States might seem like a minor problem now, it will become increasingly serious over the next ten years. When Massachusetts adopted its own law making healthcare coverage universal (the law that the 2010 "Obamacare" law is based upon), the average wait for a primary care appointment rose from 33 to 52 days almost immediately.[6] Only half of the general internists were taking new patients at all. Practices closed to new patients are already becoming more common nationwide, especially for those with poor insurance coverage. In 2008, 45% of providers in Oregon had closed their practices to new Medicare patients.[7] In the long term, the trend will be made substantially worse by the aging of the U.S. population. The American College of Physicians estimates that 40% more primary care physicians will be needed as a result of the aging population by 2020.

So we know that doctors are relatively scarce, hard and expensive to train, and are an essential key to most of the healthcare transactions that occur each day. Losing or discouraging them would probably be a bad thing. What do we know about they way they think and behave economically?

Physician Economics and Motivation

About half of the physicians in this country are small businessmen. Based upon surveys by the American Medical Association, the majority of medical practices in the United States are small—employing 10 or fewer physicians. The remaining clinicians work for larger clinics and institutions such as Kaiser Permanente, the Veterans Administration (VA), the military, medical schools and hospitals, and group practices. Collectively, small practices account for about 50% of all clinically active physicians nationwide, but have a disproportionately large impact on healthcare as a whole. That's because small and independent practices handle the majority of private-pay patients in all parts of the country. In doing so, they have far more discretion with respect to what drugs will be used, what labs will be tapped and which additional resources will be devoted to any given case than their institutional counterparts in the military, VA, or health maintenance organizations (HMOs) such as Kaiser.

Because they are businessmen, physicians react to financial incentives and disincentives in a rational way based upon how they affect net income. Probably the easiest way to think of a medical practice is as a small factory or production line, with clinical data as the raw input, the physician's time used as the processing tool, and clinical decisions leading to additional healthcare transactions as the output. In Figure 6.1, the things that doctors do are shown by the boxes labeled with bold type.

As you can see, doctors basically use their time to gather and process information from a wide variety of sources, and produce two billable types of output: (1) a clinical evaluation in which decisions dictate further actions; and/or (2) surgeries or other procedures that may or may not be done on the same visit. The only useful inventory

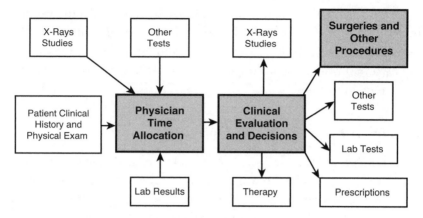

Figure 6.1   Production Process in a Medical Practice

any physician has is his or her time, exactly like attorneys, accountants, and business consultants of all types. However, unlike other professionals, doctors are not paid for their time on an hourly basis.
Instead, they're paid quite differently, according to a concept called
"procedures."

Procedures were invented as a way of bundling most or all the
tasks associated with an episode of care into one flat fee. This structure is particularly convenient for two groups. The first is insurers,
who can predetermine what any particular type of visit will cost them
simply by fixing the price they'll pay. This method allows both the
individual and cumulative cost of nearly all surgeries or other invasive
procedures to be predicted with some reliability. Paying for procedures also allows insurance companies to offload the risk of many
procedures onto doctors by a process called "bundling." A simple
example of bundling is for an insurance company to say that it will pay
a single fee for a specific surgery and all follow-up care associated
with that procedure. If the patient develops a complication as a result
of the surgery and must be seen multiple times, bundling forces the
doctor to see the patient and manage those complications on his own
dime. Because all surgeries are associated with a known risk of complication, this strategy allows the insurer to transfer the risk of caring
for the complication to the provider.

The second group is a subset of doctors, including surgeons and
radiologists, who perform procedures that are only loosely related to
time. These specialists can, under certain circumstances, work quickly

and churn out many procedures per day. This "crank-'em-out" option is not available to primary care doctors or those in the so-called "cognitive" specialties. These doctors must spend a substantial amount of time actually interacting with patients as a part of what they do. For these physicians, the value of a "procedure" is based mostly upon the time spent with the patient and the perceived complexity of the medical problem. A given doctor can see fewer sicker patients or more healthier patients and receive roughly the same compensation.

Although it might seem as if valuing office visits of different lengths as procedures is equivalent to providing doctors with an hourly rate, there are some key differences in how doctors are paid when compared to other professionals. As you can see in Table 6.1, the financial anatomy of a doctor's visit is quite different from that of, for example, a visit to an attorney. Whereas attorneys and other professionals are paid for each and every use of their time, physicians are paid only for certain uses of their time.

TABLE 6.1   Comparison of Payment for Various Activities Performed by Physicians and Attorneys

Item of Service	Doctors	Lawyers
Office consultation	Paid	Paid
"Procedures" performed (such as a surgical procedure for a doctor, or court appearance for an attorney)	Paid	Paid
Letters written to keep others informed	Unpaid	Paid
Telephone calls	Unpaid	Paid
Communication with outside parties (such as pharmacy, lab, insurers for a doctor, or plaintiff for an attorney)	Unpaid	Paid
Follow-up visits	Paid or Unpaid	Paid

Thus while time is money for everyone, a substantial portion of the time that doctors spend in the office is essentially uncompensated. The impact of these differences is actually quite important in the scheme of healthcare delivery, and its effects can be seen every day in the operation of clinics, as piles of prescriptions, lab requisitions, and referrals are processed.

Clearly the most sensitive and economically destructive use of physician time is performing administrative tasks that have little or nothing to do with actual patient care. Not only are physicians small business owners, but their personal time and skills are the *only* source of income for their business, and the *only* source of care for their customers—patients. Any unnecessary administrative burden on clinicians costs them money and deprives society of a scarce resource. As we'll see, this is a major source of healthcare cost inefficiency.

Health Insurers

There are two major sources of health insurance in the United States: private health insurance companies, and government agencies, such as Medicare and Medicaid. Private insurance has been the basis of U.S. healthcare coverage for the past 90 years, with the federal government only entering the picture in the 1960s. As a result, the vast majority of Americans are covered through private insurance. About 171 million Americans had private healthcare coverage in 2006, with about 158 million of them obtaining insurance through their workplace. This compares with 43 million Medicare enrollees, 36 million covered by Medicaid, and 44 million Americans with no insurance coverage at all in that year.[8]

Private health insurers hold sway over the lives of patients, providers, and payers as a result of the sheer numbers that they insure. Medicare and Medicaid exercise enormous influence because their policies are backed by the force and power of the federal government.

Private and public insurers differ considerably with respect to how they work as businesses. We'll look at their business structure first, and then compare their similarities and differences as actors on the healthcare stage.

Private Insurers

Private insurers are either for-profit companies such as Aetna and Metropolitan Life, or nonprofit entities such as some of the Blue Cross/Blue Shield organizations. For all practical purposes, there is little or no difference between the two. For-profit and nonprofit insurers operate under the same business conditions and behave in exactly the same way with respect to their customers, patients, and providers. In the case of health insurance, being "nonprofit" is strictly a tax status rather than a business plan.

In theory, the business of private insurance is fairly simple. Like casinos, insurers basically engage in a legalized form of gambling. Insurers take the other side of a bet that their customer wishes to place. In the case of health insurance, insurance companies are willing to bet that: (1) a whole group of policyholders won't all get sick at the same time; and (2) that the regular bets placed by their customers (in the form of premium payments) will more than cover whatever payouts do have to be made when illnesses do occur. Like "the house" in a casino, each insurance company has to weight the odds in its own favor if this mechanism is to work and a profit is to be made. And like casinos, health insurers make money in two ways. The first is by collecting "bets" (in this case, insurance premiums). The second is by investing the cash reserves that the companies must keep on hand in order to pay out when luck turns against the house. The business basis of any private insurer—including health insurers—is shown in Figure 6.2.

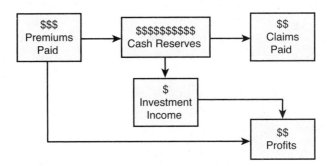

Figure 6.2   The Basic Insurance Business Model

There are several key elements that an insurance company can and must control if it's going to make a profit. First, it can decide whose bet it will take, and whose it won't. Just as known professional gamblers and card counters aren't welcome in casinos because of the likelihood that they will cost the house money, people who are likely to receive more in medical benefits than they pay in premiums will be turned away by any insurance company allowed to do so. The selection of who an insurance company will and will not insure is a powerful tool wielded by the medical underwriting department of each insurer.

Second, an insurer can limit the amount that it pays out by adjusting the conditions under which it pays out its losses. This is similar to a casino adjusting both the amount and odds of the payout on a slot machine.

Third, both insurers and casinos can enhance or diminish their returns with the quality of their investment decisions. Whereas investment income is a secondary source of income for most businesses, it's a major source of revenue for casinos, insurers, and other businesses that are required to keep large amounts of cash on hand at all times.

Of course, the comparison of an insurance company with a casino has its limitations. First, casinos have the benefit of knowing the exact mathematically determined odds for every bet they take. Dice, cards, roulette wheels, and slot machines don't have the ability to influence their own outcomes, as people often do with their health. People can and do affect their own health in dozens of ways, from diet and exercise to taking (or not taking) medications and engaging in risky behavior. Second, living organisms show great variability in their susceptibility and response to illness. Even the best efforts to screen out high-risk individuals can be foiled by accidentally covering customers with a few bad genes. Third, there is the problem of "moral hazard," in which relatively young and healthy people will avoid having to pay for healthcare insurance, while sicker individuals eagerly seek coverage. Fourth, new federal regulations will require insurance companies to write policies for anyone, no matter what their medical problems might be. This means that many people with potentially costly conditions will be entering the system. Finally, the cost of the bets insurers need to cover is affected by changes in the price of healthcare services themselves.

These differences between insurers and casinos account for a substantial difference in the way that casinos and insurers place their bets and spend their money. Although both casinos and insurers must spend money on sales and marketing, insurers must spend far more on people whose jobs are to set premium levels and minimize losses on lost bets. This is easily seen by looking at the administration cost categories of a typical commercial insurer in Table 6.2.

TABLE 6.2 Administration Cost Categories for Health Insurers[9]

General Administrative Cost Category	Category Components
Fixed Administrative Overhead	General Administration
Claims billing/payment	Claims
Other specific administration	Sales and marketing
	Finance and underwriting
	Membership and billing
	Provider services and credentialing
	Customer service
	Information systems
Major clinical elements	Utilization and quality review
	Case management
	Medical director
	Other healthcare services

Data from: Kahn JG, Kronick R, Kreger M, Gans DN. "The Cost of Health Insurance Administration in California: Estimates for Insurers, Physicians, and Hospitals." *Health Affairs* (2005); 24(6): 1629-1639.

Outflows of reserve dollars that are used to pay for healthcare goods and services are called "medical losses" in the industry, and the amount of money paid out in claims as a percentage of premiums is called the "medical loss ratio" (MLR). Medical loss ratios vary considerably from company to company and from year to year. In 2007, the medical loss ratios for a sample of 15 full-service health plans in California ranged from a low of 69.4% to a high of 95.3%, with an average of 84.7%.[10] Money left over after paying for medical losses is used to pay for administration and company profits. It should be obvious that, from a shareholder perspective, private insurance companies should be obsessed with minimizing medical losses. Medical losses eat up profits, and the goal of every insurance employee hoping for a year-end bonus will be to reduce them at every opportunity.

The drive to reduce medical losses is the source of much of the resentment that average people feel toward the current healthcare system. It is also the source of much of the inefficiency that is now threatening to topple the system itself. From a business perspective, it's important to realize that the structure, function, and behavior of private insurers are an inevitable result of the business model that we've just reviewed. Private insurance companies might want to provide healthcare coverage to everyone and work quickly and fairly with providers, but they can't do so and still remain competitive with their less scrupulous counterparts. To understand this, we need to look at the tools and processes that private insurers have at their disposal to stay in business and earn a profit.

Private Insurance Economics and Motivation

Health insurance companies have four basic tools for increasing revenues and minimizing losses:

- Increase premiums, thereby increasing premium revenue
- Clever investment of reserve funds to increase investment revenue
- Prevent high-risk individuals from entering their insurance pool
- Minimize the benefits provided to patients

Each of these presents a challenge to company management and the healthcare system as a whole.

Premiums

Setting prices would seem to be a relatively simple and straightforward way of ensuring adequate revenue for insurers. Unfortunately, it turns out to be very difficult to accurately predict what those premiums should be. The problem is that when premiums are fixed for the year to come, they are based upon cost information that is typically at least six months old. The result is an 18-month lag between increases and decreases in claims expenses and the time that those changes can be priced into premiums. This lag creates a regular and recurring imbalance between premiums and medical losses called the "health insurance underwriting cycle." As shown in Figure 6.3, the health insurance underwriting cycle is characterized by a repeated pattern of several years of insurance company profitability followed by several years of losses.

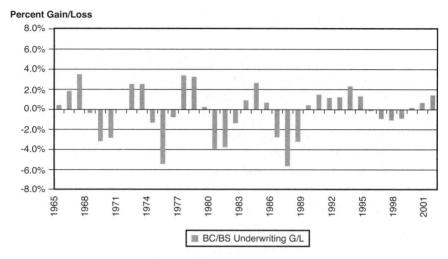

From: Kipp R, Cookson JP, Mattie LL. "Health Insurance Underwriting Cycle Effect on Health Plan Premiums and Profitability." *Milliman USA Report,* April 10, 2003. [11]

Figure 6.3 Blue Cross/Blue Shield Underwriting Gains and Losses from 1965 to 2001

The cause of the underwriting cycle is easy to understand with a good example. An excellent one is provided by Kipp, Cookson, and Mattie[12], and the process can be summarized as follows:

1. Health insurers have to set and publish their premium changes for each new year several months before those rates take effect. Because of the time lags involved with collecting and analyzing claims data, this means that the premium rates going into effect on January 1st will be based on data that is six months old. So if medical expenses had been rising at a rate of 5% per year, but doubled to 10% in the period from July to December of 2011, the premiums for 2012 would still increase by only 5%.

2. By the time insurers get around to setting rates for 2013, they have already lost money for all of 2012 *in addition to* the money lost in the latter half of 2011. Based upon their recent claims experience, rates for 2013 will now be increased by the new base increase of 10%, plus an additional 8% or so to make up for the increases that should have been implemented in 2011 and 2012. This means that their new rate increase to employers

and individuals for 2013 will be 18%, even though they are assuming that claims are rising at a 10% rate.

3. If actual claims rates in the latter half of 2012 should rise again to 12%, the insurer is now even further behind in setting an adequate level of premiums. Eventually it will try to get ahead of the curve by raising premiums even higher than its estimates of the rate of increase in medical claims. Those paying the premiums will be horrified to see their premiums rising much faster than the perceived rate of medical inflation. They will not understand that their premiums were actually too low several years ago, and that insurers are making up for that shortfall.

4. The same process will repeat itself in reverse if the rate of increase in medical claims should fall. Changes in premiums will again lag the changes occurring in medical claims by a period of several years. Premiums will be too high for a period of several years. The net result is a cycle in which insurers using time-lagged and imperfect information will tend to under- and over-charge when compared to the appropriate level of premiums.

The effect of this cycle on insurance premiums can be seen by comparing trends in the Health Cost Index with the Employment Cost Index for Health Insurance Premiums, as shown in Figure 6.4. As you can see, changes in premiums as measured by the Employment Cost Index consistently lag changes in the Health Cost by about 18 months.

Because we already know that cycles are common in many types of business, why does the health insurance underwriting cycle matter with respect to controlling costs and improving the efficiency of the health care system? The problem caused by these gyrations is not any ill intent on the part of insurers, but that each cost recovery episode of the cycle places an enormous strain on every other part of the healthcare system. During each recovery period, insurers are forced to increase premiums at a rapid rate while doing everything possible to reduce exposure to risk and payouts for medical claims. The result is a general increase in friction throughout the healthcare machine. Purchasers of health insurance see sudden and rapid rate increases. Patients see higher co-pays and deductibles, more stringent screening by medical underwriting departments, and a general

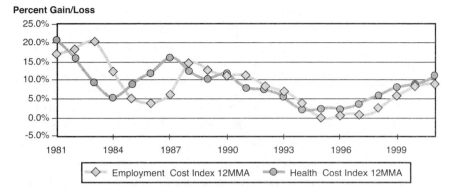

Percent Gain/Loss

From: Kipp R, Cookson JP, Lattie LL. "Health Insurance Underwriting Cycle Effect on Health Plan Premiums and Profitability." *Milliman USA Report*, April 10, 2003. [13]

Figure 6.4   Health Cost Index Versus Employment Cost Index for Health Insurance Premiums

reduction of benefits. And providers encounter intense pressure to minimize treatment expense, more administrative hurdles, and delays in payment.

Because of the lag time between setting premiums and obtaining the cost data needed for accurate pricing, the existence of an underwriting business cycle is probably unavoidable. What is useful to consider is whether the amplitude of that cycle and the friction that it creates can be minimized. This will be one of the issues addressed when we look at solutions to the current mess.

Investment Income

It should be no surprise that insurance companies are susceptible to the same ups and downs with respect to investment as the rest of us. In good times, investment income can provide a cushion against increases in healthcare costs and help moderate the need for premium increases. On the flip side, in bad economic times, the loss of investment income will—other things being equal—cause an increase in premiums above and beyond what would normally be needed to account for medical losses alone. This is because of the need to maintain a steady level of both reserves and corporate profits. The enormous fall in asset value that occurred in 2008 and 2009 is only now being fully reflected in higher premiums. In a system that relies heavily upon businesses to pay for health insurance premiums, these increases will have an additional adverse effect on company profits, cash flow and employment, prolonging the recession.

Preventing High-Risk Individuals from Entering the Insurance Pool

One of the basic tools used by both casinos and health insurers to limit their downside risk is refusing to accept bets from people who are likely to cost them money. For private insurers, this is the job of the medical underwriting department. Prior to accepting any applicant who can be legally refused coverage, the medical underwriting department reviews the application information for evidence of pre-existing conditions, a family history of illness, or any other factor that might suggest a higher-than-average risk of future medical spending. It's obvious that this behavior is just as rational for individual insurance companies as it is for individual casinos. The problem, of course, is that these are exactly the people who most need health insurance. To assist them in this effort, insurance companies have even asked physicians to help them ferret out patients who might otherwise slip through the screening process. In California, Blue Cross was recently taken to task for asking physicians to review the insurance applications of their patients and "immediately" report any discrepancies between their patient's medical conditions and the information in their applications.[14]

What's important for us to understand is that a noncustomer's need for healthcare services is not the insurance company's problem. The company's duty is to win its bets, make money, and stay in business. Doing so requires that it avoids recruiting sick people whenever possible. It is also logical that customers who become ill be dropped from covered status as soon as possible. Doing so is the business equivalent of a casino asking a card counter to cash in her chips and leave the premises.[15] It's even possible for an insurer to claim the moral high ground as part of a program to exclude patients with medical conditions from its risk pool. Insurers can plausibly argue that it's their responsibility to keep premiums as low as possible for its insured customers.

The tendency of commercial insurers to avoid patients with pre-existing conditions (or, better still, have them covered by a competitor) illustrates one of the major difficulties of a healthcare system based upon private insurers. From a business perspective, commercial insurance works best if one of two conditions exists. The first is if an insurance company is free to "cherry pick" its customers and drop the expensive ones. The second is if the population is universally required to have healthcare coverage and high-risk individuals are spread evenly among all private insurers. While premiums will inevitably be higher with mandated universal coverage, there is no other way to provide insurance for high-risk patients under a private insurance model.

Minimizing the Benefits Provided to Patients

Casinos have it easy compared to private insurers in their ability to refuse services to high-risk clients. Once a gambler starts to win, all any casino has to do is ask them to leave. State and federal regulations might require insurers to keep an expensive patient on the rolls for a variety of reasons, and the Patient Protection and Affordable Care Act[§] (PPACA) will make it virtually impossible to drop expensive patients or limit the liabilities that they incur.

On the other side of the coin, health insurers have far more flexibility than casinos in determining whether and how they will pay for a given episode of care. When a roulette wheel says that it will pay 35:1 on double zero, it's difficult to modify the payout when the ball happens to drop in the wrong slot. In contrast, health insurers possess a wide range of tools to limit both downside risk and payouts. While some of these methods are open for all to see, in his excellent book *Fixing American Healthcare*, Dr. Richard Fogoros accurately describes many of these tools as a form of "covert rationing."

Some of these corrective measures are directed at the patient, while others are directed specifically at the patient's physician. Here are some examples:

- **Raising deductibles and co-pays.** One advantage that insurers have is that coverage contracts typically last only for a 12 month period. At the end of this period, premiums, deductibles and co-pays are all subject to change. In some cases, this might be adequate to induce a business or individual policyholder to switch insurers.

[§] This is the 2,409-page 2010 healthcare law popularly known as "Obamacare."

- **Limiting access to physicians.** Since the popularization of "managed care" as a concept in the 1990s, most insurance companies have made use of either health maintenance organizations (HMOs) or preferred provider organizations (PPOs). This allows insurers to limit access to care in two ways. First, limiting the pool of providers improves the chances of having patients wait for scheduled appointments. Because many conditions are self-limited (or fatal) and go away on their own, this reduces the chances of a patient requiring tests and medications. Second, tying a physician population to an insurance plan—either by paying salaries directly or by controlling the supply of patients—makes it far easier to minimize payments, as described later.

- **Use of drug formularies.** The vast majority of people purchasing health insurance coverage are completely unaware of what medications a particular insurance plan may choose to cover. Moreover, unlike many provisions of a health policy, an insurer can choose to change its formulary at any time. Limiting access to specific medications can greatly reduce the financial impact of developing a wide variety of diseases. Removing (or failing to add) expensive medications as choices that insurance will pay for can easily save hundreds or thousands of dollars per patient per month.°°

- **Delaying payment for healthcare goods and services.** Investment income is a function of three factors: the size of the reserve pool, the rate of return, and the duration of investment. Simply waiting to pay claims is a way of maximizing the latter. Delaying payment is such a tried and true business management tool for health insurers that 47 states have had to

---

°° This is no exaggeration. Patients with multiple sclerosis (MS), rheumatoid arthritis, psoriasis, and other debilitating and complex diseases of the immune system have relatively few effective drugs to choose from. Most of the newer (and more effective) agents are extremely expensive. Patients with MS on a common health plan in Portland, Oregon were recently notified that one very effective drug called Rebif (interferon beta-1a), would no longer be included in the approved formulary of drugs. Patients would have the choice of switching to drugs known to be less effective, or paying for the drug themselves. Rebif treatment currently costs more than $1,000 per month.

pass "prompt payment laws." These laws limit the amount of time that insurers can delay payment on a so-called "clean claim"—a request for payment that is unambiguous and correct. Of course, laws are one thing, but enforcement is another. Texas has had to pass three separate prompt payment laws, yet payments from insurers to healthcare providers there and elsewhere still frequently stretch well beyond 45 days.[††] In many states, healthcare laws are pre-empted by a federal law called the Employee Retirement Income Security Act (ERISA). ERISA does not have any sort of prompt payment provision. In many of those cases, a majority of clean and accurate claims will routinely go unpaid after 90 days.[16]

There are many other ways for the creative health insurer to get around prompt payment laws. One is to simply deny that a claim was received. It's very likely that no action will be required for at least 90 days until an inquiry is made, whereupon the insurer can simply request that the claim be resubmitted. A second technique is to request more information about the claim, such as copies of the associated medical records. Simply making a request for more information stops the clock on prompt payment laws because the insurer is entitled to determine that they are "reasonably obligated" to pay for the services rendered and that no fraud is involved. A third technique is to reject an otherwise clean claim because of minor typographical errors. All these techniques are especially effective when the rejection comes at the end of a 45-day "prompt payment" window.

- **Underpaying for healthcare goods and services.** The amount that an insurer is obligated to pay on a given claim is specified in an elaborate contract that each insurer has with that provider for that particular service. Because there are thousands of insurers and a given provider might have to deal

---

[††] Athenahealth's PayerView website (http://athenapayerview.com/) regularly documents the performance (good and bad) of health insurance companies with respect to delayed payments, requests for medical documentation before payment, transparency in reasons for claims denial and other factors. In 2008, New York Medicaid had the worst record for delayed payments as measured by the number of "days in accounts receivable," at 137.3 days. The median value for all insurers included in the measure was 35.41.

with dozens or even hundreds of them, each doctor's billing office must deal with hundreds of different contracts. This provides an opportunity for insurers to shave the payments owed to providers, and there is a high probability that they won't be caught because the vast majority of providers don't have sophisticated billing or accounting systems.

- **Simply denying claims.** Another extremely effective technique for limiting losses is to simply deny payment for claims, often based upon an interpretation of payment rules or a technicality. Many denials can be based solely upon an insurance company's own interpretation of what it owes. Most of these denials are now computer-automated. Insurers use literally millions of rules (some of which are common to all insurers, and others that might be completely unique to a given insurer or even a given insurance policy) to match diagnoses, procedures, dates, authorizations, and a host of other factors.[‡‡][17] Clearly no provider is capable of knowing, much less adhering, to each of these. This imbalance has spawned an entirely new industry: "claims denial management."

  It should be obvious that the claims denial management industry has nothing whatever to do with providing care. Instead, it's entirely devoted to looking at each claim to be submitted to insurers to make sure that it passes all the tests necessary to get paid. Because these efforts try to use computers and software to anticipate and correct rules that will result in denials, the entire effort has been correctly labeled as a sort of "arms race." The Center for Information Technology Leadership has

---

[‡‡] A *Wall Street Journal* article on the growth of the "claims denial" industry documents these organized efforts: "Over the past decade, most insurers have adopted code-auditing software from companies such as McKesson and Ingenix. These advanced systems include several million coding rules to guard against overcharging, and are routinely updated with new rules to which claims must adhere." It goes on to describe cases in which properly filed claims were automatically rejected by the software anyway.

estimated the annual cost of this computerized tug-of-war to be about $20 billion per year.[§§]

- **Manipulating physician incentives.**   If you're covered by private insurance, the odds are that you've never looked at the contract that dictates whether and when they'll pay for health-care services. Few Americans ever do. There is an excellent chance that your policy contains a "managed care" component, such as enrollment in a Preferred Provider Organization (PPO), health maintenance organization (HMO), or Point-of-Service Plan (POS). Under these programs, the insurer can and does judge whether any particular treatment or diagnostic test meets its criteria of "medical necessity." Its ruling on this issue usually determines whether the given treatment or test takes place. By inserting themselves directly into the healthcare process, health insurers are in a position to limit the resources used for each case if they wish. In practice, they do so both overtly and covertly.

Overt rationing is common, straightforward, and easy to understand. A primary care physician requests a referral to a specialist for a problem she doesn't feel competent to handle, and the insurer's referral coordinator says no. A surgeon requests permission to perform a liver transplant, and it's denied. An endocrinologist recommends a newer drug to help manage a case of diabetes, and the drug is not covered by the formulary. Patients and providers might not like the ruling, but at least they know where they stand and can act accordingly.

Covert rationing is a completely different animal—one that is little known or understood by the general public. Dr. Richard Fogoros

---

[§§]   According to Athenahealth, the worst claims denier in 2008 was Health Choice of Arizona, with an overall medical claims denial rate of 37.82%. The median value for insurers examined by Athenahealth for the same period was 8.64%. In the same survey, Wellcare of Georgia scored worst in terms of "denial transparency," a measure of how clear it is as to why a given claim was denied, and what would have to be done to fix it. Only 63.23% of Wellcare's denials were well explained. The survey median across all insurers for this measure was 83.11%.

has written an entire book and maintains a blog on the subject of covert rationing, and is a keen observer of the subject.[18] In describing the role of insurers in covert rationing, we will summarize some of his findings and observations.

Covert rationing is basically a situation in which insurers (or others) do not specifically deny access to care themselves, but coerce physicians or other healthcare providers into doing it for them.[***] This coercion can take the form of positive incentives or negative incentives:

Example #1: "Bonus" pools. If the amount spent on patient care is less than projected, insurers can offer to share the savings with doctors. This, of course, gives those physicians a direct financial incentive to discourage their patients from consuming medical resources—either by not telling them about specific tests or treatments, or not prescribing them. This type of program is often operated by HMOs (now relabeled "Accountable Care Organizations" (ACOs) under the PPACA), who contract with networks of independent primary care providers. The contract states that a certain amount will be paid to the doctors for their services, but that a portion of this will be withheld and paid out at the end of the year to clinicians whose average medical expenditures were below targeted levels. The extra money serves as a positive incentive for physicians to limit the cost of care wherever possible.

There is no question that these types of programs are effective in influencing physician behavior and reducing spending. A survey of primary care physicians in California found that 57% felt pressure to limit the number of referrals, and 17% believed that this pressure compromised the quality of care.[19] An economic study found that these programs seemed to reduce medical utilization expenditures by about five percent.[20]

Example #2: Doctors can be "capitated." Under capitation, each doctor in the managed care plan is paid a fixed amount to take care of each patient in their practice. The less each patient is seen

---

[***] Covert rationing is not limited to private insurance. In its roles as a financier and regulator of healthcare services, the federal government also has a major role in covert rationing.

(and the fewer resources used on their behalf), the more each physician gets to keep. This is also a positive incentive to limit the amount of care delivered.

Example #3: Doctors can be given payment contracts that forbid them from telling patients about certain treatment options. Until the late 1990s, many prominent insurers placed something called "gag clauses" into provider contracts. A gag clause is language that prohibits physicians from relaying certain types of information to patients. The primary purpose of gag clauses was to prohibit doctors from telling patients about expensive treatment options and incentives that HMOs might provide to doctors for limiting care. Although gag clauses have since been banned from organizations working with Medicare and Medicaid patients and by many state laws, they are a profound example of a negative form of covert rationing.[†††]

Example #4. "Peer" pressure. A universal tool currently employed by insurers is to compare clinicians with "peer groups" with respect to various aspects of their practice patterns. Doctors periodically receive letters—or even personal visits from insurance company representatives—in which their medical resource utilization is compared with an insurer-defined "peer group." For example, a physician will be told that, of the top ten medications she prescribes, only two are generic, compared to five generic choices for her "peers." She might then be told that she performs several expensive diagnostic procedures at a rate that is higher than other clinicians. The implication, of course, is that she is overprescribing the

---

[†††] Interestingly enough, despite the absence of gag clauses, physicians still seem to be self-censoring what they tell patients based upon the doctor's perception of what the insurer will allow. A survey of 720 physicians found that 31% reported deciding "not to offer a useful service to a patient because of health plan coverage rules." (Wynia MK, VanGeest JB, Cummins DS, Wilson IB. "Do Physicians Not Offer Useful Services Because Of Coverage Restrictions?" Health Affairs (2003); 22 (4): 190-197.)

medications and procedures in question and should change her practice patterns accordingly.[†††]

Example #5: Physician "report cards." Publishing data on the "quality" of physician performance is usually thought of as a public service meant to protect the public. However, as Dr. Fogoros has observed, what might initially seem to be a public service can also be an effective way of discouraging physician intervention in particularly expensive high-risk cases.[21] His observations are based upon a study that looked at performing procedures on patients who had had heart attacks so severe that they were suffering from cardiogenic shock—a condition in which the heart is so severely damaged that it is not capable of supplying all the blood required by the body.[22]

New York has a system of reporting that publicizes the mortality rate of patients under the care of cardiologists and cardiovascular surgeons. This reporting does not, however, adjust the respective mortality scores of these physicians based upon the complexity of the cases they choose to treat. As a result, if you look at the treatment of high-risk cases—the cases that are most likely to result in mortality—New York heart doctors are now far more reluctant to intervene than doctors elsewhere.

Although it is unlikely that the creation of the physician-associated mortality ratings was originally intended to reduce healthcare expenses, it should be obvious that "report cards" can have important unintended consequences on physician behavior.

[†††] "Peer-pressure" comparison tactics can be quite effective in changing physician behavior, but we need to understand that this does not necessarily translate into good medical practice. The problem, of course, is that such comparisons are made without controlling for a number of important factors. First, are the patient populations being treated truly comparable? Certain specialists are often referred the toughest cases, including those in which generic treatments might have already failed. Second, generic equivalents simply do not exist for many newer drugs, and are therefore not comparable. Third, it might well be the case that the peer group is itself behind the times or is not providing optimal treatment.

Self-Insured Businesses

Many larger companies self-insure, basically pooling risk among their employees, saving money to be used as reserves against claims, and acting as their own insurance agents. These businesses often employ third-party benefits administrators (TPAs) to run their health insurance operations. These TPAs are often commercial insurers. Nationwide, about 50 million Americans are currently covered by self-insured health benefits.

Self-insured operations differ from those of commercial insurers in several ways:

- Self-insured plans do not need to make a profit from their insurance operations.

- Unlike commercial insurers, self-insured plans are governed by federal laws rather than a combination of often overlapping and even conflicting state and federal laws. One important consequence is that these plans do not need to comply with state-mandated benefits regulations, and can offer the same plan across multiple states. This can dramatically reduce both the cost of benefits and administration.

- The employer is the beneficiary of investment income, rather than a third-party insurance company.

- Self-insured employers are not subject to state health insurance premium taxes. These are typically 2–3% of premiums paid.

- Employers can contract with any providers, and offer the same health plan and benefits to all of its employees regardless of locality.

- To limit their own downside risk, many employers purchase "stop-loss" insurance from commercial insurers. Stop-loss insurance is purchased to protect the business from claims beyond a given limit, (such as. $25,000), for a single incident/occurrence, or a series of occurrences that exceed a defined annual limit.

The nature of self-insured health plans vary as much the businesses themselves, with all degrees of coverage represented. The absence of a profit motive and state regulation allows this type of program to be more cost-efficient and less expensive to provide than conventional commercial insurance. They also have a great deal of flexibility with respect to the selection of covered providers, list of benefits covered, and payment terms. Many self-insured programs historically limited the risk to employers by specifying a lifetime benefit maximum for participants, as well as benefit caps for specific expensive procedures and illnesses, such as those requiring transplants.

Public Insurers

Public insurers are government institutions that provide insurance benefits to designated subsets of the general population. The most important of these are Medicare and Medicaid. Medicare was established in 1965 to provide care to those over 65 years old. Coverage for those who are disabled and under the age of 65 was added in 1972. Medicaid was likewise created in 1965, with the original intention of providing health insurance coverage to welfare recipients. Since then the Medicaid program has grown to become the predominant long-term care program for the elderly and those with disabilities, and of insurance for children in low-income families. The TRICARE program provides health insurance for military dependents.

Public insurers differ from private insurers in several important ways. Like self-insured businesses, they do not have to contend with making a profit, nor do they need to maintain specific reserve levels or comply with state insurance regulations. For the most part, public insurance funds are financed by taxes rather than premiums, although premiums and co-pays both exist for Medicare beneficiaries. Use of taxation means that public insurers are not constrained by the same types of financial constraints as commercial carriers—especially with respect to the balance between a patient's ability to pay for premiums and co-pays and the benefits provided.

However, the most important difference between public and private insurance is that public insurers have the full weight of the government behind them. In the case of Medicare and Medicaid, this includes the power of laws made by Congress, the prosecutorial clout of U.S. attorneys, and the investigative resources of the Federal Bureau of Investigation. These powers place public insurers in a completely different league from private companies—one that can easily work its will on patients and providers through the use of carrots, sticks, and actual intimidation. Put simply, if you cross a private commercial insurer, they can cancel policies and deny payments. If you cross a public insurer, they can assess enormous financial penalties and put you in jail.

Why is this so important?

Unlike private companies whose means and motives can be readily understood in economic terms, public insurers are not only economic entities, but also instruments of political policy. The challenge to patients and providers is that political goals are inherently unpredictable. Instead of being rationally based upon the provision of care or economic criteria, political aims can vary at the whim of individuals, political parties, or interested lobbyists. Because everyone else in the healthcare system has clear motives and business needs, an arbitrary approach on the part of government—the only player with the full force and power of the state behind it—can cause serious problems for others with respect to planning, operations, and economic viability. Indeed, as we'll see shortly, government's lack of a thoughtful, broad-minded and consistent approach to healthcare has caused a considerable amount of friction for patients, providers, healthcare facilities, and even commercial insurers for the past 50 years.

Garnering Revenue

As with any insurer, public insurers need cash to provide benefits. In the case of Medicare and Medicaid, this cash comes from several different sources. As shown in Figure 6.5, Medicare is operated as several different programs, titled Parts A, B, C, and D.

- Part A pays for hospitalization expenses, including home health, which is partially funded under Part B.
- Part B pays for outpatient services, including physician visits, outpatient procedures, and durable medical equipment such as wheelchairs, oxygen tanks, and so on.
- Part C consists of the so-called "Medicare Advantage" plans, which is actually a program in which beneficiaries are enrolled in commercial insurance programs with Medicare basically

paying the premiums. In this case, all benefits are provided by those third-party insurance programs.

- Part D is Medicare's prescription drug benefit.

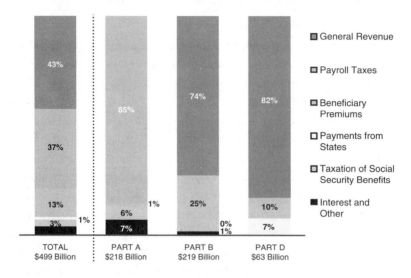

From: The Henry J. Kaiser Family Foundation. "Medicare Fact Sheet—Medicare Spending and Financing." August 2010.[23]

Figure 6.5   Estimated Sources of Medicare Revenue, 2010

As you can see, the funding for each of these programs comes from a number of different sources and in different proportions. Medicaid funding is provided by a combination of state and federal taxation.

In practical terms, this means that the administrators who actually operate Medicare have little or no control over their sources of revenue. Changes in Medicare-related taxes must be made directly through Congress. Changes in premiums and patient co-pays are more flexible, but premiums account for no more than 12% of total Medicare revenue. This is clearly a problem. Increases in taxes and premiums are always politically unpopular—especially during times of economic recession. Because of this, the future of Medicare's long-term solvency under its existing financial structure looks grim. Unless something is done to increase revenue or reduce expenses, current projections are that the Medicare Trust Fund will be exhausted by 2019.§§§

The net result is that Medicare and Medicaid administrators have little or no ability to manipulate revenue to balance their own budgets. The only tools that they have readily available are ways to minimize payouts.

Minimizing Expenditures

Public and private insurers have different constituencies and are operated by different types of people. Whereas private companies are accountable to shareholders and their executives are rated with respect to profitability, public insurers are accountable to politicians in legislatures and the executive branch. Public insurance managers are rated by two criteria: savings to taxpayers, and services delivered to patients and their families who vote.

This difference in perspective creates an important difference in the approaches taken by public and private insurers toward reducing claims-related expenditures. Private insurance executives see sick, expensive patients as a drag on earnings. If possible, eliminating those patients from the covered pool would reduce costs, increase shareholder value and maximize profits. Public insurance administrators have no choice but to retain any and all qualifying patients within their covered pool. As a result, their motivation must be to provide as much care as possible for constituents at the lowest possible cost. In real terms, this means that the savings must come from reducing payments to doctors, hospitals, and others who provide healthcare goods and services.

---

§§§ In reality, all the money earmarked for Medicare has already been spent. Medicare taxes are not held in some separate account, but are instead used to purchase U.S. government bonds. The cash is then used to pay for national defense, government salaries, overhead, and so on. Because the federal government is currently running fiscal deficits, there will be no surplus tax revenues available to buy back those bonds. The 2019 milestone simply marks the moment that the country has collectively spent more on Medicare than it has collected in taxes since the program began in 1965.

Minimizing Provider Outlays

Within the scope of limiting payments to providers, public insurers have different options than private carriers, partly as a result of their commitment to serving their constituents, and partly as a result of having the force of the government behind them. Unlike the case for private carriers, limiting access to providers is not an option for conventional Medicare. Medicare and Medicaid payments to providers are already so low that access to care for constituents is already a problem. There are no savings to be derived by steering patients to selected groups of providers under the conventional Medicare programs.

One option that public payers do have is to unilaterally reduce payments for healthcare services rendered to Medicare and Medicaid beneficiaries. In fact, a provision to routinely and automatically reduce provider payments was built into the laws that fund Medicare in 1998. In a bizarre twist, these provider payment reductions have been rescinded by Congress each year since 2003. The rescissions have been necessary because Medicare and Medicaid payments are already so low that they threaten the financial viability of healthcare providers. If these cuts were to actually go through, large numbers of physicians would be forced to drop Medicare and Medicaid patients entirely.

Despite (or perhaps because of) perceived political limitations on overt rationing, governments can and do take advantage of covert rationing. Government efforts to covertly ration care have traditionally tended to rely on complexity and fear rather than manipulating or withholding provider payments.**** There are two main tools that are used in this regard: regulatory complexity and fear of being caught up in a "regulatory speed trap."

Covert Rationing and Public Insurers[24]

Covert rationing efforts undertaken by private insurers are based upon efforts to align the financial and legal interests of physicians with those of insurance companies. In many cases, this places healthcare providers in a "no-win" situation. On one hand, the historical

---

****   Although this might be changing with the growth of so-called "pay-for-performance" programs.

doctor-patient relationship dictates that a physician has the patient's best interests in mind, first and foremost. On the other hand, financial and legal pressures applied by insurers are specifically designed to force doctors into placing the interests of carriers first.

The doctor-patient relationship is built on trust. It says that our doctors can be trusted to give us, as patients, the best possible advice with respect to what would be best for us as individuals and our own health. It should be obvious that asking doctors to consider the interests of insurers over the interests of patients poisons the doctor-patient relationship. However, this is exactly what covert rationing is designed to do.[††††]

Public insurers' covert rationing methods are somewhat different from those in the private sector. Instead of gag clauses, capitation, and sharing pools of leftover treatment money, governments covertly ration through three methods: regulatory complexity, unfunded mandates, and "standardization."

Beginning with just a few public health measures in the 1900s, the number and complexity of the healthcare rules and regulations imposed on healthcare providers has now outgrown their ability to handle them. A wide range of state and federal rules suck up enormous amounts of provider time and overhead. As time is the only inventory clinicians have, more time spent on administration means that less time will be spent on providing services to patients. Less time with patients yields fewer services and lower total bills. The de facto result is a rationing of care.

Another side effect of healthcare's regulatory complexity is fear—fear of inadvertently violating the enormous number of laws and regulations that no one can possibly keep up with and that even fewer can understand. Healthcare providers routinely fear being accused of

---

[††††] Overt rationing does not have this same destructive effect because all the information and considerations are out in the open. Whether the American people care about the doctor-patient relationship and wish to preserve it is beyond the scope of this book. Readers are referred to The *Covert Rationing blog*, *The Road to Hellth blog*, and others.

fraud or some other form of criminality—a situation that Fogoros has labeled the "regulatory speed trap":[25]

1. Over a long period of time, regulators promulgate a confusing array of vague, disparate, poorly worded, obscure, and mutually incompatible rules, regulations, and guidelines.

2. Individuals or companies, having to provide a service despite hard-to-interpret regulations, render their own interpretations (usually with assistance from attorneys, consultants, and the regulators themselves), and act according to those interpretations.

3. By their apparent concurrence with (or at least by their failure to object to) the provider's interpretation of the rules, over time regulators allow de facto standards of behavior to become established.

4. After substantial time passes, regulators reinterpret (or "clarify") the ambiguous regulations in such a way that the de facto standards now constitute grievous violations. They typically apply these clarifications retroactively.

5. Regulators aggressively prosecute the newly felonious service providers.

Any practicing clinician can testify to the fear of running afoul of government rules and regulations in their everyday lives. This fear routinely leads to under-billing for services, avoiding patient discussions of therapies that might be experimental, not covered (or covered poorly) by Medicare, over-documentation, and a general sense of paranoia when it comes to clinical care interactions.

Another important difference between private and public institutions is the government's ability to impose unfunded mandates. Unfunded mandates are requirements that healthcare providers provide additional services at the government's behest, but at no charge to the government. One example is the mandate regarding the provision of language interpreters. In 2000, the Center for Medicare and Medicaid Services promulgated a rule requiring healthcare providers to provide translators for patients with limited English proficiency. The healthcare providers themselves were required to pay for the interpreter services, and neither the patient nor Medicare could be billed for the translation. This immediately led to many financially impossible situations, such as one physician having to pay $237 to an interpreter for a single patient visit. The physician's own Medicaid reimbursement for the visit amounted to only $38.[26]

It's not hard to imagine that this type of economic punishment would eventually force doctors to drop Medicare and Medicaid patients entirely. In 2002, physicians were forced to pay $156.9 million of the $267.6 million spent on medical interpreter services. Facing the prospect of having their constituents lose access to medical services entirely, in 2003 Medicare issued a "guideline" that largely dropped the interpreter provision requirement from Medicare Part B, but retained it for other areas of Medicare and Medicaid.

This type of mandate would be inconceivable for private insurers because physicians would refuse to bear expenses that—in some cases—were greater than their medical collections. In a short period of time, none of their covered patients would be seen by providers. In contrast, the government's monopoly status, huge patient base, and the authority of state gives public insurers broad leeway. It is exceedingly easy for this power to create conditions that are expensive, economically unsustainable, and highly inefficient.

For its part, standardization is widely recognized to be one of the bases of modern industry and industrial production. In many applications, standardization has produced profound efficiencies. The standardization of weights and measures makes it simple and inexpensive to compare quantities and pricing. The standardization of computer communication brought by the Internet has reduced the cost and dramatically increased the speed and quality of shared information. It is only natural to think that the standardization of clinical care might produce enormous efficiencies in the provision of healthcare services. Some standardization has, and will have, many benefits to offer patients, providers, and the healthcare system as a whole. Like anything else, however, standardization can be taken too far.

To discuss the implications of standardization for healthcare, it is once again useful to refer to the observations of Dr. Fogoros. As he points out, "standardization is virtually a synonym for industry."

In industry, standardization is the primary means of optimizing the two essential factors in any industrial process: quality and cost.

Let's state this formally as the Axiom of Industry: *The standardization of any industrial process will improve the outcome and reduce the cost of that process.*

If you had a widget-making factory, you would break your manufacturing process down into discrete, reproducible, repeatable steps and then optimize the procedures and processes necessary to accomplish each step. To further improve the quality of your finished product (or to reduce the cost of producing it), you would re-examine the steps, one by one, seeking opportunities for improvement.... The beauty in such as system is that you only have to make one change—to the process itself—and every widget that comes off the line after you make that change will be improved.

The success of standardization in industry has spawned many efforts to introduce similar processes into medicine. One example is the use of "critical pathways," in which specific medical problems are treated according to a standard set of practices. These are often used for medical procedures such as hip or knee replacement surgery, in which the nature of the problem is elective, the scope of care is limited, and the processes involved are often mechanical. Everything from the admissions process to discharge is precisely scripted, including the questions asked, the medications given, site preparation, the way in which procedures are performed and the timing of physical therapy. Problems that seem to recur are systematically addressed, regardless of whether they are due to human or technical factors. The net result is often a progressive improvement in medical outcomes, fewer complications, shorter hospital stays and lower costs.

To the casual observer, this all seems perfect. What could possibly go wrong with such a logical and measured approach? Shouldn't all healthcare be standardized, and isn't it appropriate that both public and private insurers and government agencies of all types rapidly enforce this approach for every circumstance?

Unfortunately, there are several important problems that limit the utility of standardization in healthcare—and can even transform it into a tool of covert rationing and remarkable inefficiency.

First, as Dr. Fogoros has explained, not all medical processes are suitable for standardization. "The standardization tools of managed care work only when you're dealing with a process that can be broken down into a series of predictable tasks that generate reproducible results. In other words, industrial management tools work best when the process of care is similar to the process of making widgets."

Certain medical procedures clearly meet the criteria for standardization. Elective surgeries for hip and knee replacement have clear causes and mechanical solutions that can be broken down into a series of discrete steps. These procedures can also be reserved for otherwise healthy people admitted under controlled conditions. All these factors serve to minimize expense and potential complications.

The problem is that the vast majority of problems that doctors confront each year don't have these nice, neat characteristics. When a new patient presents to the hospital complaining of shortness of breath, there are dozens of possible causes and courses of action to be considered. These range from heart problems to lung problems; from anemia, to growths, or foreign objects physically obstructing the airways. Correctly diagnosing and managing the problem is a highly customized process in which no two patients are alike, and no standard approach is possible. Attempting to implement standardized approaches under these circumstances is highly complex, and often does far more harm than good. In the real world, "cookbook" medicine is rarely good medicine.

Second, standardization does not always improve outcomes and reduce costs. Why? Because patients are not widgets.

If you're a widget maker, deciding between two manufacturing processes is a matter of economics. Nobody expects you to consider the widget itself. The outcome by which you are judged has nothing to do with how many individual widgets get discarded during the manufacturing process or even the quality of the widgets that pass final inspection. Instead, it's the bottom line: how much profit do you make with relation to whatever level of quality you put into the widget. So the quality of the widget is not necessarily maximized, instead it's optimized, tuned to the optimal quality/cost ratio as determined by the market forces of the day....

If instead of running a widget company you're running an HMO, the calculus is different. You're supposed to be more interested in how things turn out for individual patients than you are in the bottom line. So an expensive process that yields a better clinical outcome is one most people (patients, at least) would expect you to use, even though it only gets you a healthier patient and doesn't make your money back for you. A process that increases patients' mortality rate by five percent is one you should disregard, even if it is substantially cheaper than the alternative. The clinical outcomes experienced by patients—the measure of success you're supposed to be concerned about—might move in the same direction as costs, or in the opposite direction.[27]

It's easy to see that any public insurer is going to be torn between using standardization to minimize cost, and using it to maximize health benefits to constituents. One can't do both.

The third problem with medical standardization by public agencies is a problem that anyone who has ever dealt with government will immediately appreciate: bureaucracy.

Some standards need to last forever. Civilized life requires that we all drive on the same side of the road, use uniform measures and adhere to the same laws. But as we have just seen, many standards that can be applied to healthcare—such as critical pathways, medical guidelines and even formularies—must be living, flexible and ever-changing. Medicine should be based upon science, and that science changes as our knowledge grows over time.

In contrast, standards set by government agencies are notoriously inflexible and slow to change. Even worse, rigid standardization historically tends to stifle innovation and improvement. Guidelines and other standards promulgated by public insurers have the force and power of the state behind them. Violations and variances are, almost by definition, punishable events; otherwise insurers have no way of enforcing desired behavior and discouraging behaviors they wish to avoid. Healthcare providers who wish to maintain their licenses, income, and good standing in their professional communities will instinctively tend to toe the official line no matter what circumstances might present themselves. Second, bureaucracies are themselves notoriously slow to change. Anxious to avoid mistakes, eschewing controversy and reluctant to do anything that might have unforeseeable effects on the cost of care, their standards tend to change at a snail's pace, if at all.

A final problem presented by mandated standards is one of politics: Namely, whose standard do you use? "Dueling" healthcare standards in healthcare are becoming increasingly common as a direct result of the importance being attached to them. As the government begins to pick winners and losers by virtue of its mandates, medical lobbying has begun to twist and distort healthcare, just as it has twisted much of the rest of government policy. Different factions of the medical establishment are now pushing to have their own guidelines accepted as the last word in patient care.[28] Who is better qualified to dictate the standard for the management of attention-deficit hyperactivity disorder (ADHD) in children: pediatricians or psychiatrists? Who should determine what heart studies should be done and how they should be interpreted in ADHD patients about to begin therapy: pediatricians or cardiologists?

In the context of our current discussion, we are most interested in efficiency and the runaway cost of healthcare. Guidelines of care, critical pathways, and other managed care tools are widely seen as ways to reduce costs and increase efficiency. How is it possible for overuse and over-reliance on standards by public insurers to actually damage the *economic* efficiency and effectiveness of our healthcare system?

The answer is that many "standards" in healthcare rapidly make the transition from being flexible guidelines to rigid rules, regulations, and mandates. The existence and proliferation of these rules directly affects the budgets and performance of providers and insurers alike, just as well-intentioned over-regulation can destroy the viability of small businesses of all types. Regulations that add to administrative overhead are inflating the cost of every single healthcare good and service provided in the United States today:

- Standardization measures don't implement themselves. Every guideline, critical path, and formulary requires time and money to create, disseminate, learn, and implement. The more numerous and specific they are, the more time and money is required—often diverting time and resources away from other aspects of patient care.

- Guidelines need to be maintained. Outmoded guidelines not only waste time but money and lives, as better (and sometimes less expensive) methods of care are found. Each time a guideline is altered, each of the costs incurred by its creation, dissemination, education, and implementation is repeated.

- Standards reduce clinical flexibility, and can actually incur additional costs with little or no benefit to the vast majority of people they affect. Part of this is a result of creating guidelines or other standards that simply cannot be practically implemented in the clinical setting, no matter how logical and beneficial they might be in theory.

- Standards have ways of proliferating, often beyond those relatively "widget-like" applications for which they can be most useful. Proliferating standards can overwhelm providers and their support systems.

- Under many circumstances, standards grow to become mandates. These divert resources from other elective uses that might have a much higher return on investment to the patients involved. One example is a formulary that will pay for an older, well-established, but relatively ineffective drug that is part of a treatment "standard," but not for a newer and more effective drug that would be more cost-effective in a given patient.

The bottom line is that public insurers and other government agencies covertly ration healthcare by underpaying for services and creating so much overhead and complexity that administrative overhead simply overwhelms the actual provision of expensive healthcare services. But is covert rationing on the part of government intentional? Is it plausible that regulators and administrators periodically get together to purposely reduce the efficiency of healthcare and intimidate doctors into turning away patients with the riskiest conditions?

It simply doesn't matter. The ultimate impact of these government initiatives is to reduce the amount of time and energy that clinicians can devote to providing actual healthcare services. Whether this occurs as the result of clever forethought or with absolutely no forethought at all, the end result is the same. The only way to stop this type of covert rationing and its adverse economic impact is to rethink any and all government healthcare regulations and limit the ways in which they are used and/or abused.

Government

Our goal in characterizing the four primary players in healthcare (physicians, commercial insurers, government, and patients) is to understand how and where they fit into the healthcare machine. We want to know their role in the overall healthcare system, what motivates them, and how they view the business of healthcare. Knowing this, we can explain the current situation and figure out where it should be possible to go from here.

While this is a relatively straightforward process for providers, insurers, and patients, the situation for government is quite different. The problem is that the roles of government (both state and federal) are so massive, varied, and pervasive that they are hard to even list, let alone fully describe. It is possible to categorize several critical areas of government interest and intervention. The extent to which these interests and activities are coordinated is an important determinant of the efficiency with which governments can meet their various goals.

We've already examined the motives and behaviors of the portions of government represented by public insurers such as Medicare and Medicaid. How do other branches of government exert their own influence and why?

How Government Works with Respect to Healthcare

Only two branches of government really matter for healthcare purposes—the legislative and executive branches. Let's consider them separately.

Legislative Branch Priorities

Elected officials in America have two critical constituencies: the citizens who elect them, and the people and institutions that fund their campaigns. Legislators need them both. One important consequence of this two-pronged dependence is that each legislator will see healthcare differently depending upon exactly who's providing their campaign financing, and the elected official's perceived importance of contributors versus constituents.

From the perspective of constituents, the legislative ideal is to give consumers exactly the level and quality of healthcare they desire, at no cost to the government, patients, or their families. Each legislator's desire to provide goods and services for constituents without immediate cost explains why we currently have high levels of deficit spending. The "we'll give you this now, someone else will pay later" mentality is also a major reason as to why unfunded mandates have become increasingly common, and why the treasured ideal of employer-sponsored healthcare coverage is so completely ingrained in legislative thinking.

Of course, there is an inherent problem with providing free healthcare legislatively: in the long run, it's economically unsustainable. Healthcare providers simply can't work for free, and deficit spending simply forces future generations to pay for today's healthcare at inflated prices. These constraints mean that it's not entirely possible for legislators to work the unfettered will of patients and their families—or at least not in the long run. For legislators, the needs of constituents have to be balanced against the needs of contributors and the economic carrying capacity of healthcare providers.

Given the balance between providing unlimited services to constituents at no cost and having to maintain the financial viability of providing healthcare services, one would think that every legislator should desperately want to increase the efficiency of the healthcare system as a whole. This is not necessarily the case.

For one thing, change is hard. Change makes most people uncomfortable, including voters, contributors, and the legislators themselves. Change contains an element of risk and the unknown, even if that change is ultimately necessary. For another, a more efficient healthcare system might require voters to be more responsible for many aspects of their own healthcare, including assuming some degree of personal financial responsibility. Most voters would prefer to avoid that responsibility. Finally, legislators must also consider the interests of their financial contributors, who might not want a more efficient system.

It might seem hard to believe that there are companies that would want inefficiency in healthcare, but this is clearly the case. There are even companies whose entire businesses depend upon it. Of the hundreds of billions of healthcare dollars spent annually on administration and overhead, the vast majority is spent on goods and services provided by companies in the private sector. These companies provide everything from the software used to look for reasons to reject insurance claims, to the people creating and monitoring clinical care guidelines, to the billers who are needed to make sense of unbelievably complex insurance payment and coding rules. All those companies will protect their revenue with any means at their disposal. Much of the time, that means lobbying and political contributions.

There are many examples. When Congress created the Medicare Part D drug benefit in 2003, it took the unusual step of expressly forbidding Medicare from negotiating prices with pharmaceutical manufacturers. An attempt to repeal this law and allow Medicare to negotiate for lower drug prices failed again in 2007, with lobbying by pharmaceutical companies getting much of the credit.[29] A second example is America's inability to pass meaningful tort reform. Fear of medical malpractice lawsuits is a continual drag on the practice of medicine. Each year billions of dollars are spent on surplus testing, documentation, procedures, and insurance whose sole function is to protect clinicians from lawsuits. From 1995 through 2001, tort reform measures that would have limited non-economic damages passed the House six times, yet only once did a similar bill reach the Senate, where it was defeated 56–44 in 1995. The primary reason is effective lobbying by the Association of Trial Lawyers of America, who oppose even minor revisions in tort reform laws "because it is a bread-and-butter issue for them."[30]

Legislators can also be afraid of what's ultimately best for their own constituents. As we'll see, creating and maintaining an efficient healthcare system inevitably involves forcing healthcare consumers to take responsibilities that they might not want. These include putting their own money into purchasing decisions, taking responsibility for learning about the healthcare system, and learning about and consistently treating their own medical conditions. Regardless of how necessary they are, it's easy to understand why many of these responsibilities might be unpopular, especially for healthcare consumers who might be used to playing a passive role in their own care.

Executive Branch Priorities

Compared to legislators, members of the executive branches of government represent a more diverse and complex group. These include elected officials, such as the president and governors, political appointees, and career civil servants. Each of these is subject to a separate set of incentives and constraints.

Elected officials in any administration are very similar to legislators with respect to constituents, political concerns, and the need to balance the interests of contributors with those of voters. Whether their policies converge or diverge from those of other elected officials or legislators depends, of course, upon the degree to which they share contributors and similar voting populations. Political appointees to state and federal agencies are, for all practical purposes, the agents of elected officials. Their motives, incentives, and concerns are identical to those of whoever appointed them. The real difference occurs when we consider the case of career civil servants.

Career civil servants are not directly accountable to voters and don't have to think about fundraising. As a consequence, the motives and measures of success are profoundly different for those who operate our funding and regulatory agencies. Instead of votes, contributions, and policies, civil servants who fund and regulate healthcare have three basic concerns:

- A desire to protect the public's health, welfare, and finances
- A suspicion that providers can't be trusted to do the right thing
- Benefits derived from the exercise of power and control

The good work undertaken by government officials to protect the health, welfare, and finances of patients and the public is one of the most valuable services we derive as taxpayers. In an ideal world, it would be obvious how this is best achieved and all programs, rules, and regulations would be structured accordingly. Unfortunately, in an industry as complex and dynamic as healthcare, this is rarely the case. Even the scorecard that should be used to measure success can be difficult to clearly delineate. What does it really mean to protect the health and welfare of Americans? Does this mean that everything medically possible should be done for each individual American, even if this is financially unrealistic? Or does it mean that healthcare should be optimized for all Americans based upon the total financial resources available? Is length of life a better measure of health than quality of life? If we have a limited budget, how do we decide how to ration or otherwise allocate the resources that are available? If we're to protect the financial well-being of the public, are we talking about minimizing the amount spent by individual patients, or by state or federal governments?

Given the ambiguities involved and the honest differences of opinion that they foster, it's easy to see how each career employee of the executive branch might have a different idea of what it means to protect health, welfare, and spending. Unless an extremely clear set of definitions, goals, and objectives are established and then backed by political leadership over time, the many possible directions the healthcare system can or should take will tend to be cancelled out over time. The sheer number of people working in different directions simultaneously will see to that. In practice, this means that the real impact of civil servants on healthcare will inevitably be governed by the two remaining concerns—suspicion of providers and a desire to expand and protect the influence of their own section of government.

Regulators and Providers: Friend or Foe?

Except for the military and the Veterans Administration, the U.S. government does not directly provide healthcare services. Medicare and Medicaid are payers, not providers. As a result, nearly all the interactions that the executive branch of government has with the healthcare system are in the form of rules and regulations. These dictate what hospitals, clinics, doctors, and others are required to do and are prohibited from doing. For better or worse, the overall relationship between state and federal regulatory agencies and healthcare entities is an adversarial one.

One of critical functions of any government is to protect its citizens. Many of the healthcare-related rules, regulations, and processes developed by the executive branch are intended to fulfill this function. However, a need to *protect* the public implies that some or all healthcare providers and institutions will *harm* the public if given the opportunity. This harm can be a result of either action or inaction, but there is no question that most employees of the executive branch see their relationship with providers in an adversarial light.

Adversity is understandable and even constructive in many regulatory settings. Regulatory initiatives typically begin in response to violations of the public trust. For example, the Environmental Protection Agency was created after it became clear that unfettered pollution was harming millions of people and animals. Unfortunately, the situation becomes more complex when regulating an industry whose entire premise is based upon making people well.

As one might expect, the initial abuses leading to the regulation of healthcare providers were the result of deliberate falsehood and criminal deception. The presence of unqualified, abusive, incapacitated, or criminal doctors created a need for licensure and monitoring. When the federal government began paying for the delivery of healthcare services, a few unscrupulous hospitals, clinics, and others chose to game the system by billing for services that were never delivered. This naturally led to efforts by state and federal governments to identify and curtail "waste, fraud, and abuse" in healthcare.

The problem is that, once kindled, suspicion is hard to contain. Once government agencies begin to carefully scrutinize every aspect of healthcare delivery, it becomes routine to see misdeeds everywhere. Under intense public scrutiny, civil servants have to wonder if they themselves be held responsible if they miss any opportunity to regulate more "safety" into the healthcare system.

The most important result of this adversarial relationship has been the headlong regulation of all aspects of clinical behavior. Many rules have created operating inefficiencies and overhead that far outweighs any practical benefit that they might have. From the perspective of a civil servant, over-regulation is a far safer alternative than under-regulation.

Government As a Growth Industry Within the Healthcare System

Everyone who is a part of the healthcare machine is ultimately concerned about their jobs. Frankly, it's part of the problem that makes the healthcare machine difficult to fix.

Regulation itself generates jobs, power, and access to money. Although there is no readily available data on the number of state and federal jobs directly tied to healthcare regulation, there is no question that they have expanded dramatically over the past two decades. Federal rules and statutes—CLIA, HIPAA, the False Claims Act, and proposed regulations to require electronic prescribing, electronic medical records, and adherence to clinical guidelines have become part of everyday life for healthcare providers.[††††] States have added many rules of their own. Each rule and regulation requires that the number of offices and employees in the executive branches of government be increased to answer questions, promulgate opinions, assess compliance and enforce the rules. The net result is that all these rules and regulations turn large portions of the executive branch itself into a major part of the healthcare system, with its own substantial budget, workforce, and momentum for growth. In this context, it is easy to see that reducing regulations—and therefore regulatory overhead—cannot be a popular topic among the regulators themselves. Given the way the civil service works and the difficulty of cutting state and federal programs, administrative overhead associated with government regulation is among the hardest to eliminate. To do so requires a concerted, conscious, and active effort on the part of elected officials and political appointees.

[††††] CLIA stands for the Clinical Laboratory Improvement Amendment, which directly affects approximately 200,000 clinical offices and dedicated clinical laboratories. HIPAA stands for the Health Insurance Portability and Accountability Act, which affects every medical provider and facility in the United States.

Patients

The role of patients in the healthcare system is unique. Not only does the healthcare machine exist entirely for their benefit, but every patient and family is also an essential component of the machine itself. In one respect, this means that each patient should have a vested interest in seeing the entire system function smoothly and efficiently. An efficient healthcare machine is in the best position to provide the best possible care to the greatest number of patients at the lowest possible cost. On the other hand, when illness does strike, each patient also has an incentive to obtain the most possible care at the lowest possible personal cost.

We are all schizophrenic with respect to our own healthcare motives and incentives. We each want the system as a whole to be lean, mean, and low-cost; but when we are sick, we would like unlimited access to the best possible care without regard to cost. Because patients are voters, consumers, and a key component in the occurrence and treatment of their own diseases, their opinions, thoughts, and actions largely determine what's possible and impossible when it comes to optimizing healthcare.

For our purposes, three elements of patient behavior define their actions in the healthcare machine:

- **Economic behavior.** What will patients and their families pay for or refuse to pay for? What influences their economic behavior with respect to healthcare? How does this potentially affect the quantity of healthcare goods and services that they consume?

- **Health behavior.** What will patients and their families do, or not do, on their own behalf to maximize the efficiency and effectiveness of the health care services that they receive?

- **Political behavior.** What determines whether patients and their families will reward or punish elected officials based upon decisions those officials make regarding the structure and function of the healthcare system?

Economic Behavior

In most respects, the American public sees healthcare as a good or service like any other. People want it, they will use more if it is readily available, and—other things equal—they will pay for it if it is not available for free. A great deal of time and effort has been spent trying to figure out what people believe healthcare services are worth by trying to measure their "willingness to pay." Willingness to pay (WTP) research is primarily used as an attempt to describe the *value* of a specific healthcare intervention to the public, as opposed to its *cost*. This type of study is especially useful when looking at goods or services that do not currently have a free-market price.

WTP studies are done by describing a healthcare intervention and then asking people if they would themselves be willing to pay various amounts for the good or service if necessary. Although it's entirely possible that study subjects might not be telling the truth, such measurements can be useful. For example, a WTP study in Canada, Spain, and Denmark demonstrated that, although citizens of those countries did not enjoy waiting an average of four to six months for government-sponsored cataract surgery, only about one-third of them were willing to pay $500 to have their procedure done immediately.[31]

More usefully, WTP analysis makes it possible to gauge many factors that might be difficult to tease out by looking at market data alone. For example, would patients be willing to pay more to see a doctor who had more experience with a particular surgery, or who has been in practice longer than another? Would they be willing to pay more to see a doctor who was open at more convenient hours? What about a doctor who specialized in the treatment of their specific medical condition? None of these questions can be readily answered by looking at the existing U.S. healthcare marketplace because clinicians are not currently paid according to their experience, availability, or special expertise.

Although Americans are willing to pay for healthcare services if they have to, they clearly have a strong aversion to doing so. Unlike virtually any other goods or services provided by the private sector, a majority of Americans now believe that it is someone else's responsibility to see that this good is provided to them. In recent nationwide surveys, 60% or more of those polled believe that it is the government's responsibility to provide healthcare for those who do not have it, 56% believe that all employers should provide health insurance to every employee, and 70% believe that the federal government should pay for catastrophic coverage.[32]

Of the approximately 50 million uninsured people in the United States, about two million are uninsured not because they cannot afford or obtain health insurance, but because they choose not to.[33] Many of these are younger people who have few existing medical problems and who do not believe that health insurance is a worthwhile investment. In many respects, this attitude is completely rational. To use our analogy of health insurance as a casino-type bet, the expected payoff for relatively young, healthy people is simply too small to be worth the gamble.

That said, what do we know about how asking patients to pay for care influences their behavior, and how can we use this information to improve the efficiency of the healthcare machine itself?

Patient Economic Behavior As a Way to Control Resource Utilization

The broader market for healthcare services will never truly be consumer-driven. Unlike food, clothing, and entertainment, medical goods and services are often too diverse, complex, and specialized to be navigated without the assistance of doctors and other healthcare providers. On the other hand, there is no question that we collectively drive a great deal of our own demand for medical services. Each of us decides individually when pain, discomfort, functionality, or appearance becomes intolerable. At some point, we decide that enough is enough and begin consuming medical goods and services. At each stage in the process, and with or without the advice of clinicians, we decide whether to consume the next set of tests, drugs, or therapies and incur the next set of expenses.

All efficient markets balance the desire for consumption with some level of economic pain. Providing anything free of charge—whether it is food, water, electricity, or medical care—leads to over-utilization of the resources offered. Not only do we have to feel physically uncomfortable to see that doctor or take that pill—but we have to be uncomfortable enough to be willing to part with money that could be spent on food, clothing, shelter, or entertainment as a check on pulling the medical spending "trigger" too quickly.

These economic restraints usually take the form of medical co-payments for services. These include insurance deductibles, flat co-pays (such as $15 per visit or $5 per prescription), and co-insurance payments that are a percentage of the total bill (such as 20% of any charges incurred after the deductible amount is met.) Patient co-payments are an incredibly important part of a properly functioning healthcare machine. Failing to charge consumers the right amount for healthcare will produce poor and inefficient results, many of which exist in the present system. Charging too little causes patients to pull the trigger too soon, wasting medical resources with trivial complaints. Charging too much prevents people from securing care in a timely fashion, and produces more severe and expensive episodes of illness than would otherwise be the case. Indeed, as a practical matter the proper use of patient co-payments is the *only* way in which we can use the invisible hand of the free market to correctly balance the use of healthcare services.

Co-payments do work, and properly structured co-pays lubricate the wheels of the healthcare machine. Much of what we know about the utility and effect of co-pays comes from the forward-thinking RAND Health Insurance Experiment (HIE) performed in the 1970s. In this experiment, the HIE randomly assigned 2,000 non-elderly families to health plans that were deliberately structured with widely different co-insurance and maximum out-of-pocket dollar expenditure (MDE) amounts. Five types of co-insurance arrangements were used:

- Free care (with no co-insurance requirement)
- 25% co-insurance (that is, patients were liable for 25% of any medical bills)
- 50% co-insurance
- 95% co-insurance
- A flat deductible of $150 per person, or $450 per family (equivalent to $600 and $1,800 in 2005 dollars, respectively), that applied to *outpatient care only*.

For all plans with co-insurance, the maximum that patients were required to pay was varied between 5%, 10%, and 15% of income, with a maximum liability for any family of $1,000 (which is equivalent to $4,000 in 2005 dollars). All medical services were covered and the families were followed for up to five years after enrollment.

The important lessons learned from this research are as follows:[34]

1. **The co-insurance rate has a clear and statistically significant impact on medical utilization and expenditures.** Patient co-payments reduce the likelihood that patients will both obtain medical care and be admitted to a hospital or other inpatient facility.

   Increasing the co-insurance rate from zero to 25% in the HIE reduced the probability of patients seeking and receiving medical care from 86.8% to 78.8%. Increasing the co-insurance rate to 50% brought this down to 77.2%, while the 95% co-insurance rate reduced the probability of care to 67.7%. Asking patients to pay the flat deductible amount was equivalent to a co-insurance rate of between 50% and 95%. A similar result was seen in the probability of hospitalization.

   Not only does the probability of any medical encounter fall with use of co-pays, but the absolute number of face-to-face visits and hospitalizations per capita fall as well. A 50% coinsurance rate reduces the number of face-to-face visits by more than 33%, and the number of inpatient admissions by more than 28%.

   These reductions in medical visits and hospitalizations had a tangible effect on medical spending. Total per capita medical expenditures for the group with no co-payments was $749, while a co-insurance rate of 25% reduced this by more than 15% to $634. Oddly enough, having only a flat deductible for outpatient services alone reduced total expenditures even more to $608—almost a 19% difference. The HIE also demonstrated that the restraining effect of co-payments applies to a wide range of healthcare goods and services, including physician visits, dental care, prescriptions, and more.

   The bottom line is that American consumers—like their healthcare providers—do what they're given financial incentives to do. Wisely crafted co-payment programs can have a considerable impact on all types of medical resource use and expenditures.

2. **Consumer co-payments don't have any impact on the health of the average person, although those with pre-existing conditions and specific low-income populations probably need special consideration when crafting co-payment programs.** One of the visionary elements of the HIE was that it followed a substantial number of useful health indicators, including mortality, vital signs, health practices, and monitoring critical indicators for a wide range of organ systems. One of the important findings was that for the vast majority of participants, the use of co-payments had essentially no adverse impact on health when compared to care provided free. There was no significant difference between the free care and co-payment groups across any of the medical indices measured.

The situation was somewhat different for those with severe chronic diseases. Those in high-risk groups, such as patients with high blood pressure and diabetes, are significantly more likely to forego medications, have unfavorable disease-related parameters such as blood pressure and blood sugar levels, and have worse clinical outcomes if co-payment requirements are imposed.[35,36] There is also some concern about the potential impact of co-pays on poor children and preventive care.[37] This suggests that the exact design and structure of consumer co-payments might best be crafted to work as a scalpel rather than an ax to optimize care and minimize expenditures simultaneously.

Health Behavior

Americans are clearly ambivalent about whether individuals are responsible for their own health behaviors and should be held responsible when it comes to changing them or paying for them. According to a recent survey, fully 82% of the U.S. population believes that they alone are responsible for their health. They also agree that lifestyle decisions such as smoking and exercise have a direct impact on healthcare costs. However, 44% of these same people believe that they should not bear any part of the responsibility for paying for their own healthcare.[38]

A different survey portrays a slightly different story—one in which some self-inflicted health insults are deemed to be acceptable, and others less acceptable:

- A 46% to 37% plurality of adults say we should not require people with unhealthy lifestyles to pay higher premiums than people with healthy lifestyles, and a virtually identical 47% to 36% plurality feel that we should not require people with unhealthy lifestyles to pay higher deductibles or co-payments for their medical care.

- However, when questions were asked about different types of health risk, attitudes vary depending upon which risk is involved. Majorities believe that smokers should pay more than nonsmokers (by 58% to 31%) and that people who do not wear seat belts should pay more than people who do wear seat belts (by 53% to 33%). On the other hand, majorities do not believe that people who are overweight (by 52% to 27%) or people who do not exercise regularly (by 52% to 27%) should pay more."[39]

There are two important lessons that we can learn from these studies and others like them with respect to consumer attitudes toward health behavior in the United States:

1. **Americans are as fiercely independent about their perceived "right" to engage in lawful but unhealthy behaviors as they are about their constitutionally delineated rights to free speech and peaceable assembly.** Measures that threaten financial, legal, or civil penalties for personal behaviors that increase health risk will be opposed roughly in proportion to the fraction of the population that engages in that behavior.

   On the other hand, it may well be the case that financial or other *incentives* can be used to encourage and enforce appropriate health behaviors without running afoul of the public's "perceived rights" objections. Studies have shown that paying people to stop smoking is significantly more effective in recruiting smokers into smoking cessation programs and getting them to complete the course than equivalent programs without payment.[40]

2. **Education itself might be the best tool that we have available with respect to improving the personal health behaviors of Americans.** The link between education and known risk factors such as smoking, obesity, lack of exercise, and a number of other behaviors is unambiguous, strong, and well documented. It might be far more effective in the long run to invest in education than to purchase healthcare services. (Furthermore, investment in education is truly an investment in human capital, unlike the outright consumption of medical services.) From a "healthcare machine" perspective, education has the effect of reducing friction between patient and providers, and increasing the probable effectiveness of most medical interventions.

Political Behavior

Even in modern society, there are still a few fears and desires that can be considered primal. Fear of starvation is one. Fear of becoming destitute is a second. Fear of illness or injury without recourse to treatment, (or the specter of destitution if treatment is to be had) is a third.

Patients, prospective patients, and their families—that is to say, *voters*—are more desperate for a simple, efficient, rational, and affordable healthcare system now than at any time in our history. Without question, part of the reason is fear. Since 2000, the cost of employment-based health insurance premiums has risen at four times the general rate of inflation as a whole. The average premium for a family of four is currently more than $12,000 per year, or about one-fifth the median family income of $67,000. Historically, it is nearly impossible to buy medical insurance at any price if you have a pre-existing condition. Each dip in the economy, every group of faltering small businesses, and every corporate reorganization means that thousands more Americans will lose their insurance coverage. Each year, fewer and fewer have faith that they will readily get it back.

So what do voters want? Based upon polling data, election results, news reports, and common sense, it's relatively simple.

1. **Americans believe that the U.S. healthcare system is in a state of crisis, and they want fundamental change.** Figure 6.6 is from Dr. Lawrence Jacobs's comparison of public opinion in 2008 as compared with the early 1990s.[41]

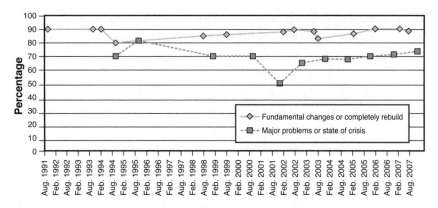

Negative Public Attitudes toward the U.S. Health Care System, 1991-2007.
Data for "fundamental changes or completely rebuild" are from surveys conducted by CBS News and the *New York Times*, which asked, "Which of the following three statements comes closest to expressing your overall view of the health care system in the United States?" The data points reflect the percentage of respondents who answered either "There are some good things in our health care system, but fundamental changes are needed" or "Our health care system has so much wrong with it that we need to completely rebuild it." Data for "major problems or state or crisis" are from surveys conducted by Gallup, which asked, "Which of these statements do you think best describes the U.S. health care system today?" These data points reflect the number of respondents who answered either "It has major problems" or "It is in a state of crisis."

From: Jacobs LR. "1994 All Over Again? Public Opinion and Health Care." *New England Journal of Medicine.* May 1, 2008. 358(18):1881-3.

Figure 6.6   Public Opinion with Respect to the Need to Reform the U.S. Healthcare System

The vast majority of Americans want change, while the belief that the current system is fatally flawed has been growing steadily since 2001. The combination of a high rate of healthcare inflation with economic uncertainly has generated fear, and people tend to vote as their fears dictate. In the case of healthcare, the current fear will not subside until: (1) health insurance coverage becomes more consistent and certain; (2) healthcare costs are brought under control; and (3) there is reason to believe that governments and businesses will be able to sustain the rate of healthcare expenditures required over the long term.

2. **Oddly enough, most voters want continuity along with their healthcare revolution.** As mentioned previously and shown in Figure 6.7, most Americans clearly see their own situation as being more manageable than the situation facing the country as a whole.

The key observation that explains these findings is that individual families are deeply concerned that any system created by politicians to "fix" things will make their own situation worse.

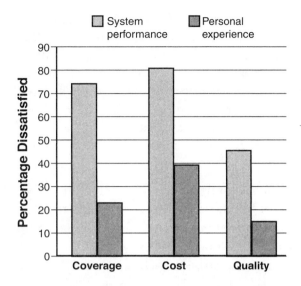

Dissatisfaction with National and Personal Experiences with Health Care. Data are from Gallup polls conducted in November 2006 and November 2007. For coverage and quality, the data represent the percentage of respondents who said these aspects of care were "only fair" or "poor"; for cost, the data represent the percentage who indicated they were "dissatisfied."

From: Jacobs LR. "1994 All Over Again? Public Opinion and Health Care." *New England Journal of Medicine.* May 1, 2008. 358(18):1881-3.

Figure 6.7 Disparities Between Public and Personal Perceptions of Healthcare Delivery in the United States

Immediately after the election of President Obama, 60% of voters surveyed said that they believed that it was the "government's responsibility to ensure that everyone in the United States has adequate healthcare."[42] However, since 2001, when voters were asked whether they would prefer to "replace the current healthcare system with a new government-run healthcare system, or maintain the current system based mostly on private health insurance," voters have consistently said that they would prefer to maintain the current system by an average plurality of 55% to 37%, with 8% unsure.[43]

Jacobs found that:

Although a 2006 poll conducted by ABC News, the Kaiser Family Foundation, and *USA Today* found that 56% of Americans favored government health insurance over the current system, support eroded when these respondents were told that such a program could mean reduced access to some medical treatments (64% of initial supporters became opponents), limits on the choice of doctors (49% became opponents), increased waiting times (40% opposed), and greater cost sharing (36% opposed). Whether these downsides would actually materialize and, even if they did, how much the resulting system would differ from current managed-care practices are matters of debate. The point is that public perceptions appear fragile and susceptible to change.[44]

What we can gather from these polls is that the public really wants the benefits of a healthcare system that utilizes private (that is, non-government-run), providers and practices, but in a setting in which payment for health coverage is not subject to the vicissitudes of personal income and employment. These desired benefits specifically include

- The ability to personally choose one's physician, hospital, and other healthcare providers
- Minimized waiting times
- Access to the widest possible variety of treatments
- Opportunities to reduce cost sharing
- Assured access to health insurance for individuals and families wherever and whenever needed, without regard to pre-existing medical conditions

It is also worth noting what is *not* high on the priority lists of American voters, despite being cited continuously as high priorities by the media and politicians: improving the quality of care and reducing overall healthcare spending nationwide. These results are illustrated in Figure 6.8.

While improving the quality of care, reducing medical errors, and reducing overall spending are all useful and desirable goals, they are simply not the highest priorities for the majority of Americans. Most of them seem to believe that the quality of the care currently available is "good enough," and that the current level of total healthcare spending is manageable as long their personal share of it does not increase.

Which ONE of the following health care issues is most important in your vote for president? (among registered voters in October 2008)

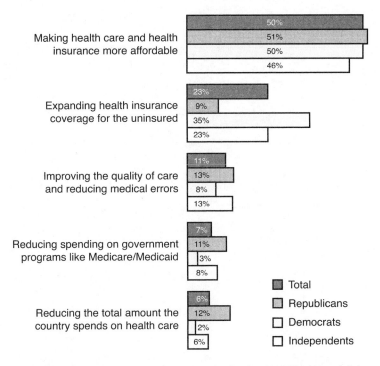

From: *Kaiser Health Tracking Poll—Election 2008.* Issue 11, October 2008. The Henry J. Kaiser Family Foundation.[45]

Figure 6.8 Voter Perspectives on Healthcare Costs, October 2008

Fear is a call to action, but it is hardly a plan. Voters might know the results they desire, but there is no public consensus whatever as to how to bring it about, even after the passage of the 2010 healthcare "reform" law. Fortunately, this situation has some advantages when it comes to repairing the country's currently inefficient healthcare machine. Because the public still does not have any specific strategy in mind, there is actually a greater opportunity for politicians to be creative when it comes to solutions. Many of the measures that we will discuss subsequently as ways of improving efficiency have never been generally proposed or even discussed. While this means that they will require public explanation and education, they are also unlikely to be rejected out of hand as "more of the same old tired ideas."

Part II

Why the Machine Is Breaking Down

"Machines built by human beings will function correctly if we provide them with a very specific environment. But if that environment is changed, they won't function at all."

—*Ralph Merkle*

7

Too Many Parts

"Simplicity is the ultimate sophistication."
—*Leonardo da Vinci*

One of the guiding principles for building efficient and stable systems is moving toward simplicity at every opportunity. No engineer would ever build a machine that has more parts than required—especially moving parts that create wear and tear on other parts of the machine simply by virtue of their existence. Given this, why does our healthcare system have so many parts? Which parts are the most troublesome, and how can they be removed—or if they can't be removed, how might we mitigate any adverse impact that they might create?

Why So Many Parts?

No one actually planned the U.S. healthcare system. Rather than being laid out and constructed in an orderly fashion, it was left to grow organically over time. From the perspective of healthcare providers, American healthcare literally began as a cottage industry. Cottages were the places where doctors visited and services were performed. Fees for services rendered were universally paid in cash or in-kind goods and services. Science began to have a substantial impact on the type of medical services that could be rendered beginning only about 100 years ago. Because not much could be done for the average patient and the costs that could be incurred by an individual were relatively limited, there wasn't much need for health insurance. This had changed dramatically by the 1930s and 40s, when

scientific advances, the invention of antibiotics, and progress in surgery brought about by World War II meant that far more could be
done than ever before. The cost of these new treatments sparked the
need for health insurance—that is, a financial cushion to help pay the
bills and prevent medically induced poverty in the event of unfore-
seen illnesses and hospitalization.

When the need for health insurance developed, workplaces started
to supply it as something of a historical accident. Wages and prices were
strictly controlled by the federal government during the Second World
War, but health benefits were not. As a result, Kaiser Shipyards and
other companies began to offer health benefits as a means of attracting
employees. President Truman attempted to develop a national health
insurance program beginning with coverage for children and mothers.
This would be followed by a national health insurance plan that was
open to, but strictly optional for, all Americans. Citizens would pay premiums into the plan just as they would for private insurance.

The Truman proposals were rapidly attacked by the combination
of the American Medical Association and Republican legislators. The
predominant concern was that national health insurance would
become equivalent to "socialized medicine"—a situation in which
doctors would be told where and when to work and how to practice
medicine by politicians and bureaucrats. In response, the AMA
launched the most expensive lobbying effort in American history up
to that time. In 1949 it spent $1.5 million to defeat the Truman initia-
tive.[1] It did not help that organized labor—the main public advocate
of Truman's healthcare legislation at the time—chose to antagonize
the public with a series of disruptive and unpopular strikes.[2] Blurred
lines between a federally run national health insurance program,
socialism, and communism effectively killed any prospect of a uniform national health insurance program through the remainder of the
20th century and up to the end of the Bush administration in 2008.

With the science of medicine and treatment options expanding
rapidly into the 1950s, 60s, and 70s, private insurers expanded in
both numbers and size to meet the growing need for health coverage.
The number of Americans insured by the nonprofit Blue Cross/Blue
Shield companies rose from 28 million in 1945, to more than 61 million in 1953. By the mid-1960s, there were more than 700 companies

selling health insurance. Federal and state governments stepped back into the picture with the development of the Medicare and Medicaid programs for the elderly and disabled, and the poor, respectively. Even these were not strictly government-run efforts, however. Rather than develop its own administrative processes for Medicare, the federal government decided to rely upon private insurers to process and pay Medicare claims. The role of private insurers in the administration of patients covered by Medicare expanded dramatically with the institution of the Medicare+Choice program in 1997, and the Medicare Advantage program that replaced it in 2003. Under these programs, the federal government basically agreed to use Medicare to pay for enrollment in health plans that were completely created and administered by private insurers. Nearly one-quarter of Medicare recipients (totaling 10.1 million people) were enrolled in these private plans by early 2008. More than one-third of Medicare recipients are enrolled in Medicare Advantage in several states, including California, Oregon, Arizona, Pennsylvania, Colorado, and Nevada.

In 2010, President Obama and a Democratic majority in Congress altered the landscape of American healthcare yet again by passing a sweeping piece of legislation they called the "Patient Protection and Affordable Care Act" (PPACA). This legislation significantly expanded the power of the federal government over the private health insurance market, mandated broad expansions of insurance coverage (largely through expanding Medicaid), and created more than 120 new boards, commissions, and federal programs. Most importantly, it gave the federal government broad new powers to establish medical guidelines of care and to regulate the terms under which healthcare providers will be paid for their work. Putting so much unchecked power in the hands of government regulators (the vast majority of whom have little or no medical training) has profound implications, and is a cause for serious concern among healthcare providers. Although many aspects of the law do not come into effect for years, it will clearly result in a substantial tilt away from free-market forces, along with literally thousands of new healthcare regulations. These will affect all parts of the healthcare system, beginning with private insurers.

Thousands of Insurers

The single most important characteristic of private health insurance plans today is that there are a lot of them. According to the Insurance Information Institute, there were 1,257 life/health insurers in the United States in 2006.[3] Each company is different with respect to size, geographic region in which it does business, the populations that it will insure, the conditions under which it will grant coverage and how and when it will pay claims. In addition, any given health insurer might have dozens or even hundreds of unique health plans, each of which has its own provisions with respect to deductibles, co-payments and co-insurance, referrals, pharmaceutical coverage, and a host of other factors. Simple math suggests that 1,200 insurers each sponsoring ten different plans will force providers to cope with more than 12,000 different possible combinations of billing, clinical, and administrative provisions when seeing and treating patients. Getting any one of these wrong could easily result in delayed or denied payment for services rendered. Adding to the complication is the fact that nearly one-third of patients change their health plans every year. Whenever they do, they change all of the forms, deductibles, referrals, test and treatment vendors that their healthcare providers must use. From the physician perspective, each new insurance company and each new plan represents yet another gear they need to engage to deliver and pay for an episode of care.

Variability in insurance plans even extends to "single payer" programs such as Medicare. Medicare's coverage of newer therapies is inconsistent from state to state because Medicare benefits themselves are administered by private insurers. A recently reported example is payment for "CyberKnife"—a new but fast-growing radiation treatment for prostate cancer. CyberKnife's primary advantage is the reduction of treatment time for patients. It reduces treatment time from eight weeks (for conventional prostate cancer radiation) to five days. And it's less expensive than many comparable treatment alternatives that are covered. Nevertheless, as of December 2008, Medicare's regional private insurance company administrators had decided to pay for the procedure in 33 states, but not in 17 others.[4] Imagine the confusion and frustration that you or any other patient would feel upon having the same federally funded Medicare insurance as an acquaintance in a neighboring town, but completely different insurance coverage for treatment of the same clinical condition. Millions of patients and healthcare providers must deal with this administrative nightmare each and every day.

As important as it is, the tangled web of public and private insurance is just one set of excessive gears in the healthcare machine. The past 20 years have seen enormous growth in both governmental and quasi-governmental agencies whose stated goals are to "certify" that the quality of the healthcare goods and services meets some arbitrary standard. The sheer number of state, federal, and private agencies and requirements that providers must contend with has become truly staggering.

Medical Licensure

It is particularly strange that the provision of healthcare services is licensed and regulated on a state-by-state basis without reciprocity. Human anatomy, physiology, pathology, and psychology are all exactly the same in every part of the nation, just as the rules of the road are the same for every driver and the laws of gravity and aerodynamics are the same for every pilot. But while American drivers are licensed by their state to drive anywhere, and airplane pilots are nationally tested and licensed by the Federal Aviation Administration, American doctors, nurses, pharmacists, and other healthcare providers are licensed and regulated separately by each individual state.

State-by-state licensure comes at a considerable cost. Because there are so many of them and they are all different, state-specific medical licenses are time-consuming and inconvenient to obtain, and expensive to keep. The hurdles for obtaining a medical license vary from state to state. Some states require that providers take a state-specific test to be granted licensure, despite the fact that all physicians trained in the United States have attended medical schools that are nationally inspected and accredited; have taken (and passed) nationally recognized medical board examinations; and have attended nationally accredited internship, residency, and fellowship programs. Virtually every state requires its own fingerprinting, criminal background checks, submission of credentials, and other records. Some states require the submission of personal references and even in-person interviews with members of the board of medical examiners, regardless of how many times an applicant has already been licensed by other states. Other states conduct their own separate program of testing in addition to nationally accredited board examinations.*

In 2008 the Milbank Memorial Fund and two federations of medical boards published a study of 56 medical licensure and regulatory boards in the United States and Canada in an attempt to provide an overview of the current system. Their primary findings:[5]

- Although each authority examines competency at initial licensure, there is substantial variation in what authorities do to monitor competence at re-licensure.

- Although each authority accords high priority to investigating complaints about physicians' behavior, and each imposes sanctions, the scope and methods of programs of remediation vary significantly.

- Many authorities have programs to improve quality, and many others report that they would like to begin such programs. But a considerable number of authorities report that they are not interested in or lack the capacity to offer new programs to improve quality or do not have the statutory authority to do so.

The cost and consequences of state-by-state licensure for healthcare providers add up. A physician who wants to be licensed in all 50 states plus the District of Columbia will have to spend more than $26,000 in application fees alone—not including the cost of her time or supporting documentation. The time cost for an older physician with lots of history to document can be almost as much as the application fees themselves.† Patients are losers in this system.

---

* Perhaps one of the oddest aspects of the current system is just how similar the applications and licensing processes are in each state, despite the fact that none of them are the same. If one compares the medical license applications from any two states, there will be at least 95% overlap in the questions, document requests, and necessary qualifications. The result is that clinicians are more or less equally qualified everywhere in the United States—just as they would be if a national or reciprocal state licensure program were in place—but with 50 times the overhead.

† If we assume four hours of work per application at an opportunity cost of $100 per hour to prepare, submit, and follow-up; 51 medical license applications would cost $20,400 to prepare. This does not include the cost of travel and interviews, or the licensing fees themselves.

Non-reciprocal state-based licensure directly reduces the mobility and flexibility of healthcare services. The vast majority of clinicians are licensed in only one or two states. By increasing the cost associated with moving to new locations, the flow of clinicians to areas of need is impaired. New "telemedicine" services made possible by progress in communications have been slow to catch on, largely as a result of state-centric licensing and reimbursement practices.

Professional Credentialing

Fragmentation of quality control for medical professionals goes well beyond state licensure. There are few better examples than a process that is ubiquitous but little known to the general public. It's called credentialing.

Credentialing (and re-credentialing) is a process in which all health plans, hospitals, surgery centers, and other medical facilities require doctors and other health professionals to submit their professional histories and credentials for review and verification. Each organization seeking these credentials—*and there are tens of thousands in the United States*—asks its providers to submit all of this information annually or semi-annually. Not just the incremental changes that might have occurred since last time; they want *everything* submitted all over again. As is the case for state licensure, the questions asked and answered in the credentialing process are almost exactly the same for each of the thousands of organizations asking for the information. These include personal demographics, business demographics, education and training, (including all institutions and training including the month and year of attendance, complete addresses, and names of program directors), all hospital affiliations, (past, present, and pending), work and practice history, professional certificates and license numbers, (including all state licenses currently held or held in the past), professional liability insurance information, and a host of other documents and details far too numerous to list.

With more than a million providers and each credentialing document requiring anywhere from a few minutes to many hours of time to prepare and submit, the annual credentialing burden in the United States runs into many millions of person hours and billions of dollars per year for providers alone. This burden is almost certainly matched by that of the thousands of health plans, hospitals, and other credentialing organizations that must process, store, and sometimes verify the information provided. Some efforts have been made to reduce this burden by taking the simple and obvious step of asking providers to submit this information once, and only once, to a centralized data repository. Unfortunately, nearly all these initiatives have been either half-hearted or ill-conceived. Several states have developed "standardized" credentialing forms, but they are, of course, all different.

The process and progression of credentialing is just another milestone in a long history of government, health plans, and the American public asking for ever more assurance that their healthcare professionals are trained, competent, and not frauds or imposters. To the objective observer and those outside the United States, the need for public reassurance has come to resemble paranoia at best, and institutionally incited panic at worst. Still more pieces of expensive administrative overhead have been added by the requirements surrounding healthcare provider "certification."

Gilding the Lily: The Multi-Billion Dollar Certification Industry

Prior to the 20th century, there was little standardization in the training of American healthcare providers. This changed in 1912 with the formation of the Federation of State Medical Boards (FSMB). The FSMB voluntarily began to base accreditation of medical schools on the highest academic standards. By the 1930s, the results of standardization were being felt in the form of fewer, but more arduous, scientific, standardized, and better endowed medical schools. Medical training became much harder, but also far more expensive as result. Fewer physicians could be trained with any given level of resources, and the cost of attending medical school in the United States rose markedly. In 1915, the National Board of Medical Examiners was founded to create a nationwide, voluntary examination to be taken after medical school to qualify graduates for medical licensure. These national board examinations were meant to assure state licensing boards and the public that their physicians were well trained and qualified to practice medicine by the time of their entry into the medical marketplace.

By the 1940s, additional training had been formalized into clinical internships and residencies, in which recent medical graduates could begin to specialize and practice their skills while still under the supervision of experienced physicians. Under these programs, the medical school graduate would work in one or more residency programs for an additional one to seven years of supervised instruction; the total number depended upon their field of specialization. At the end of residency, the hospital residency program would certify that the trainees had received adequate experience and achieved sufficient skills to be experts in their respective fields.

This worked well until guilds of specialists began to create their own specialty boards. In 1933, four specialty boards (for Ophthalmology, Otolaryngology, Dermatology, and Obstetrics and Gynecology) established what would later become the American Board of Medical Specialties (ABMS). Specialty boards were formed partly to maintain a monopoly on the training and supply of physicians (as only specialty boards could sanction training programs), and partly as a way of generating revenue from the process of certification. In the process, they have become big businesses. There are now 200 certifying medical boards *in addition to* ABMS members, while the 24 ABMS member boards oversee 37 general specialty and 94 sub-specialty certificates. Virtually every aspect of the practice of medicine now carries a specialty requirement, and board certification is a common requirement to be eligible for health plan membership and insurance reimbursement.

With the formation of specialty boards, the quantity of mandatory medical training increased, as did the number of moving parts and the cost to both healthcare providers and the health system itself. Specialty boards began to require providers to take rigorous one-time specialty examinations in addition to years of residency and fellowship training to become "board certified." These were accompanied by requirements for ongoing "continuing medical education" (CME).

This state of affairs lasted until approximately the 1970s, when many specialty boards realized that requiring periodic recertification of providers would boost both specialty board revenues and their claims of insisting that only the best quality of care be provided to

American consumers. Board certification was quickly redesigned to expire every six to ten years, and providers were required to take (and pay for) board-sanctioned training and recertification courses to maintain certified status. Once again, clinicians were forced to forego practice, take up pens, and open their wallets to reassure payers and the public of their medical competence.

The pursuit of continuing medical "excellence" is now a huge business unto itself. CME in the United States consumes more than $3 billion annually, and 35 states now mandate that physicians obtain a specific amount of CME annually to retain their medical licenses. Unfortunately, it's not at all clear that any of this is currently worth the cost and loss of system efficiency that it entails. Many studies have been undertaken regarding CME and "continuing professional development" (as it is known in the United Kingdom). Under certain circumstances, CME can clearly have a positive impact. One review of CME studies found that 70% were able to document a change in physician performance as a result of the intervention, while almost half (48%) were able to produce a change in healthcare outcomes.[6]

However, not all CME is created equal, and much of what is currently being required in the United States has little or no effect on improving the health of patients. In 2004, researchers at Duke University found that state-mandated CME appeared to have little or no impact on improving outcomes for heart attack patients, or in increasing the use of therapies proven effective by clinical trials.[7] Another recent study that looked at CME research over a 20-year period concluded that: "Even though the most effective CME techniques have been proven, use of least-effective ones predominates. Such use of ineffective CME likely reduces patient care quality and raises costs for all, the worst of both worlds."[8]

The final stages in the evolution of professional vetting is now taking shape within the halls of medical boards, Congress, and government administrative buildings. Still unsatisfied that American clinicians are being trained, tested, and monitored enough, both the healthcare industrial establishment and state and federal governments have initiated new programs designed to up the ante once again. For all practical purposes, all clinicians will soon be quizzed, examined, and monitored virtually all the time. The assumption, of course, is that the new and continuous cost of all these new steps would be worth whatever benefits might be derived—even though measuring actual benefit of raising the bar is *not* part of the plan. The strategy for the future is perhaps best described by the ABMS itself:[9]

> The ABMS Maintenance of Certification (ABMS MOC) is the most recent advance in the board certification process. Like medicine and science, certification is evolving. Originally, the physician passed a rigorous one-time exam and was considered board certified for life. Beginning in the 1970s, individual ABMS Member Boards began implementing time-limited certification; physicians had to pass the certification test every six to 10 years (depending on the board) to become recertified. But even this requirement seemed insufficient given the increasing pace of research and technological advances and the drive to improve patient care and safety.
>
> The ABMS Maintenance of Certification program replaces recertification and assures that the physician is committed to lifelong learning and competency in a specialty and/or subspecialty *by requiring ongoing measurement* of six core competencies:
>
> - Patient Care
> - Medical Knowledge
> - Practice-based Learning and Improvement
> - Interpersonal and Communications Skills
> - Professionalism
> - Systems-based Practice

It's easy to see that most providers will be spending more time studying, being tested, and documenting their activities and performance, as opposed to taking care of patients. Meanwhile, the federal government has taken a different approach to "quality" that promises to add many parts to the system. It is based upon using provider payments as a means of introducing new complexity, monitoring programs, and technology hurdles into the process of care. These will be discussed at greater length in the next chapter.

There is no question that quality is important. All of us have the right to expect that the system that provides our healthcare will be knowledgeable, well-trained, competent, and exercise an appropriate level of care in the conduct of its operations. But when we ask whether we're being adequately protected, at some point it's important that we take "yes" for an answer. Any regulatory initiative eventually reaches a point of diminishing returns. Once that point is reached, the net cost of regulation rapidly increases, efficiency falls, and services begin to suffer.

The extensive fragmentation and profusion of parts in American healthcare has finally become dangerous to our health as well as our economy. The machine must be simplified.

8

Sand in the Gears

"The insurance industry communicates through codes and check-off boxes. If there's no check-off box for you, you don't exist."

—*Jack Anderson*

Anyone who has ever had an opportunity to work with motors or machinery knows the impact that foreign bodies such as sand or grit can have on gears and other moving parts. Not only do they make it hard for the gears to turn, but the damage they cause is expensive to repair. If the foreign objects are big enough, they can stop things entirely. A "wrench in the works" is the definitive example of a large foreign body, and symbolizes the externally introduced problem that makes it nearly impossible for a mechanical system to engage in productive activity.

For the purposes of our discussion, we can define "sand," "grit," or any other foreign body gumming up the healthcare system as discrete, substantial, and externally introduced impediments to the normal process of providing healthcare services. "Sand" in the system incurs a major economic cost, and greatly reduces the efficiency of providers and patient-provider interactions.

Pricing and Billing for Medical Services

No single aspect of the healthcare system is more inefficient, destructive, and harmful to the average American than the way in which medical services are currently priced, billed, and paid for. It is hard to conceive of a system that is harder to understand, more difficult to adhere to, more expensive to implement and operate, and less conducive to the public welfare than the one that currently burdens patients and providers alike. Even explaining how the process works is a challenge.

In most businesses, how a vendor gets paid will have little or no impact on the overall efficiency of the industry at large. This is not the case when it comes to physicians and other healthcare industry providers. Instead, the complex and byzantine ways in which bills are generated and paid has forced the creation of a new and completely separate industry with no purpose except to broker the process. Its impact goes well beyond the typical concept of "administrative overhead."

Our discussions regarding billing and physician payment will often use Medicare as the prototypical example. Medicare is the "800-pound gorilla" in the world of health insurance. The vast majority of private health insurance companies follow Medicare's terminology, methodology, and example with respect to billing and payment.

How American Clinicians Get Paid

Healthcare providers provide a wide range of goods and services to millions of patients every day. Unlike the vast majority of professionals who are allowed to bill by the hour, doctors are paid according to an extremely complex system based upon something called "CPT codes." CPT coding is an attempt to pre-establish a single payment for anything that a doctor might do.

This was not always the case. From Medicare's inception until 1992, clinicians were paid on the basis of something called the "customary, prevailing, and reasonable charges" (CPR). The CPR system was originally designed to pay clinicians based upon their actual fees. This pricing mechanism was similar to one called the "usual, customary, and reasonable" payment system that was already being used by private insurers when Medicare was created in 1965. The retention of a "customary" charge system was part of the promise that President

Johnson made in exchange for the AMA dropping its opposition to the creation of Medicare.[1] Like so many of the promises government has made with respect to healthcare, this one was soon broken.

The CPR system was relatively simple in both concept and execution. "Customary charges" were defined as the median of a given physician's charges over a given period of time. The "prevailing charge" was defined as being the 90th percentile of customary charges of all similar physicians in a specific geographic area. Using these first two definitions as a base, Medicare would then pay the lowest of: (1) the actual charge; (2) the physician's customary charge; or (3) the prevailing charge for a given service. The lowest of these three was known as the "reasonable charge."[2]

The CPR approach had some advantages, as well as some qualities that were felt to be disadvantages by those in charge of Medicare. It was easy to understand and relatively simple to implement. This kept administration costs relatively low. Another advantage was that the price of medical services could, at least theoretically, change in conjunction with the supply and demand for services and the cost of doing business. If physicians were scarce in the Southwest and population growth and building costs in that area were rising quickly, physicians could gradually raise their fees and the increases would eventually be reflected in the reimbursement that they would receive. One problem was that the private insurance companies that administered Medicare benefits on behalf of the government often used different methods of calculating the various elements of the CPR. This led to purely administrative differences in the way charges were calculated and paid in different regions, even if the charges submitted were otherwise identical. Needless to say, this seemed unfair to a large number of the affected providers.

The demise of the CPR system occurred over a roughly ten-year period beginning in the mid-1970s . Medical costs were not immune to the high inflation of the late 1970s, and it rapidly became apparent that Medicare costs were increasing faster than the program's creators had expected. In response, Medicare began to unilaterally dictate prices. It started by gradually reducing the prevailing charges rate from the 90th to the 75th percentile. A wage and price freeze was then imposed on physician services. The freeze was lifted in 1976, but prevailing charges remained artificially limited by a growing number of payment regulations. The net effect was to lock the country into the pattern of medical reimbursement that prevailed in the early 1970s. Increasing costs that might occur in a given region were no longer covered by a gradual increase in the CPR for that region. Charges began to fall behind the cost of providing care, and inequities in payments for identical services delivered in different areas began to increase. A new set of CPR changes was implemented by Medicare in the 1980s, along with a new price freeze, limits on the physicians charges, and rollbacks in payments that Medicare deemed to be "excessive." In short order the relatively simple, understandable, and adaptable CPR was rendered complex, impossible to understand, unpredictable, and failed to reflect anything related to market-based changes in the cost of providing care.

Having essentially destroyed the logical basis of the CPR with regulatory tweaking that had little or nothing to do with economic reality, Medicare began to look for an alternative payment mechanism. As a national insurer, Medicare wanted three elements in its new payment mechanism: (1) a "standardized" way of calculating an approved amount to pay any given provider; (2) something that might be perceived as having a rational basis in science or economics; and (3) a system in which the reimbursement rate could be unilaterally controlled by Medicare over time. Government regulators were only willing to consider three alternatives:

1. Using an HMO-type model to "capitate" physician payments. Capitation involves paying a fixed amount to a physician or other healthcare provider for every patient that they accept into their practice. They are then obligated to provide any services that patient might need from them and cannot charge an additional fee for doing so. Although it can work for clinicians in primary care, this system is difficult to implement for specialists who might only see a given patient once.

2. Using a system of lump-sum payment for services that is based upon a given patient's diagnosis. This is similar to the "diagnosis related group" (DRG) methodology that is used to determine payment for hospitals and other inpatient facilities.

3. Inventing a brand new concept called a "relative value scale" (RVS), with which providers would be paid a fixed amount for any particular service, regardless of what each provider might otherwise charge. This would be a profound change, because under the RVS system, Medicare would essentially be establishing a federally dictated price for healthcare services. That price would have nothing to do with the economic realities of medical practice or market conditions.

In 1985, Congress ordered the U.S. Department of Health and Human Services (HHS) to develop a "resource-based relative value scale" (RBRVS), in which the value of healthcare services provided to Medicare could be assigned different values based upon a measure of the clinical resources required to perform them. The ultimate result of this effort was the Medicare RBRVS. In 1989, Congress passed the Omnibus Budget Reconciliation Act of 1989, which ordered Medicare to implement an RBRVS payment system beginning on January 1, 1992.

To reiterate, the Medicare RBRVS is an attempt to "scientifically" determine a fixed value for each of the thousands of different services provided by clinicians—fully recognizing that these values are established by a government-mandated formula rather than the marketplace. Medicare, TRICARE, about 85% of private insurance, and 69% of Medicaid programs currently use this system as their method of determining provider payments. Let's look at this system more closely, first by looking at how it was supposed to work, and then by looking at what it's actually become.

Initially, the Medicare RBRVS system was supposed to work like this:

• Every single service that can be provided by clinicians—from the lowliest throat culture to the most complex brain surgery—is ranked by the amount of "work" that it is supposed to entail. (Generically, these services are known as "procedures," regardless of whether they consist of simply talking to a patient or performing a complex surgery.) In theory, provider "work" consists of four key elements:

- The time required to perform the service
- The technical skill and physical effort involved
- Mental effort and judgment
- Psychological stress associated with the provider's concern about doing harm to the patient

In most cases, the majority of the provider payment would be made as a result of the work component of the payment equation. This component is generally known as the "relative value component for physician work," or RVU_{work}. Each RVU for any task is supposed to be objectively and quantifiably comparable to that calculated for any other task. A task with an RVU of 2.0 should be twice as hard (based upon the four elements listed previously) as a task with an RVU of 1.0. And, of course, a task with an RVU of 30.0 will be fifteen times harder than the task rated at 2.0.

- Because the work component does not take into account whatever overhead might be required to maintain the clinician's practice, a second "practice expense" component is added into the equation. This is generally known as the RVU_{PE}. Because all RVUs are relative to one another, a practice with an RVU_{PE} of 2.0 will have twice the overhead of one with an RVU_{PE} of 1.0.

- A third component of cost taken into account is medical malpractice liability expense. This varies considerably from procedure to procedure; doing spine surgery is obviously much riskier than treating a cold. This component of relative value is known as the "RVU for professional liability insurance," or RVU_{PLI}.

- Before being added together, each RVU component would then be multiplied by a factor that takes into account the differing costs of doing business in different parts of the country. Medicare currently identifies 89 distinct regions for this purpose. This factor is known as the Geographic Practice Cost Index (GPCI), and each region has three different GPCIs—one for each of the three RVU cost components.

- Finally, the total of the geographically adjusted RVUs are multiplied by a monetary conversion factor (CF) to convert the whole total relative value of each given procedure into a fixed dollar amount. In mid-2010, the Medicare conversion factor was $36.0791.

Let's illustrate with the example shown in Table 8.1. These calculations are based upon performing an office visit of moderate difficulty (CPT code 99213) on a person who is an established patient of a practice in Portland, Oregon:

$$RVU_{Total} = (RVU_{work} \times GPCI_{work}) + (RVU_{PE} \times GPCI_{PE}) + (RVU_{PLI} \times GPCI_{PLI})$$

$$Payment = RVU_{Total} \times CF$$

TABLE 8.1   Some Factors Involved in a Medicare Payment Calculation[3]

	RVUs	GPCIs (Oregon)
Physician Work	0.97	1.002
Practice Expense	0.88	1.015
Prof. Liability Ins.	0.05	0.472
2010 Conversion Factor	$36.0791	

$$RVU_{Total} = (0.97 \times 1.002) + (0.88 \times 1.015) + (0.05 \times 0.472) = 1.889$$

$$Payment = 1.889 \times \$36.0791 = \$68.14$$

The RBRVS system was created by Harvard academics, approved by the AMA, placed into law by Congress and implemented by Medicare as a "scientific" answer to the question of how much any given healthcare service should cost. With credentials like this, what could go wrong? The answer is just about everything.

From Theory to Practice—The Failure of RBRVS

From the very beginning, the RBRVS system was (and is) a purely artificial creation. That doesn't necessarily make it bad, but it does make it something that would never exist without the need for thousands of seemingly arbitrary decisions and an underpinning of politics. Unfortunately, politics and economic efficiency rarely, (if ever) peacefully co-exist.

The first challenge with the relative value scale for physician work appeared almost immediately. Because no such scale exists in nature, how could the relative difficulty of completely different procedures be compared? There are nearly 15,000 different procedures, each with its own CPT code. Who decides how many throat swabs a brain surgery is worth, and how each of them relates to the number of endoscopies? Attempts to directly measure the theoretical underpinning of physician work in the real world—the time, complexity, skill, physical effort, and stress involved—were unsuccessful. As a result, Medicare contracted for a series of surveys in which a selected group of doctors came up with their own estimates. In the first stage physicians within a given specialty were asked to personally rate the amount of "work" for each of the procedures that they might perform. In the second stage, panels of participants were asked to come up with procedures in one specialty that they felt represented an equivalent amount of work as procedures in a different specialty. After these comparisons were made, all the procedures between specialties were placed in a single giant global ranking. After some final tweaking, the RBRVS was then legislated into existence as Medicare's payment basis. From that point on, the problems that grew from its adoption were inevitable.

The first and perhaps most important problem with the RBRVS system is its very premise. The system was created to calculate and reimburse *cost* rather than *value*. What's the difference? The difference is that value is the monetary equivalent that a market would place upon a service if it had a chance to do so. Value takes into account all sorts of factors that cost cannot, such as the relative supply and demand for different services, the worth that the recipients of the services themselves place upon what they receive, the relative skills, personality and experience of the providers themselves, and the relative importance of the various different services to society as a whole. Value is something that is measured automatically by the invisible hand of the marketplace, and is very difficult (and often impossible) to calculate in any other way. Value is a unique quality that allows goods and services to be prioritized efficiently, and is the only thing that can really allows millions of suppliers and customers to dynamically balance supply and demand.

Second, no matter how rigorous the survey process might be, it is inherently a process of subjective assessment and political negotiation. This is perhaps best illustrated by the way in which relative values are determined for new procedures and re-evaluated for existing ones.

Medicare does not itself create or maintain CPT codes and the relative value scales. Instead, this lucrative franchise is owned and operated by the American Medical Association. Despite the fact that it represents only one out of every five American physicians, the AMA has a virtually monopoly on recommending CPT and RVU additions or changes to Medicare. RVU updates are created by the AMA's AMA/Specialty Society Relative Value Scale Update Committee (RUC). As the AMA itself says on its website:

> The AMA established a process in the course of its activities to develop relative values for new or revised CPT codes. This process was established in the course of the AMA's normal activities and as a basis for exercising its First Amendment right to petition the Federal Government as part of its research and data collection activities, for monitoring economic trends and in connection and related to the CPT development process. In addition, CMS [i.e., Medicare] is mandated to make appropriate adjustments to the new RBRVS in response to the Omnibus Budget Reconciliation Act of 1989 to account for changes in medical practice coding and new data and procedures. The purpose of the RUC process is to provide recommendations to CMS for use in annual updates to the new Medicare RVS.[4]

The RUC has 29 members, with 23 of these nominated by various major national medical specialty societies and approved by the AMA. Three seats rotate on a two-year basis, with two reserved for an internal medicine subspecialty and one for any other specialty. The RUC Chair, the Co-Chair of the RUC Health Care Professionals Advisory Committee Review Board, and representatives of the AMA, American Osteopathic Association, the Chair of the Practice Expense Review Committee and CPT Editorial Panel hold the remaining six seats. Each RUC member has one vote. The total composition of the committee is shown in Table 8.2.

This approach might seem reasonable until one realizes that representation on the committee does not reflect the number of doctors in each field, numbers of patients using each class of specialty services, the quantity of services rendered, or even the total value of services. As some have aptly observed, this arrangement is rather like having the Senate without the House of Representatives in the U.S. Congress. A large number of important medical specialties are unrepresented, including endocrinologists (who are experts in diabetes, one of the most common, expensive, and fastest-growing diseases in America), oncology (the second-leading cause of death in the United States), or pulmonary medicine (specialists in the treatment of asthma and smoking-related chronic lung disease).

TABLE 8.2   Makeup of the AMA Relative Value Scale Update Committee in 2008

Chair (Appointed by the AMA Board of Trustees)	
American Medical Association Representative	
CPT Editorial Panel Representative	
American Osteopathic Association Representative	
Health Care Professionals Advisory Committee Representative	
Practice Expense Review Committee Representatives	
Anesthesiology	Ophthalmology
Cardiology	Orthopaedic Surgery
Dermatology	Otolaryngology
Emergency Medicine	Pathology
Family Medicine	Pediatric Surgery*
Gastroenterology*	Pediatrics
General Surgery	Plastic Surgery
Geriatric Medicine*	Psychiatry
Internal Medicine	Radiology
Neurology	Thoracic Surgery
Neurosurgery	Urology
Obstetrics/Gynecology	

Source: American Medical Association
* (Indicates rotating seat)

In practice this has meant that the real relative value of various procedures is determined not by any patient need or market-based economic consideration, but instead by what amounts to political horse trading by RUC members. This might work if there weren't so much at stake, but the flow of healthcare dollars inevitably determines the makeup of the health services that we have available. It determines how many providers we have of each type, both by directing new trainees into higher paying specialties and by discouraging the retention of providers in those that pay less. Primary care specialties—those that see the most patients, take care of the vast majority of the elderly, patients with multiple conditions, and chronic diseases—have only about 5 votes out of 23. One result has been that specialties with lots of relatively expensive procedures dominate the negotiations when RVUs are put up for consideration. This is natural and predictable given the financial interests of the parties involved, but it's no way to operate an efficient healthcare system.

The RVU differentials between various procedures are often understandably large. A complex brain aneurysm repair (to fix a defective and potentially fatal blood vessel in the brain) has an assigned relative physician work value that is 50 times higher than that of moderately complex office visit. However, in other cases, one would be hard pressed to understand how the comparisons are made. Here's just one 2010 example:

- A return patient visit of moderate complexity (CPT code 99213) is the most common type of patient encounter in any given year. The assigned Medicare RVU_{work} is 0.92, and the visit would normally be expected to take about 30 minutes. At a medical office in Portland, Oregon in 2010, this would be reimbursed at a rate of $57.09.

- Removing two skin tags (benign fleshy outcroppings of skin) by snipping them with a pair of scissors (CPT code 11200) will usually take less than five minutes. Medicare rates the Medicare RVU_{work} as being 0.79, and will pay $68.99.

Both of these procedures require skill and expertise, but it's unlikely that market forces—were they allowed to function—would rate a moderately complex 30-minute office visit and a 5-minute skin tag removal as being nearly equivalent in terms of work, and then pay more for the shorter procedure. This indifference to the market has had a profound effect on the availability and composition of the clinical workforce.

The third and perhaps most serious problem with the CPT code system of payment is its mind-boggling complexity. Perhaps more than any other factor, the complexity of medical billing, the opportunities that it provides for potential accusations of provider abuse and fraud, and the sheer time and cost of abiding by its resulting regulations has created a mood of complete despair in the healthcare provider community. The same system leaves patients clueless about what they owe and why, even while it wastes billions of dollars annually.

The essence of the CPT code system is that it pays for procedures (that is, *things*), rather than *time*. In 2009, the CPT system defined 14,592 procedures in its Physician Fee Schedule. The system's complexity therefore arises as a result of three elements. The first is simply picking the right procedure code. The second is defining exactly what has to be done by providers to qualify their efforts as a billable procedure. The second is a whole set of additional rules that determine whether Medicare will pay for each procedure, based upon a welter of additional documentation, codes, code modifiers, and other conditions that must be satisfied before payment can take place. The combination of these requirements creates a world in which paperwork grows exponentially, ambiguity rules, suspicion abounds, and our healthcare dollars are spent paying hundreds of thousands of people whose only job is to wrestle with claims.

Many surgical procedures are relatively simple to define. When a doctor removes an appendix using an open abdominal incision and there are no other complicating factors, there is little need to describe the procedure beyond a relatively simple code—in this case, a CPT code 44950. However, so-called "cognitive" procedures—patient visits in which the patient presents with a complaint that the doctor has to diagnose and manage by taking a medical history and doing a physical exam—are different. These are billed using something called "Evaluation and Management" (E&M) codes.

Some patients are more complicated than others, and so some E&M visits are harder than others. Because Medicare pays clinicians according to what they actually did rather than the time it took them, it means that each E&M CPT code is a function of many different tasks performed during that visit. Medicare ranks each of these visits on a difficulty scale of 1 to 5, with Level 1 visits being the most cursory (and lowest paid), and Level 5 visits being the most complex (and highest paid). To determine which level of visit they will be allowed to bill for, Medicare requires doctors to record exactly what they did with and for each patient during each visit. The key areas of the visit that need to be documented are the length and comprehensiveness of the patient history taken, the comprehensiveness of the physical examination, and the complexity of the medical decision making involved. Based upon this information, the provider is then supposed to consult a variety of tables and requirements and identify the proper CPT code to be used in billing. Medicare has published a 27-page reference manual that describes this process (to go along with the 48-page definition of the rules themselves), including exactly how much history, physician examination, and medical data has to be reviewed (and how) in order to qualify for any specific level of visit.

It's pretty much impossible to understand what we're talking about without an example. Here is one straight from the front lines of American healthcare. The *Happy Hospitalist* is a weblog that is published by a doctor who takes care of patients in the hospital full-time.[5] In this piece, he outlines the E&M coding process in his own practice:

> I will attempt to walk you through an example of the payment system, and how it relates to relative value units (RVUs) and ultimately how that affects physician reimbursement. The number of codes is massive. For all imaginable procedures, encounters, surgeries. Any possible health care interaction.
>
> Hospitalist medicine is limited (thank goodness) in the types of codes we use. So I only have to remember a few.
>
> 95% of my billing is based on about 20 codes:
>
> 3 admit codes (99221, 99222, 99223)
>
> 3 follow up codes (99231, 99232, 99233)
>
> 2 critical care codes (99291, 99292)
>
> 5 consult codes (99251–99255)
>
> 5 observation codes (99218–99220, 99217)
>
> 2 discharge codes (99238, 99239)
>
> ...These 20 codes determine my very financial existence. Medicare says so.

Every single [detail] has a code. There are even codes for codes: modifiers for codes, add-on codes, disallowed codes, V-codes, M-codes. It is endless...

And you have to get it just right. Every time. Or you don't get paid, or you are accused of "fraud." It is an impossible feat. The process of taking care of patients has turned into a game of documentation...

Let me walk you through a 99223, the code for the highest level admit for inpatient care...

There is no actual law, as I understand it, on the Medicare books that definitely defines the requirement for the codes. There are [two] generally accepted "guidelines"; 1995 and 1997 guidelines. Even the guidelines...are different, and you are allowed to pick and chose from both... This is my understanding of what Medicare requires to bill a level 3 admit, a 99223. You must have every one of them or it's considered "fraud," "overbilling," "waste"...pick your favorite *New York Times* tag line:

1) HPI: The history of present illness. It requires 4 elements (for example, character, onset, location, duration, what makes it better or worse, associated signs and symptoms) or the status of three chronic medical conditions.

2) PMH: Past medical history. It requires complete personal medical (medical problems, allergies, medications), family medical, and social (do you smoke or shoot up cocaine?) histories.

3) ROS: Review of [body] systems. A 12-point review in which ask you every possible question in the book, separated by organ system.

4) A complete physical exam of all organ systems.

5) A high complexity of "medical decision making." This one is great. It is broken down into 3 areas and you must have 2 of 3 components as follows:

(Pull out your calculator...)

5a) Diagnosis. 4 points required to get high complexity. Self-limiting, established stable, established worsening, new problems with no work up planned and new problems with work up planned are each defined a different point value and some have maximum additive amounts, and some don't. Add up the points to get your total.

5b) Data. 4 points required for high complexity. Different components are worth different amounts on such things as reviewing or ordering labs, reviewing x-rays or EKGs yourself, discussing things with other "health care providers" (which I have never been able to define), reviewing radiology or nuclear medicine, obtaining old records, etc. Each element is worth a different number of points. Add up the points to get your total.

5c) "Concepts" I call this the basket. Predefined, sometimes vague medical processes that are defined as "high risk." Such as close monitoring of drug levels, de-escalating care, severe exacerbations with threat to "life or limb" changes in neuro-logical status.

You must have 2 out of 3 components of high risk for medical decision making for #5...

This is ONE PATIENT. ONE ENCOUNTER. ONE DAY... And I have to do this for every single patient I see. Every day. Over 2,500 times a year. And I am expected to get it right 100% of the time.

I am good at coding because I took the time to learn the rules. I know exactly what I'm doing. But it took me along time; I would say a good 2 years to really grasp it. And that is with a limited arsenal of 20 codes. Imagine trying to do this with an outpatient arsenal of hundreds of codes. This is the state of medicine.

I carry around cards that help me. There are multi-billion dol-lar industries that do coding, submission, denials, software. It is built on the premise of Medicare's rules, not medical care. And it adds billions to the system in lost productivity...

The Happy Hospitalist isn't kidding when he says that failure to do all this properly or document each and every step *every* time places our healthcare practitioners in legal peril. A basic premise of the current CPT-based system is that "if you didn't document it, it didn't happen." This means that a doctor might do every part of a his-tory and physical exam, but if she fails to write down every required element for a certain level of billing, the claim is considered to be unsupported. Federal law defines billing for a higher visit than your records support as a form of health care fraud, punishable by repayment, a $10,000 fine and/or imprisonment of up to five years for *each instance*.[6] In the back of the mind of nearly every physician in the United States is the thought that a few confused chart notes or billing calculations, an aggressive prosecutor, and ambiguities in the way Medicare laws and regulations can be interpreted can ruin him for life. There are whole sections of the federal government devoted to ferreting out and prosecuting "Medicare fraud," beginning with the Office of the Inspector General of the Department of Health and Human Services. Although real criminal activity and health insurance fraud does exist, this is not what we're talking about here. It is absurd that the penalties for getting lost in the "coding jungle" should be as severe as those for setting up fake clinics and billing for services rendered on imaginary patients.

Those of us who are not in the business of actually delivering healthcare services might have a hard time understanding this paranoia. Supposedly, no one is going to be prosecuted simply for following the rules. But what if the rules are so complicated and vague that they really can't be followed by half of the provider workforce? And if doctors are really worried, why don't they just code at a lower level than they think they deserve?

As it turns out, they do. A study of more than 200 family practice doctors specifically looked at the question of how well providers could follow the E&M coding rules in practice. These doctors—who knew that they were being studied—were each sent complete records for six hypothetical patient visits. They were then asked to code each visit to the best of their ability based on the information provided for each visit. Two-thirds of the doctors had received at least six hours of coding training, and they were allowed to use any reference materials they wished to help with the process. Their findings were compared with those of a panel of five expert coders, who reviewed the same materials. The results were absurd. Even the coding experts did not agree with each other, so a majority opinion was taken as the "real" code for each case. When compared with the expert coders' results, the physicians matched the expert coding only 52% of the time for established patients, and 17% of the time for new patients. Almost one-third of the cases involving established patients were under-coded. *Fewer than one-third of the doctors were able to code half of the cases correctly.*

In 2001, then Secretary of Health and Human Services Tommy Thompson convened a blue ribbon Advisory Committee on Regulatory Reform to recommend specific ways in which federal regulations could be eliminated, reduced, or modified to improve the efficiency and effectiveness of the healthcare industry. As Secretary Thompson said at one committee meeting: "When we flood doctors and hospitals with excessive paperwork, patients suffer the consequences." In 2002, the committee published a 198-page final report titled "Bringing Common Sense to Health Care Regulation."[7] It contained more than 250 specific recommendations, most of which have yet to be implemented. Recommendation #99 was brief and to the point: "CMS should eliminate the Evaluation & Management Documentation Guidelines."

A decade later it still hasn't happened.

The medical claim coding process is actually far more complex than we've depicted, although to go into significantly more depth is probably not a good use of our time. Suffice it to say that, in addition to the difficulty of E&M coding, a host of other factors go into creating a fully coded "clean claim." Procedure codes have to match correctly with diagnosis codes. Special code modifiers must be used in many cases. And most importantly, doctors have to take enormous amounts of time to specifically document large amounts of information that is largely irrelevant except for coding purposes. Indeed, the clinical function of the medical chart has largely become subordinate to its legal alter ego. Figure 8.1 is an increasingly typical example.

From the perspective of a clinician actually trying to take care of a patient, a good medical note should be brief, to the point, and concentrate on pertinent positive and negative findings. What we see instead is a computer-generated note that highlights the "cover your ass" mentality created by Medicare billing and medical malpractice considerations. Like an increasing number of notes, it's a product of an electronic medical record program. The doctor selects various parts of the exam from a multiple-choice menu. The software then automatically generates the note with all the requisite legalese. Every single observation

PHYSICAL EXAM:
   CONSTITUTIONAL:
      VITAL SIGNS:
         VS-TEMPERATURE: 98.2°f Tympanic
         VS-PULSE: 76 Right Radial, Regular
         VS-BLOOD PRESSURE: 138/86 Right Arm Sitting
         VS-RESPIRATION: 16
         VS-HEIGHT: 5ft5in
         VS-WEIGHT: 202lbs
         BMI: 33.61

APPEARANCE: I personally examined the patient's general appearance (state of dress, state of grooming, state of conduct, affect).

GENERAL EXAMINATION: I personally examined each of the following: left and right carotid pulses (intensity, symmetry, bruit); lungs (adventitious sounds); heart (rhythm, rate); left and right radial pulses (intensity, symmetry); extremities (edema).

MENTAL STATUS: I personally examined each the following: level of alertness; orientation (self, circumstance, location, time); memory (recent and remote); language fluency; fund of knowledge.

CRANIAL NERVES: I personally examined each of the following:
   II: Visual acuity (hand-held card); left and right optic fundi (disk sharpness, arterial and venous appearance); left and right conjunctiva (appearance); left and right pupils (symmetry, shape, reaction to light and accommodation)
   III/IV/VI: left and right ocular movements (ocular vergence in each cardinal direction, presence or absence of nystagmus)
   V: left and right jaw strength, and left and right facial sensation
   VII: left and right facial expression (symmetry, ptosis)
   VIII: left and right hearing (finger rub)
   IX/X: left and right palatal elevation (symmetry)

   XII: left and right shoulder shrug (power)
   XIII: left and right tongue protrusion (symmetry)

MOTOR: I personally examined each of the following: left and right upper limbs, and left and right lower limbs (power, muscle bulk, muscle tone); left and right pronator drift.

COORDINATION: I personally examined each of the following; Left and right finger-to-nose (accuracy, fluidity, rhythm); left and right foot tapping (rhythm, fluidity, amplitude).

REFLEXES: I personally examined each of the following: left and right brachioradialis and left and right patellar reflexes (amplitude, symmetry); left and right plantar response.

SENSORY: I personally examined each of the following: Left and right upper limb and left and right lower limb (sensation to light touch).

GIAT: I personally examined each of the following: Casual gait (stride length, arm swing, 180 degree turn).

ABNORMAL/INVOLUNTARY MOVEMENTS: I personally examined for the presence or absence of abnormal or involuntary movements.

I found each of the above elements to be within normal or expected limits with the following exceptions or addenda:

Cushingoid appearance. Obese.

Unable to examine fundi due to extreme refractive error. Balance of cranial nerve examination is unremarkable.

IMAGING STUDIES: I personally reviewed the patient's neurodiagnostic imaging studies (imaging and radiologist's interpretation). I am not credentialed to interpret nor do I receive compensation derived from interpretation of, neurodiagnostic images, and my comments do no represent an interpretation of the patient's radiologic findings.

Figure 8.1   Excerpt from a Modern Medical Chart Note

says that "I personally examined…" because Medicare requires that you do everything yourself for the encounter to be billable. The perseveration on this point adds no medical value whatever. Instead it adds to the paperwork, clutters the real findings, and makes one wonder if all of this really was done or whether it's just computer-generated boilerplate for a billable encounter. The Imaging Studies section is pure legalese.

Imagine this additional wasted effort replicated millions of times each day, every day of the year. The cumulative effect is tens of millions of pages of excess records. The existing system replaces real medical communication with "bureaucratese," wastes time, adds overhead expense, and contributes nothing to patients or providers. All of this costs money; billions of dollars each year.

Regulatory True Grit

Groucho Marx once said that "politics is the art of looking for trouble, finding it everywhere, diagnosing it incorrectly, and applying the wrong remedies." This succinctly describes government policy with respect to American healthcare today.

It's no secret that voters are unhappy with the way healthcare is going in the United States. It costs too much. Health insurance is expensive and hard to get. Many people aren't insured at all. Healthcare costs keep rising more rapidly than GDP even as access to care declines. Doctors have stopped going into primary care specialties. Health plans and insurance policies are difficult or impossible to understand. And nothing in the 2010 PPACA law does anything to help lay a sound, sustainable medical or economic foundation for the future.

When things aren't going well and voters are angry, governments automatically respond with legislation and regulation. Given the role of the government, this is only logical. After all, it's supposed to be responsive to its constituents. But virtually all state and federal responses to "crises in healthcare" have themselves become major problems. Reactive government initiatives intended to save money, improve quality, and protect patients using the healthcare system almost always increase cost and reduce efficiency while failing to provide the intended benefits. One typical mistake is trying to regulate an intricate industry with crude and inappropriately standardized tools. Let's look at just a few examples.

Quality Improvement

Everyone would like to ensure that the quality of care we receive is as good as it can possibly be. Mistakes should be few and far

between. We want our care to be cost-effective and efficiently provided. The use of medications and surgeries should have a rational
and scientifically sound basis. And most of all, we would like the care
to be tailored to the needs, resources, and preferences of each specific
patient. Why? Because, as we established in previous pages, patients
are not widgets. In a nuanced, diverse, and complex setting such as
healthcare, one person's remedy might be bad news for another.

Virtually any government-mandated program is going to be too
blunt, too crude, and insufficiently adaptable to improve the system
as a whole. On the other hand, it's certain to create new provider documentation and reporting requirements, legal headaches, and compliance costs. Far from saving money and increasing quality, there is
substantial evidence that, in many cases, they have increased healthcare expenditures with little benefit to patients. And, of course, they
have boosted the size of the healthcare bureaucracy. Let's examine a
couple of quality improvement programs that have been implemented in just the past couple of years:

Guidelines of Care

We've already discussed some of the problems associated with
government-mandated guidelines of care and critical pathways,
including: (1) all insurers (public and private) often have a conflict of
interest when it comes to choosing between quality and cost; (2) conflicting dueling standards originating from different special interest
groups; and (3) standards often change far too slowly to keep up with
medical innovations. However, a couple of additional considerations
are worth mentioning here.

The first is that standardized guidelines simply aren't appropriate
when considered in light of the special circumstances presented by
many patients. As a result, incentives or punishments meted out for
their use or non-use will often miss the mark—either punishing or
rewarding inappropriate behaviors. Here's a simple example:

One "best practice" pay-for-performance guideline is checking
the urine of diabetic patients for microalbuminuria (that is, evidence

of small amounts of protein leaking into the urine as a result of kidney damage). It's important to know if this happens because kidney damage can be minimized by beginning to treat the patient aggressively with certain medications. The cost of this test ranges from $15 to $90. As you can see in Figure 8.2, each provider is judged based upon the total number of diabetic patients who have had this test done as a percentage of the total number of diabetic patients in their practice.

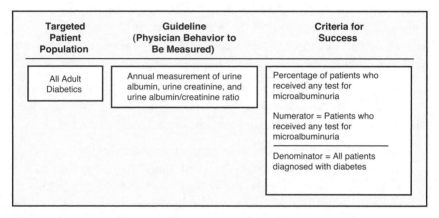

Targeted Patient Population	Guideline (Physician Behavior to Be Measured)	Criteria for Success
All Adult Diabetics	Annual measurement of urine albumin, urine creatinine, and urine albumin/creatinine ratio	Percentage of patients who received any test for microalbuminuria Numerator = Patients who received any test for microalbuminuria Denominator = All patients diagnosed with diabetes

Figure 8.2   Pay-for-Performance Criteria for Microalbuminuria Measurement in Diabetic Patients[8]

Notice that the guideline is quite simple. It has to be if it's going to be widely promulgated as a regulation or pay-for-performance measure. If guidelines become conditional and complex, they become hard and expensive to devise, promulgate, follow, track, and change over time. So what happens when guidelines such as this one are applied in the real world?

Probably the best example is a study published in 2001 (a virtual lifetime ago in what should be a rapidly changing and updated field). Researchers looked at the "best practices" behavior of 85 internists who volunteered to participate in a study group designed to improve clinical practice.[9] Astonishingly, these highly motivated physicians failed to do microalbuminuria tests on their diabetic patients 46% of the time. The reason wasn't a lack of interest in quality, but instead that these clinicians made a conscious decision to skip the test when getting it would not be helpful in the care of their patients. There are many circumstances where this is the case, including when the treatment for urine protein is already maximized, the patient has known renal failure, or the patient has protein in the urine for other reasons. In a substantial proportion of cases, patients declined to be tested even when the need and purpose was described to them. Several other "best practice" guidelines had similar problems. In 2007, a careful search of the medical literature found *absolutely no* direct evidence that monitoring for microalbuminuria improved outcomes in patients already being treated with kidney-sparing medications.[10]

Despite these findings, the guideline regarding microalbuminuria and the physician incentives or punishments for not complying still remain in place. As the authors of the study observed:

> Because the physicians provided explanatory remarks, we gained insight into clinicians' patient-specific reasons for providing care that diverged from best practices. Although the reason most often discussed in the literature has been physician oversight, we found that a substantial amount of non-compliance was attributable to other factors, such as systems issues and patient non-adherence. Furthermore, our research clearly indicates that physicians occasionally made a conscious decision not to comply with a best practice. This raises questions about the appropriateness of the term *best practice*.

The result in cases like these is a lose-lose situation. If all providers were to mindlessly follow the guideline for microalbuminuria that has been dictated to them, almost half of the tests ordered will result in additional expense that provide little or no benefit to anyone. (In fact, if the guidelines were not originally promulgated by the government, one wonders if the extra testing would be classified as a prosecutable form of "waste, fraud, and abuse"?) On the other hand, if providers do *not* follow the guidelines, they are scored by the system as providing substandard quality care. The point is that: (1) guidelines simply can't be detailed enough to apply to every circumstance; and (2) simple, standardized guidelines espousing "best practices" are simply not going to be the most efficient, least expensive, or highest quality way to take care of every patient. Making them into laws and regulations simply increases costs and overhead.

A second problem with mandating that doctors follow clinical guidelines is that some of them simply can't be followed given the time and financial resources typically available. Consider the case of the 196-page federal guideline on smoking cessation.

Smoking is clearly a major cause of serious disease and premature death, and the vast majority of physicians regularly advise their patients to quit. Patients who express an interest in doing so are generally offered whatever assistance the clinician might be able to provide. But the federal guidelines go further, and require that physicians try to "promote [their patients'] motivation to quit." This is supposed to be done using "Brief Strategy B," a small portion of which is shown in Table 8.3. (The complete "Brief Strategy B" is reproduced in the Appendix.)

One has to wonder where any busy provider could possibly find the time to engage in these otherwise uncompensated discussions. In 2005, a study of family doctors showed that each saw an average of 20.1 patients each day. The average amount of time that family practice physicians had to spend with patients was 17.5 minutes. This included the time available for obtaining a history, doing a physical examination, clinical decision-making, providing counseling, writing prescriptions, and arranging for follow-up. Charting and administrative overhead consumed an average of an additional seven minutes for each patient seen. Even the most casual observer will notice that the "brief" guidelines described in the Appendix could easily consume more time than is generally available for an entire patient visit.

TABLE 8.3   "Brief Strategy B," from the Federal Guidelines Regarding Smokers Who Report That They Are Unwilling to Quit[11]

Strategy B1. Motivational Interviewing Strategies

Express empathy	• Use open-ended questions to explore:
	  - The importance of addressing smoking or other tobacco use (e.g., "How important do you think it is for you to quit smoking?")
	  - Concerns and benefits of quitting (e.g., "What might happen if you quit?")
	• Use reflective listening to seek shared understanding:
	  - Reflect words or meaning (e.g., "So you think smoking helps you to maintain your weight.").
	  - Summarize (e.g., "What I have heard so far is that smoking is something you enjoy. On the other hand, your boyfriend hates your smoking, and you are worried you might develop a serious disease.").
	• Normalize feelings and concerns (e.g., "Many people worry about managing without cigarettes.").
	• Support the patient's autonomy and right to choose or reject change (e.g., "I hear you saying you are not ready to quit smoking right now. I'm here to help you when you are ready.").

Develop discrepancy	• Highlight the discrepancy between the patient's present behavior and expressed priorities, values, and goals (e.g., "It sounds like you are very devoted to your family. How do you think your smoking is affecting your children?").
	• Reinforce and support "change talk" and "commitment" language:
	  - "So, you realize how smoking is affecting your breathing and making it hard to keep up with your kids."
	  - "It's great that you are going to quit when you get through this busy time at work."
	• Build and deepen commitment to change:
	  - "There are effective treatments that will ease the pain of quitting, including counseling and many medication options."
	  - "We would like to help you avoid a stroke like the one your father had."

Roll with resistance	• Back off and use reflection when the patient expresses resistance:
	  - "Sounds like you are feeling pressured about your smoking."
	• Express empathy:
	  - "You are worried about how you would manage withdrawal symptoms."
	• Ask permission to provide information:
	  - "Would you like to hear about some strategies that can help you address that concern when you quit?"

Support self-efficacy	• Help the patient to identify and build on past successes:
	  - "So you were fairly successful the last time you tried to quit."
	• Offer options for achievable small steps toward change:
	  - Call the quitline (1-800-QUIT-NOW) for advice and information.
	  - Read about quitting benefits and strategies.
	  - Change smoking patterns (e.g., no smoking in the home).
	  - Ask the patient to share his or her ideas about quitting strategies.

Providers, patients, and the public already strapped by medical expenses therefore have a grim choice if such elaborate guidelines are to be followed each time a smoker is seen. They can (1) endure shorter patient visits on average to make up for the time used in such counseling; (2) endure longer waiting times to see their physicians; or (3) pay physicians more in an effort to spend more hours seeing more patients.[12] All these options will reduce increase cost and/or reduce access to care for the large majority of patients—smokers and non-smokers alike.*

A third and philosophically troubling aspect of centrally dictated standardized guidelines—whether government mandated or not—is that they threaten to replace patient choice and provider judgment with a biased perspective based upon imperfect data. As we've seen, "critical pathways" recommendations are most valuable when the clinical situation is relatively standardized, controlled. and the evidence is clear. Relatively few situations in non-elective clinical medicine fit this description. Do we really want to enact and enforce standardized guidelines that cause our providers to engage in rote behaviors, whether these behaviors are in our personal best interests as patients? If physicians are paid more to order useless tests, or if they are punished if they do not, they will surely order more useless tests and increase healthcare costs. The same principle applies to prescribing useless or potentially harmful drugs, performing surgeries or any other intervention potentially dictated centrally. Is it in the best interests of

---

* Fogoros has pointed out another questionable benefit of mandated guidelines: their ability to increase providers' legal risk. He describes the case of John Banzhaf, Executive Director and Chief Counsel for Action on Smoking and Health (ASH), "who bills himself as the 'law professor who masterminded litigation against the tobacco industry.' Mr. Banzhaf "sent a letter to each of the 50 state health commissioners warning them that he will soon begin instigating medical malpractice suits, on behalf of smokers who continue to smoke as the result of their doctor's refusal to follow federal guidelines. Mr. Banzhaf informs the commissioners that 'physicians are killing more than 40,000 American smokers each year by failing to follow federal guidelines.' That's right, doctor, you're killing them. (Cigarettes don't kill people; people kill people.) Specifically he invokes the doctor's obligation to 'warn the smoking patient about the many dangers of smoking and provide effective medical treatment for the majority who wish to quit.' That is, it's your job not just to counsel them and treat them, but also to see that they actually quit smoking."

Americans to allow these types of policies to interfere with personalized care and the doctor-patient relationship?

"Never" Events

Good healthcare practices try to minimize the number of bad things that happen to people as a result of taking care of them. It also makes sense that people shouldn't have to pay for poor quality care. Medicare began to apply both of these principles in 2007 by working with other agencies to come up with a list of serious and preventable hospital errors nicknamed "never events." Never events are things that should rarely, if ever, happen if high quality care standards are applied. Medicare has made it policy to refuse to pay for the care required as a result of never events, thus encouraging hospitals to adhere to high standards and saving the government money. As generally happens, private insurers and Medicaid agencies have followed Medicare's lead.

The concept of never events is a good one where a condition is truly preventable, and the initial list of "hospital-acquired conditions" (HACs) that Medicare and other insurers declined to pay for was quite reasonable. The original list included things such as operating on the wrong person or the wrong body part, leaving foreign objects in patients after surgery, or giving patients the wrong medicine. From there, however, Medicare has gone on to declare as never events some conditions that can be only partially prevented even with the best care. Infections associated with urinary catheters are one of these. Some percentage of patients who require the constant use of catheters to drain their urine will inevitably get urinary tract infections regardless of what hospital personnel may do.[13]

But the real problem is that it's all too easy for regulators to lose sight of reality in their quest for perfection.

As part of their most recent proposal for new "never events," Medicare included several complications that—far from being thoughtless errors—are actually known and unavoidable risks of being treated for certain specific conditions. One of those complications was accidentally nicking and collapsing a lung in the course of certain important diagnostic and therapeutic procedures. (In medical parlance, this is known as an "iatrogenic pneumothorax.") The vast majority of the time this has nothing to do with carelessness on the part of the provider. A small percentage of patients requiring these procedures will suffer a collapsed lung no matter how skilled or careful the doctor may be. In fact, a collapsed lung is specifically listed as a potential risk on every consent form for these procedures for exactly that reason. And this is where the march to "quality" becomes a problem. If doctors and hospitals are afraid to perform important procedures that have known risks, aren't they being discouraged from providing quality care to those who might need those procedures? Withholding timely and appropriate care increases total risk and healthcare costs for the population as a whole.

A storm of protests halted the classification of iatrogenic pneumothorax as a "never event" in FY2009, but the basic problem persists. Once we've addressed common sense issues such as patient misidentification and gross negligence, broad and nonspecific government efforts to reduce payments and "increase quality" for some patients will inevitably conflict with what is best (and represent acceptable risks) for others.

Pay-for-Performance

Pay-for-performance, commonly abbreviated as P4P, is the newest truckload of regulatory gravel being poured into the healthcare machine. More than half of health maintenance organizations and 126 health plans now have P4P programs in place for physicians and/or hospitals, and Medicare has no fewer than 11 P4P demonstration projects currently underway.[14] While it is not yet mandatory for U.S. physicians to participate in most Medicare P4P programs, this will change in the near future.

Briefly stated, P4P is a payment incentive program in which doctors and other healthcare providers are given financial rewards or penalties based upon some measured parameter in their practice. In theory, this measured parameter could be anything, ranging from patient satisfaction to the adjusted mortality rates of their patients. In practice, however, P4P measures are usually based upon some type of testing that the government or private insurer wants them to perform. For example, for Medicare's hospital-based Health Quality Incentive (HQI) demonstration project, 27 out of 34 of the "quality indicators" used measured compliance with dictated processes rather than outcomes measures such as mortality, complication, or readmission rates.[15] In the outpatient setting, P4P performance criteria are nearly always limited to "processes" (such as performing a test or prescribing a medication), rather than a health outcome. There are three reasons for this.

First, process parameters are far easier to measure. All one has to do is ask whether the test was done or the medication was prescribed. Second, virtually all P4P programs are based upon some sort of standardized guidelines of care. Because the guidelines are themselves simply a set of processes (for example, if the patient is diabetic, get a microalbuminuria test each year), the success of the P4P program is generally a function of how well providers adhered to the guidelines. But most importantly, even under the best of circumstances, healthcare providers can only be partially responsible for the outcomes of their patients. A great deal depends upon the patient's compliance with the provider's attempts to diagnose and treat, as well as the nature of the disease itself. As we've seen previously, "report cards" that simply describe outcomes that are not adjusted for patient compliance or the severity of illness will cause rational providers to avoid seeing high-risk patients. Thus, P4P programs that specifically target outcomes might have the paradoxical effect of denying care to those patients who need it most.

The pay-for-performance movement is a recent outgrowth of something called "evidence-based medicine," the philosophical origins of which extend back to the mid-19th century. Evidence-based medicine is

> ...the conscientious, explicit, and judicious use of current best evidence in making decisions about the care of individual patients. The practice of evidence-based medicine means integrating individual clinical expertise with the best available external clinical evidence from systematic research. By individual clinical expertise, we mean the proficiency and judgment that individual clinicians acquire through clinical experience and clinical practice."[16]

The emphasis on the use of both scientific evidence and individualized clinical judgment is vital, because patients are not widgets. It is extremely rare that the exact clinical situation faced by a given physician and patient was identical to that studied in any clinical trial.

There are too many variables of age, sex, ethnicity, family history, social history, medical problems, and treatments for this to be the case. This means that even the best medical guidelines can and should be trumped by individual circumstances....

> "Evidence based medicine is not "cookbook" medicine. Because it requires a bottom up approach that integrates the best external evidence with individual clinical expertise and patients' choice, it cannot result in slavish, cookbook approaches to individual patient care. External clinical evidence can inform, but can never replace, individual clinical expertise, and it is this expertise that decides whether the external evidence applies to the individual patient at all and, if so, how it should be integrated into a clinical decision."[17]

The underlying idea behind evidence-based medicine is clearly a good one. In practice, however, the real question is whether evidence-based medicine can be successfully linked to a pay-for-performance mechanism. Because they have to rely on relatively simple rules to determine whether providers are rewarded or punished, there is no good means by which a P4P program that relies on process measures can take provider judgment into account. And as we've seen, P4P programs that rely upon outcomes can't allow for patient cooperation or severity of disease without careful and time-consuming risk adjustment. The result is that these programs are inevitably based on mindless, centralized standard guidelines rather than the appropriate use of evidence-based medicine.

There are many reasons to be skeptical of pay-for-performance initiatives. Dolinar and Leininger have done a good job of summarizing the most important of these.[18] They include the limitations of evidence-based medicine itself (including the lack of good randomized controlled trials as a basis for making decisions), the dangers of replacing patient choice and physician autonomy with central planning, undermining personalized care and the physician-patient relationship, and actually worsening the quality of care by forcing physicians to "game" the system to get paid.

There is also a surprising lack of evidence to suggest that P4P even works. Although many P4P programs report increases in the desired parameters with time, most fail to compare these gains with a control group: a comparable sample of providers that are not participating in the P4P program. At least two studies that did do this type of comparison found that increases in the majority of program "success" indicators were not significantly different between the P4P and control groups.[19,20]

How can P4P efforts like these cause headaches for doctors, hospitals, and other providers, and actually hurt the efficiency of the system as a whole? Once again, the real-life experiences of the Happy Hospitalist are revealing:[21]

> ...Here's how the program works. [Medicare] has a list of over 100 indicators that physicians can choose to report on. Things like checking HgbA1C for diabetics, monitoring blood pressure, assessing fall risk, evaluating for beta blocker use in heart failure... But we physicians don't need to report all of them. How many?
>
> Just three. But here's the catch. You must report at least 80% of the time on qualified patients on all three of those indicators or you don't get any money. None. If you meet the qualifications for two of them with 100% and the third indicator is 79%, you get nothing.
>
> For the reporting period of July-December 2007, Dr. Happy was the only physician in his group of almost 20 that successfully achieved the 80% mark on three indicators. And with that, Dr Happy took home a walloping $1,100 bonus, before taxes. For all the time and energy spent by our billing company. For all the time and energy spent by me and all my partners. $1,100. That's what we had to show for it.
>
> So what does it take to qualify?... Let's look at coronary artery disease (CAD). The quality indicator was: 'Is a patient with coronary artery disease being prescribed anti-platelet [medications]? For simplicity, anti-platelet will mean aspirin in this discussion.
>
> How does one report?...
>
> 1. Which CPT code is the quality indicator good for? This is one of the most important aspects. Just because I saw the patient does not mean I can report to the PQRI system on that patient. Only certain CPT codes qualify. Remember CPT

stands for Current Procedural Terminology. Whenever you have any possible billable encounter, your doc must submit the CPT code to the insurance company... So you have to know which CPT codes your quality indicator is good for... Let's say... that I discharge a patient from the hospital, using CPT code 99238. [Medicare] says this CPT code *can* be used to report aspirin use for CAD to PQRI. The PQRI system does not care how many qualifying patients you report. If you only submit one patient all year for aspirin use in CAD and if you document it appropriately, then you have 1/1 on your report card. You are 100%. You meet the threshold of 80% for that one indicator [of the three needed] and you are successful. It seems easy, but it's not really. It gets a lot more complicated.

2. Are you linking the ICD code with the qualifying CPT code? The ICD code or International Classification of Disease is the disease... Whenever a doctor submits a CPT code to the insurance company to get paid, that CPT must be linked to an ICD code... So all diseases have their own ICD code. In this case the ICD code for coronary artery disease [CAD] is 414.0. Now here's the kicker. If you submit a claim to [Medicare] to be paid for a 99238 (a hospital discharge code *and* an allowable CPT code for PQRI for the quality indicator for aspirin use in CAD) and you link the CPT code to ICD code 414.0, but you FAIL to report to PQRI, you have just lost a patient on your numerator. For example, let's say you have 2 patients all year with CAD who you saw and whose CPT code would qualify them for PQRI reporting. Let's say [that for] patient 1 you link ICD code 414.0 (CAD) to your claim to Medicare for CPT code 99238 and you report to PQRI. You have successfully completed 1/1 claims. You are 100% successful on your reporting for that one quality indicator. Now, let's say patient number 2 has CAD and you successfully link your ICD for CAD, 414.0, to your CPT code for discharge, 99238, but you *fail* to fill out the appropriate reporting...to PQRI. Your have now increased your denominator to 2, but you have only reported on 1/2 patients. So your successful reporting is only 50%.

Remember PQRI requires you to report on 80% of your qualified patients. In this case, because you failed to report to PQRI on just 1 of 2 patients, even though you submitted to

[Medicare] to get paid for your office visits, your 50% does not qualify, and this quality indicator thus fails... Another common area to fail in the reporting game is failure to link the [qualifying] ICD to the CPT code when submitting to PQRI. Many patients we see have 10, 15, or 20 medical problems/ICD codes. When you submit a claim to [Medicare], they will only accept four ICD codes. If a patient has pneumonia, hypertension, chronic obstructive pulmonary disease, and diabetes, *and* CAD, and you submit your CPT code to [Medicare] on discharge code 99238 using the ICD codes for pneumonia, hypertension, COPD, and diabetes, BUT you fail to include the ICD code for CAD (414.0), then [Medicare] will not include this patient in your denominator for PQRI reporting. For [Medicare's] reporting purposes, it is as if this patient does not exist... In the course of a year, this can hurt you because the fewer patients that you qualify, the fewer screw-ups you can tolerate and still hit 80%...

3. What exactly are we reporting? Good question. Now that we've gotten past to first two steps of making sure you know what the qualifying CPT codes are *and* then making sure you link the qualifying ICD code to the CPT code, what exactly to we do next? Well, in the case of the aspirin use in CAD, it's not simply reporting yes or no... For each possible quality reporting indicator, we docs have the choice of 3, 4, 5 or more choices to report to PQRI. And each choice has its own code. Of course it does. In the case of aspirin use we can report...

- Aspirin prescribed code 4011-F
- Aspirin not prescribed for medical reasons 4011F-1P
- Aspirin not prescribed for patient reason (social reasons or declined) 4011F-2P
- Aspirin not prescribed for a system reason (insurance/resources unavailable) 4011F-3P
- Aspirin not prescribed, reason not specified 4011F-8P

...But it's not that simple. If you have a patient that would qualify in the denominator (appropriate CPT code for the quality indicator) *and* has the appropriate ICD code to report, but you choose not report to PQRI, your denominator increases and your numerator stays the same. This would put you at risk for not meeting the 80% requirement.

This is what happened to the vast majority of folks in Happy's Hospitalist group. We all met the required number of patients for each quality indicator... Most of Happy's partners linked the ICD code to the appropriate CPT code, but [may have]... failed to circle one of the five 4011-F codes. So most of the quality indicators came in under 80%. Most denominators were in the 5-15 patient range. So you can see, failure to submit just 1, 2, or 3 PQRI claims can destroy a whole year's worth of effort. And keep you below the 80% threshold.

...There is no way to know where the errors are occurring. Medicare does not tell you which patients qualified, which didn't. Which patients you failed to submit but should have. It's a giant black hole of faith. Faith that paper pushers in the entire data trail have done their job correctly, so you, doc, get your $600 bonus, the average paid out last year.

It's no wonder why less than 1/3 of doctors have chosen to play the game. So much time. So little money. And no way to verify that everyone else is keeping up their end of the bargain.

So, the problem with P4P, guidelines, and other relatively simplistic "quality" efforts is that they consume huge amounts of resources—both in time and dollar terms. The P4P program itself uses resources, of course, to set up and administer. But more importantly, every new "quality" program produces more overhead for physician offices in terms of billing, data collection, and reporting. A recent study found that the administrative overhead for P4P reporting can be as high as $11,000 per clinician in the start-up phase, and then $4,300 per clinician annually.[22] All these expenses eventually end up being translated into higher costs and higher insurance premiums.

Medical Malpractice Liability

Politicians, academics, special interest groups, and pundits have argued about the U.S. medical malpractice liability system for decades. Doctors complain that the vast majority of claims are bogus, while plaintiff attorneys insist that more doctors must be punished. Unaffected by the debate, malpractice premiums skyrocket regularly in line with that industry's own insurance cycle. Patients typically find little or no justice and the root causes of errors are fearfully concealed, lest they generate more claims. Laws, awards, and insurance premiums are a hodgepodge, varying dramatically from state to state. But despite the bellowing and jawboning—or perhaps because of it—little or nothing changes from year to year. Doctors live in fear, patients suffer, and dollars are misdirected. It is more than grit in the system; the current medical malpractice system is universally corrosive.

What Is the Current System Trying to Accomplish?

Doctors make mistakes. They always have and they always will. The underlying basis of the medical malpractice system in the United States today is based upon two separate objectives.

The first is that when patients suffer harm as a result of a medical error, most people feel that something should be done to mitigate the medical and financial consequences. We want them to get well, and it seems unfair to ask them to pay for expenses incurred as a result of the error.

The second objective—most commonly invoked by the legal community—is to punish negligent providers. The idea is that the ever-present threat of lawsuits will reduce the number of mistakes providers make by acting as a sort of Sword of Damocles. Knowing that any mistake will subject them to swift and certain retribution, providers will always do their best. Those who do not will be called forward for public trial and face the prospect of personal and financial ruin. Incompetent doctors and hospitals will thereby eventually be removed from the system, and incentives for providing cheap or shoddy care will be minimized.

Given these motivations, the real questions are whether the current system efficiently accomplishes its intended purpose, and at what cost to the healthcare system as a whole?

Medical Malpractice Liability—The Existing System

Like just about everything else in the U.S. healthcare system, little or nothing about the management of medical errors was planned. Instead, it has been improvised through the tort system—the part of the legal system that allows citizens to seek redress for alleged injury through the courts. And like medical licensure itself, much of medical malpractice law is regulated at the state level. Most states require physicians to purchase medical malpractice insurance as a condition of practice, and both the insurance industry and malpractice litigation are regulated quite differently from state to state. Under the current system, a claim works something like this:

1. Patients perceive that some harm was done to them as a direct or indirect result of the healthcare goods or services that they received. They seek out a malpractice trial attorney to take their case. This is almost always done on a contingency basis.

2. A plaintiff attorney reviews the case to decide whether she believes that it's worth taking. Generally speaking, this decision is based upon whether a good case can be made that a mistake was made, that the mistake resulted in harm, and that the value of a potential judgment or other settlement provides the attorney with a good return on their investment.[23,†]

3. If the plaintiff attorney accepts the case, a long period of discovery and investigation ensue. Much of the time, the case is settled out of court. If not, and if the case is not dropped, a civil trial is held with a jury. In most cases, the defense is led and financed by the provider's malpractice insurer.

4. If the jury finds in favor of the defendant, the patient gets nothing. If it finds in favor of the plaintiff, an award is made and paid by the provider's insurance company. All attorney fees and expenses are paid first. The remainder of the judgment goes to the patient.

---

† This last condition is critical because law firms are inherently businesses just like the medical practices and hospitals they sue. Plaintiff attorneys working on a contingency basis (that is, they only get paid for their time and expenses if they win) still lose their cases most of the time. The American Bar Association reports that only about 25% of medical malpractice actions are won by the plaintiff either pre- or post-trial. Thus, each successful case must not only generate enough income to pay for the time and costs associated with the current case plus a profit margin, but also the three-quarters of malpractice cases that are unsuccessfully prosecuted. Plaintiff attorney medical malpractice fees vary, but tend to cluster around 33% of the total award made.

On average, it takes four to five years to resolve a claim from the date of the original incident.

Given this background, it is reasonable to ask just how well the current malpractice system achieves its goals, whether it does so efficiently, and whether there are undesirable consequences that result from this mode of doing business. If the system does a poor job of achieving its goals or does so inefficiently or with lots of undesirable consequences, our efforts to repair healthcare needs to take this into account.

So how does the existing system perform? Frankly, it's not looking good.

The largest and most thorough study to date on the relationship between malpractice claims, medical errors, and the resulting compensation was published in 2006.[24] This effort reviewed a random sample of 1,452 closed malpractice claims to determine how the claim was resolved, whether a medical injury had occurred, and, if so, whether it was due to a medical error.

Some observations on the results are instructive:

- Patients are certainly not being well-served by the current system. In cases that both involved an injury *and* a medical error, no payment was made to the patient over one-fourth of the time (27% of these cases). Because the patients in this study had all filed claims, even this number probably overstates the number of injured patients receiving appropriate compensation. Only 1 in 15 patients who suffer an injury because of medical negligence receive compensation, and those who do have to wait years to resolve their claim.[25] While up to two years was average in this study, other sources claim that four years is more typical.[26]

- Providers are not being well served, either. Claims without errors were actually more likely to reach trial than claims with errors (23% versus 10%), and payments were made in almost one-third of the cases in which no error occurred. In fact, as we can see in Table 8.4, the evidence suggests that, for many physicians, the current system resembles a lottery more than a system designed to deliver justice.

TABLE 8.4   Comparison of Malpractice Claims With and Without Clinician Error in the 2006 Study

Characteristic	"Error" Claims (N = 889) No. (%)	"No Error" Claims (N = 515) No. (%)	P Value*
Severity of Injury			
Psychological or emotional	25 (3%)	26 (5%)	0.04
Minor physical	106 (12%)	81 (16%)	0.05
Significant physical	372 (42%)	201 (39%)	0.31
Major physical	147 (17%)	72 (14%)	0.22
Death	239 (27%)	135 (26%)	0.80
Type of Claim			
Surgery	258 (29%)	163 (32%)	0.30
Obstetrics	209 (24%)	123 (24%)	0.90
Missed or delayed diagnosis	259 (29%)	155 (30%)	0.72
Medication	163 (18%)	74 (14%)	0.06
Indemnity paid	653 (73%)	145 (28%)	< 0.001
Mean defense costs	$50,966	$55,233	0.50
Mean time from injury to filing claim	1.6 years	2.2 years	< 0.001

* A "P-value" of more than 0.05 means that the difference between the "error" and "no error" percentages is not statistically significant.

From: Studdert DM, Mello MM, Gawande AA, et al. "Claims, Errors, and Compensation Payments in Medical Malpractice Litigation." *New England Journal of Medicine* (2006); 354: 19: 2024-2033, Table 2.

- Resources are clearly wasted on meritless claims. Non-error claims accounted for 16% of total system costs, 12% of indemnity costs, and 21% of administrative costs.

- Enormous amounts are directed away from healthcare and into purely administrative costs. The study found that for each dollar paid to patients in compensation, $0.54 in additional costs are incurred for attorney fees, experts, court costs, and other overhead expenses.

What providers see in these numbers is that they are equally likely to be sued whether or not they make a mistake. All that is required is that the patient has an undesirable outcome, (and sometimes even that is optional). Still worse, even if no error was made, the patient still has a 28% chance of winning. Trial lawyers are quick to point out that claims with errors have a much higher compensation rate than those without, but this blessing is largely lost on providers. Much of the real harm that is done to them occurs the moment that the claim of malpractice is filed. At more than $50,000, the cost of defending a meritless claim is no different than defending a credible one. The time spent, anxiety incurred, loss of sleep, and heartache are all the same.

Although some might argue that claims keep doctors sharp and prevent negligence, a siege mentality inevitably leads to defensive medicine. We'll look at this more closely in a bit, but from both a patient and system perspective, one has to ask whether we really want to foster an adversarial relationship between patients and caregivers? Mello, et al looked at a natural experiment in which several Pennsylvania malpractice insurance carriers abruptly left the market. Almost overnight it became extremely difficult for many providers to buy malpractice coverage. Malpractice insurance premiums skyrocketed. The researchers then compared the satisfaction rate of Pennsylvania physicians with those of other states, and asked Pennsylvania providers how the malpractice situation was affecting their lives and medical practices.[27]

Not surprisingly, physicians in Pennsylvania were significantly less satisfied with their careers than physicians elsewhere—about half as satisfied on average. Of potentially greater importance was their attitude regarding their patients and ability to deliver appropriate care. This is described in Table 8.5.

"Wounded" physicians in this study are defined as those dropped by their insurer and/or sued in the prior three years. The important finding is that doctors—especially those who have been "wounded" in a malpractice sense—change as a result of the process, and not for the better. They are less open and candid, more paranoid, and less able to provide what they believe to be the best possible care. The physician-patient relationship operates less smoothly and efficiently as a result. This is exactly what we would expect to occur with "sand" in the gears.[‡]

TABLE 8.5 Effects of Liability Pressures on Pennsylvania Specialists' Interactions with Patients

Number of physicians who believe that, because of concerns about malpractice liability...	"Wounded" Physicians	"Non-wounded" Physicians
They are less candid with their patients	26%	17%
They view every patient as a potential lawsuit	81%	71%
The malpractice system limits their ability to provide the highest quality care	91%	92%

Data from: Mello MM, Studdert DM, DesRoches CM, et al. "Caring For Patients In A Malpractice Crisis: Physician Satisfaction and Quality of Care." *Health Affairs* (2004): 21(4): 42-53.

Finally, there is the sheer economic cost to clinicians—something that becomes important when we discuss the supply and appropriate distribution of providers, and the market's ability to constrain the cost of providing care. These costs vary considerably depending upon medical specialty. In 2003, average obstetricians paid 6.7% of their gross revenue for malpractice insurance, general surgeons 4.3%, and internists 2.9%.[28] Because physicians have an average overhead rate

---

[‡] In many respects, it doesn't matter whether the paranoia doctors feel is backed up by true risk and valid statistics, or whether it's simply all in their heads. If they *feel* that a Sword of Damocles is hanging over their heads, they will behave accordingly. Otherwise rational providers will change their practice patterns to avoid risky behaviors or perceived "problem patients," choose to practice in less affected medical specialties, move to locations where the perceived risk is lower, and cover their tail with additional costly tests to make sure they're not missing anything, regardless of how small the likelihood of those tests turning out positive. It hardly matters that their real chances of being sued for negligence are low, or that their chances of prevailing are high–in or out of court. Their behavior is inevitably changed in far more ways than simply trying not to be negligent. One of the most important conclusions of the 1994 OTA study "Defensive Medicine and Medical Malpractice" was that: "Physicians are very conscious of the risk of being sued and tend to overestimate that risk. A large number of physicians believe that being sued will adversely affect their professional, financial, and emotional status."

of about 50% of revenues, medical malpractice costs as a percentage of the physician's salary are about twice as high as the percentages shown. For example, a obstetrician will have medical malpractice costs equivalent to about 13% of his take-home pay.

Larger studies suggest that the overhead cost of uncompensated claims is actually higher than that of claims involving compensation. In 2006, the Ohio Department of Insurance found that no award was made in almost 80% of all claims filed. A very large cumulative study by the Physician Insurers Association of America (PIAA) found that the total administrative and defense expenses of unpaid claims actually exceeded the amounts spent on those resulting in compensation by more than $275 million over a 20-year period.[29]

To what extent does the current system fulfill its second mission of preventing negligence on the part of providers? The fact is that no one has any idea. In 1994, the U.S. Office of Technology Assessment (OTA) reviewed this topic and concluded that: "The role of the malpractice system as a deterrent against too little or poor-quality care—one of its intended purposes—has not been carefully studied." Little has changed since then. There appear to be no credible measures or studies that document the extent to which the tort system has contributed to the safety of American healthcare. One thing that seems certain is that it's probably not helping much. Attorneys seeking to justify the role of the tort system have pointed out that: "...even with...conservative methodology, the [Harvard Medical Practice] study found that doctors were injuring one out of every 25 patients—and that only 4 percent of these injured patients sued."[30] Given this evidence and the high rate of medical errors reported by the Institute of Medicine and others, it's clear that the existing tort system is a crude and inefficient way to protect patients.

Although the current system has many undesirable attributes, its proponents take consolation in statistics that show that the total cost of malpractice insurance, overhead, and litigation is a relatively small percentage of the total healthcare budget. The Congressional Budget Office has estimated the direct costs of medical malpractice insurance, legal costs, compensation, and litigation to be approximately $24 billion in 2002, which was just under 2% of all healthcare spending in that year.[31] Tillinghast estimated these costs to be $30.3 billion in 2006, but noted that they were growing at an average of 11.1% per year, compared with an average annual increase of 8.2% per year for all other tort costs.[32] "The compounded impact of this 28-year difference in growth rates is that medical malpractice costs have risen by a factor of 23 since 1975, while all other tort costs have grown by a factor of 12."[33] This average rate of growth implies that the direct costs of medical malpractice was nearly $40 billion in 2009. However, none of these estimates take into account a critical factor: the cost of defensive medicine.

Defensive Medicine

Defensive medicine has been defined in various ways. One definition is "a deviation from sound medical practice that is induced primarily by the threat of liability."[34] The Office of Technology Assessment (OTA) defined defensive medicine as follows:[35]

> Defensive medicine occurs when doctors order tests, procedures, or visits, or avoid high-risk patients or procedures, primarily (but not necessarily solely) to reduce their exposure to malpractice liability. When physicians do extra tests or procedures primarily to reduce malpractice liability, they are practicing positive defensive medicine. When they avoid certain patients or procedures, they are practicing negative defensive medicine.
>
> Under this definition... the motive need not be conscious. Over time some medical practices might become so ingrained in customary practice that physicians are unaware that liability concerns originally motivated their use...

Thus, concern about malpractice liability pushes physicians' tolerance for uncertainty about medical outcomes to very low levels. Stated another way, concerns about liability drive doctors to order tests, procedures, and specialist consultations whose expected benefits are very low. There is no doubt that defensive medicine does exist, and that it is a universal part of the daily life of every healthcare provider. To the extent that defensive medicine wastes resources, it reduces the efficiency and effectiveness of our healthcare machine.[§] A 2005 study of more than 800 physicians found that 93% of them report practicing defensive medicine.[36] Among practitioners of defensive medicine who detailed their most recent defensive act, 43% reported obtaining imaging studies of questionable clinical necessity. Forty-two percent reported avoiding patients and procedures that would increase their potential liability risk. A 2008 survey of more than 830 physicians (in eight specialties) conducted by the Massachusetts Medical Society had similar results, with 83% of physicians reporting that they practiced defensive medicine.[37] Both studies showed that the number and types of defensive medicine practiced varied considerably by provider specialty. Some of the results from the Massachusetts study are shown in Table 8.6.

[§] It's quite possible for paranoia and intensive diagnostic efforts to do actual harm as well. This can happen in at least two ways. The first way is that many diagnostic procedures carry some risk of harm as part of the procedure. Radiographic tests such as CT scans and ordinary x-rays all make use of ionizing radiation that is known to increase the risk of cancer in humans. The typical chest CT scan subjects patients to the radiation equivalent of about 175 regular chest x-rays, and the number of CT scans has risen rapidly over the past 25 years. More than 62 million CT scans are done annually in the United States today, compared with just 3 million in 1980. The 2008 conference of the Society for Academic Emergency Medicine heard presentations from researchers who found that "a typical patient who visited the emergency room received a cumulative radiation dose of 40 millisieverts over a five-year period. Ten percent of patients ended up with a staggering 100 or more millisieverts. Both levels are well above the safety threshold for lifetime radiation exposure." One radiation expert has suggested that "in a few decades, 1.5 to 2 percent of all cancers in the United States might be due to radiation from CT scans done right now."

Another potential hazard is that testing will produce a result that requires still more testing. By definition, medical laboratory tests will turn out to be out of the "normal" range about 5% of the time, even when nothing is wrong. Many of these "abnormal" results will be repeated just to see if they are real. Still other tests will find abnormal results that are the result of benign conditions that can easily be confused with something harmful. A simple example is the finding of a nodule on a chest x-ray taken for some other reason. The nodule could be cancer, an infection, or an old scar left over from many years ago. In a paranoid clinical climate, these findings will require yet more procedures and tests to rule out the worst possible case. Each of these procedures (such as a lung biopsies) can carry its own serious risks, and lead to medically induced complications, or even death.

TABLE 8.6   Average Percentage of Medical Interventions Undertaken With Liability Concerns As a Major Motivating Factor

Medical Test or Intervention	Average % Performed for Liability Reasons (All Doctors)	Specialty with Highest Defensive Percentage	Specialty with Lowest Defensive Percentage
Plain Film X-Rays	22%	OB/GYN (–25.8%)	Neurosurgery (–18.6%)
CT Scans	28%	OB/GYN (–32.7%)	Neurosurgery (–18.9%)
MRI Studies	27%	General Surgery (–34.4%)	Neurosurgery (–18.4%)
Ultrasound Studies	24%	Orthopedic Surgery (–33.2%)	Neurosurgery (–5.7%)
Specialty Referrals and Consultations	28%	OB/GYN (–39.8%)	Neurosurgery (–15.6%)
Laboratory Tests	18%	Emergency Medicine (–24.0%)	Neurosurgery (–7.0%)
Hospital Admissions	13%	Family Medicine (–17.7%)	Orthopedic Surgery (–6.0%)

Data from: Massachusetts Medical Society, "Investigation of Defensive Medicine in Massachusetts." Informational Report I-08, November 2008.

Although many of us might be horrified that so many "unnecessary" tests are being ordered, it's important to remember that no one really knows that they were unnecessary until they came out negative. Instead, there was simply a very low (and sometimes vanishingly small) probability that something seriously wrong could have been going on. It's really a question of incentives. The psychological, social, professional, and financial incentives of the current tort system cause providers to have a zero tolerance for certain types of catastrophic errors. And, as we've seen, incentives work. The behavior of one emergency room physician is typical:[38]

"I recently treated a very old and pleasantly demented gentleman who had slipped and fallen at home, sustaining a laceration to the back of the scalp. It was a witnessed fall, his

second in less than a month, and there was no report of syn-
cope [i.e., fainting] or loss of consciousness. Other than the
laceration, the patient was without complaint and neurologi-
cally intact, at his baseline mental status. He just wanted me
to hurry up and close his wound so he could go home.

I briefly considered not ordering a CT scan; after all, his
recent head scan (reflexively ordered by one of my risk-
averse colleagues) was normal, he wasn't on any blood thin-
ners, and he seemed to be OK. Apparently there are some
ivory tower physicians who think we ER docs order too many
imaging studies, and I heard them murmuring like a chorus
in the back of my mind. Fortunately, I ignored them.

I'm certain that if I had NOT ordered a CT scan on this
patient with a seemingly benign injury, the Multidisciplinary
CT Scan Rationing Committee would have had a meeting
with the Quality of Care Committee and they would have
jointly supported my decision...even after his subdural
hematoma [i.e., bleeding into his head] and hemorrhagic
cerebral contusions had become clinically apparent and possibly devastating. Maybe they would have even given me an
award for my outstanding clinical judgment or my superior
rationing of resources.

In the real world outside of academic conference rooms,
nobody ever gives you a pat on the back for ordering fewer tests
or practicing more cost-effective medicine. But one thing that
academia and private practice have in common is that administrators in both arenas have a very low tolerance for missed or
delayed diagnoses, particularly when the outcome is bad.

So we'll continue to order as many damn CT scans as we
want. Personally, I'd rather order 1,000 "unnecessary" CT
scans than face the question of why I didn't order the one that
might have mattered."

How much does all of this defensive medicine cost? It depends
upon who you ask.

One of the key findings of the OTA study was that "accurate
measurement of the extent" of defensive medicine is impossible.
While physician surveys are helpful, they are to some degree subjective. Clinicians might feel compelled to inflate or deflate the numbers

for a variety of reasons, and some of their defensive behaviors are almost certainly subconscious rather than deliberate.

Another approach is to try to estimate the impact based upon differences in medical expenditures in parts of the country with different medical malpractice law. This was the approach taken by the Congressional Budget Office (CBO) in 2006. It looked at the history of healthcare spending in states that imposed various sorts of malpractice tort reforms (such as caps on non-economic damages, caps on attorneys' fees, caps or bans on punitive damages, and modification or elimination of joint-and-several liability). Taking the historical data from these various state experiments, the CBO performed regression analyses in an attempt to determine what, if any, impact on per capita medical spending might have been attributable to the tort reforms. The results were equivocal. Spending went up in some states and down in others. Although the CBO concluded that "the estimated effects of implementing a package of previously proposed tort limits is near zero," it provided a caveat to this conclusion. "The mixed results...demonstrate the difficulty of disentangling any effects of tort limits from other factors that affect levels of healthcare spending."[39] In other words, the CBO really has no idea. Katherine Hennesy at Ursinus College attempted a similar analysis limited to defensive medicine practices in skull fracture patients and came up with similarly equivocal results.

So do these studies mean that defensive medicine has little net impact on healthcare costs and efficiency? Hardly.

The biggest problem associated with these types of malpractice analyses is that they assume that "conventional" types of tort reform will have an impact on provider behavior. This approach is inherently flawed from a provider's perspective. Capping awards or attorney fees or removing punitive damages really only affects the price that malpractice insurers charge for coverage. The social, personal, professional, and financial impacts of being sued remain unchanged, and the process itself is still an adversarial one. To the average provider, it makes little difference if the maximum non-economic damages are $2,000,000, $500,000, or $250,000. Being accused of malpractice is still a miserable and traumatic experience. It's difficult to imagine that any provider would change her practice patterns simply because their insurance company would, on average, be paying less in claims compensation. A far more profound change in the way the system works will be needed for that to happen.

The result is that we're left with estimates. Not surprisingly, these vary considerably depending upon the source. Table 8.7 shows a number of these estimates along with their source and methodology, if provided. With the exception of the last one, all these estimates are limited to the effect of current malpractice law on high-risk specialties only. They do not include costs associated with all other specialties or non-physicians.

TABLE 8.7   Prominent Estimates of the Cost of Defensive Medicine in the United States

Source	Estimate of Annual Cost*	Methodology
Congressional Budget Office (2004, 2006)	"Very Small", Uncertain	"Existing studies and [CBO's] own research"
Hellinger and Encinosa (2006)[40]	At least $40 billion	Multivariate analysis of data from states with different limits on medical malpractice cases
Kessler and McClellan (1996)[41]	$60-108 billion	Economic modeling based on data for cardiac care in states with different tort limits
Massachusetts Medical Society (2008)[†]	$70 billion	Data extracted from physician surveys
PricewaterhouseCoopers' Health Research Institute (2008)[42]	$210 billion	Interviews with industry and government experts

Notes:

* As of the year published.

† Original amount calculated for Massachusetts extrapolated to the United States as a whole based upon that state's proportionate share of the U.S. population.

Just as physician surveys and "expert" assessments might be expected to be biased upward, estimates based on state tort law reform are almost certainly biased downward. Assuming that the CBO numbers are zero, the average of these estimates is $80 billion annually. This is as good an estimate of the cost of defensive medicine as we are likely to get for now.

Only two-thirds of the $28 billion spent on medical malpractice claims, insurance, and overhead goes to patients. This implies a total medical malpractice overhead cost of nearly $10 billion per year. Adding this overhead to the cost of defensive medicine means that our current approach to medical malpractice is costing us $90 billion per year, or a total efficiency loss of about 4% of the total that we're spending on healthcare. This is enough to insure about seven and one-half million people annually. There has to be a better way.

9

Friction

"It's not the work which kills people, it's the worry. It's not the revolution that destroys machinery, it's the friction."

—*Henry Ward Beecher*

"Friction" within the healthcare machine can be defined as the wear, tear, and loss of efficiency caused by aspects of the system that are poorly designed or operated. Friction typically isn't the fault of any individual part of the machine, nor is it typically a clear defect imposed from the outside. Instead, elements of friction are more likely to be structural defects that keep the wheels of healthcare from turning smoothly, efficiently, and economically. Some elements of friction are relatively simple and easy to fix, but can have a disproportionately large effect on all the elements in the system. Others are more complex but still manageable with a little cooperation, will, and common sense. Let's look at a few of these.

Unique Patient Identifiers

Properly associating individuals with their insurance, medical records, laboratory tests, billing, and hundreds of other medical and administrative functions is one of the most vexing challenges in all of healthcare. This is because the United States has no single identifier that can be used to uniquely and universally identify each and every one of us as medically distinct individuals.

There is currently no way to reliably know that a given medical item (be it a chart, fluid sample, radiograph or report) is uniquely associated with a given human being. Instead, the process of mapping a person to all other objects in their medical world is known as "statistical mapping." One tries to collect pieces of indentifying information about each patient—none of which are necessarily unique by themselves. These include names, gender, dates of birth, Social Security numbers, addresses, and anything else that seems useful. The hope, of course, is that if enough of these elements match, you have a good chance of distinguishing one John Smith from another.

There are many drawbacks to the statistical matching approach. The first and most obvious problem is that this approach might not work to distinguish two individuals. This is of special concern in healthcare, where errors resulting from a case of mistaken identity could easily prove fatal. As discussed in a RAND Corporation report on patient identification, statistical matching will inevitably create errors in the form of both "false positives," in which the wrong patient is identified, and "false negatives," where not all of a patient's records are found.[1] Either situation can result in serious errors in medical management. Indeed, many duplicated tests, laboratory errors, and medication errors are the direct result of false positive and false negative patient identification.

The second problem with statistical identification is that it's highly inefficient. That makes it expensive. Every medical facility is forced to collect many pieces of information about every patient, and associate that information with every specimen, medical record, and communication. The more pieces of information one has, the more accurate and reliable the statistical matching process becomes. On the other hand, each additional piece of information adds to administrative overhead cost. Not only is the process tedious, it is also prone to human error. Misspelled names, incorrect dates of birth, changes in names, addresses, and telephone numbers all add to the obvious difficulty of making each match and keeping identities straight. Each specimen needs to be labeled with multiple pieces of information. Even supposedly unique nonmedical identifiers such as Social Security numbers are less helpful than one might think.

All this overhead accrues to anyone and everyone who has anything to do with patients. All hospitals and providers are, of course, affected. However, all insurance companies, government health agencies (including Medicare and Medicaid), clinical laboratories, billing offices, pharmacies, vendors of medical equipment, research efforts, nursing homes, and hospices are as well. Patients and their families are ultimately most affected because they must inevitably deal with each of these entities.

A more subtle hazard of the existing statistical identification system is that it places each patient's privacy and identity at risk. By forcing so many people to collect so much information again and again, all our personal details become widely distributed on a regular basis. This is the same information that must be used for our personal business—from bank accounts to credit cards, mortgages, employment, and Social Security. After this data is misplaced or stolen, it's a herculean effort for patients to recover and start over.

The intelligent alternative to statistical identification is a unique patient identifier that is specifically created for, and dedicated to, healthcare use only. Unique medical identifiers would almost instantly correct nearly all the friction inherent in the current patient identification system. They would reduce medical errors, save time and money, improve privacy, enhance security, and facilitate healthcare research. In terms of the healthcare machine, unique patient identifiers would lubricate virtually every healthcare transaction—hundreds of billions of them each year. These identifiers already exist in several European health systems (such as Norway, the United Kingdom, and Canada). There they have functioned smoothly, been associated with few, if any, privacy or security concerns, and have performed as advertised. None of this is a secret. One has to wonder why the United States has not followed suit.

The answer is a combination of short-term thinking, popular misconceptions, and political timidity.

The original Health Insurance Portability and Accountability Act of 1996 (HIPAA) law mandated that the Secretary of Health and Human Services (HHS) adopt standards providing for "a unique health identifier for each individual, employer, health plan, and health care provider for use in the healthcare system." As the RAND report describes:

> Although an analysis completed for HHS in 1997 suggested a number of practicable options for a national patient identifier, subsequent hearings conducted by the National Committee

on Vital and Health Statistics (NCVHS, 1998) revealed significant concerns that the privacy and security of patient information could be threatened if it were networked beyond local healthcare information systems.

Very few comments at those hearings were directed specifically at the relative merits of the UPI as a patient identifier, but Congress subsequently prohibited HHS from expending funds in further study of a UPI without its explicit approval. This prohibition effectively stopped HHS from further considering or experimenting with a UPI as a means of linking health information in a national or regional network.[2]

Based upon testimony presented by those opposed to unique identifiers at the time, the overriding concern was not that the IDs were inherently risky, but instead that no "comprehensive privacy protections" were in place to govern their use. The most strident objections were that unique IDs would be used to aggregate all medical information without the patient's consent, and the aggregate information would be placed at the disposal of government agencies.

Placing complete personal medical information in the hands of bureaucrats and/or political operatives is clearly a valid concern. So is allowing personal health information to be used for commercial purposes that are of little or no benefit to patients themselves. But instead of implementing unique IDs and severely limiting their use by nonmedical personnel, Congress took the opposite approach. It banned research into the best way to devise and implement unique identifiers, and left issues pertaining to their use unresolved. Having made this decision more than a decade ago, Congress has never seriously reconsidered the matter. Instead, the healthcare system has been subjected to ten years of unnecessary friction—excess errors, overhead, and duplicated tests.

Medical Recordkeeping and Transaction Processing

Creating, maintaining, and sharing medical records and transactions (such as prescriptions, orders, consults, and referrals) are among the most basic and essential healthcare processes. Healthcare records are the starting point for clinical evaluation, an archive for future reference and legal documentation for legal, administrative, and billing purposes. If the process of creating medical records and transactions does not go quickly and smoothly, nothing goes quickly and smoothly.

In recent years the electronic creation, storage, and dissemination of medical records has become a multibillion dollar industry and a focal point for politicians, businessmen, and academics looking for a quick fix to the dysfunction present in healthcare. It's comforting to imagine that simply adding more technology can solve most, if not all, of the knotty problems that healthcare presents. There is certainly no shortage of bullish projections to support this notion. A 2004 study by the RAND Corporation concluded that fully implementing electronic medical records (EMRs) in the United States would save $77 billion annually, and a cumulative total of $371 billion over a 15-year implementation period.* Their estimated cost to implement these systems over that period of time is about $115 billion. That's a return on investment of more than 100 percent. The logical conclusion of this type of analysis is that we might want to drop everything and simply implement more technology—at gunpoint if necessary. With returns like that, how can we possibly go wrong?

The answer is simple: friction.

Medical records provide an interesting study in friction because of the technological contrast presented by pieces of paper and computerized medical records. They are the classic examples of the antiquated and the futuristic, the physical and the ephemeral, the unfashionable and the stylish.

The vast majority of medical records in the United States are currently created and maintained in paper form. Your basic medical chart is a heterogeneous collection of information of varying degrees of interest and importance. Its contents will differ depending upon whether it reflects inpatient or outpatient records. In an outpatient office, the chart will contain insurance information, records of histories and physical exams, progress notes, vital signs, x-ray, pathology

---

* The terms "electronic medical record (EMR)" and "electronic health record (EHR)" are used interchangeably in healthcare.

and lab results, surgical notes, prescriptions, records of phone calls and missed appointments, patient correspondence, and of course, insurance and billing information. Inpatient records will have much the same information, but will also contain nursing notes, physician orders, and notes from the various inpatient departments, such as physical therapy and the pharmacy. Most paper charts are organized like file cabinets—each type of information is maintained in chronological order in a different tabbed portion of the medical record folder.

If we think of a paper record as a physical book or a file cabinet, electronic medical records are the computer equivalent. Instead of creating and filing pieces of paper, all notes and records regarding history, physical exams, surgical labs, progress notes, vital signs and all other pieces of information are stored as bits in a computer. As we all know, computers have a number of advantages over paper when it comes to sharing data remotely, searching for specific pieces of information, duplicating information quickly and easily, and downloading data (such as digital radiographs, lab results, and pictures) that are already in electronic form.

One would imagine that electronic records would be rapidly embraced as the standard way in which medical information would be recorded and stored. Indeed, the federal government is placing a great deal of pressure on healthcare providers to do exactly that. Beginning at least as early as 2006, legislators began proposing legislation that would mandate the purchase and use of EMRs. Even before taking office, President Obama set a goal of computerizing all America's healthcare records by the end of 2014.[3] And one aspect of electronic healthcare data management—electronic prescribing—is already the law of the land. Beginning in 2012, physicians who fail to switch to electronic prescribing will be penalized 1% of their Medicare payments, with the penalty rising to 2% after 2013.[4]

But for millions of smart, well-informed, and well-educated healthcare providers, the case for electronic medical everything isn't so clear cut. In spite of government cheerleading, mandates, and threats of payments and/or penalties, only 6% of American doctors currently e-prescribe, and just 2% of the prescriptions written annually are electronic.[5] Electronic medical record use is not a great deal better. A large 2008 survey of physicians practicing in office environments found that 4% reported having an extensive "fully functional" electronic medical record system, while 13% reported having a "basic system".[t,6] How is it possible that there could be such a disconnect between what's apparently "good for healthcare," and what clinicians are willing to purchase and use voluntarily?

The reality is that both paper-based and electronic healthcare information systems have serious drawbacks. As with so many other aspects of the healthcare machine, the current push to force clinicians to switch to electronic systems is motivated at least as much by vested political and economic interests as by any potential benefits of the systems themselves. If we're going to understand where friction occurs in healthcare and try to reduce the inefficiency it causes, it behooves us to examine the role, format, and agendas behind medical information in more detail. Why are some people so anxious to force healthcare into electronic records and transactions, while so many providers are reluctant at best? And what's the best course of action for us to take as patients and those financing the system?

---

[t] On a nationwide basis, this survey underestimates the total percentage of physicians using EMRs because the study excluded doctors working in federal hospitals such as those in the Veterans Administration and on military bases. All providers at these facilities are required to use federally provided electronic record systems that were developed (and sometimes completely scrapped and redeveloped) at a cost of billions of dollars. Ironically, even in these environments, the distribution of the technology exceeds its actual use. One example is the "Joint Patient Tracking Application" (JPTA), which cost $320,000 to develop and $2 million per year to operate. The system was designed to allow providers in Iraq and Afghanistan to document care provided in those theaters of war—thereby creating medical records that could be accessed for healthcare purposes by doctors in the United States when those patients returned stateside. However, in 2007 it was reported that only 13 of 70 military treatment centers in the United States used the system, even though they were required to do so beginning in 2005. The problem was that the JPTA was implemented as a parallel system to the larger primary EMR system already present and in use at military facilities. Providers were therefore forced to remember to look for patient information in two places instead of one. Integration of the two systems has proven difficult—costing more than $230 million and counting. The presence of two incompatible record systems—one of which did not fit into the ordinary workflow of stateside physicians—allowed patients to fall through the cracks, resulting in the unnecessary duplication of tests and even the deaths of some soldiers. (Urbina J, Nixon R. "Disuse of System is Cited in Gaps in Soldiers' Care." *The New York Times*, March 30, 2007.)

Paper-Based Healthcare Information Systems

Despite their age, pen and paper are still among the most convenient and efficient recording and communication devices known to man. They are fast, cheap, and portable. Moving parts are few. Paper systems don't crash, don't depend upon electricity or the Internet, and don't require much in the way of skill to maintain. Almost every type of visual information can be recorded on paper, from writing to drawings to photos and electrocardiograms. A clinician can take paper into an exam room and easily listen and talk to patients and families while writing. Because our current healthcare system is based upon paper, the infrastructure investments needed to handle it have already been made. Most importantly, pen and paper require no introduction or training, and their applicability is universal. No one receiving a paper record or prescription has to worry about learning how to use it, or whether it's compatible with the software or systems they happen to have. Provider workflow is already optimized for paper, even as computers are used for many non-provider clinic tasks such as scheduling, billing, and accounting.

These qualities give paper-based records and transactions enormous flexibility and versatility. Roughly the same materials and equipment can be used in clinics and hospitals catering to completely different groups of patients, illnesses, and specialties. Patient records can be copied and transferred with relative ease, and prescriptions can be carried to any pharmacy in the country without special provisions or equipment. This type of flexibility is invaluable when dealing with large numbers of independently held and disparate organizations, as in the United States. Millions of offices, clinics, labs, imaging centers, pharmacies, and hospitals know that they can rely on paper to communicate reliably and effectively. In a world where hype is routine and technology is often incompatible, these are valuable attributes and should not be taken lightly.

Of course, paper is hardly perfect. Although paper is cheap, convenient, and a universal input medium, it leaves much to be desired as a means of storing, searching, recalling, and transmitting data.

Paper is bulky and takes up lots of space. It's relatively labor-intensive. In large clinics and hospitals, the physical size and number of records to be managed require whole rooms and medical record staffs to operate. Because paper is a physical entity, it can only be in one place at a time, making it difficult for many providers to share information simultaneously. On average, a provider looking for a paper hospital chart will be unable to obtain it immediately about one-third of the time. Paper can be slow to send. Finally, paper is far from ideal with respect to searching for and tabulating data. Looking at a pile of charts, there is simply no easy way to extract which patients have what condition or how they're being treated.

These drawbacks are the reason that electronic medical records are of considerable interest to payers and government agencies. If you want to know about a patient, you can simply look at his chart. On the other hand, if you want to *track* and *control* things such as diagnostic tests, formularies, referrals, and other forms of resource utilization, it really takes a computer. Let's look at the corresponding advantages and disadvantages of electronic media in healthcare.

Electronic Healthcare Information Systems

Computers have now been used in healthcare for almost 50 years. Initially computers were used in purely business and administrative roles. Mainframes were adopted by insurers and large hospitals to run their billing and accounting systems, while mass production facilities such as clinical laboratories and pharmacies used them to track orders and results. The first efforts to use computerized records for patient care in the United States came in the late 1960s, when the University of Vermont began to develop the "problem-oriented medical record," or POMR. POMR was first used on a medical ward in 1970, and the 1970s and 1980s saw the development of other EMRs in both clinical and research settings. Beginning in the late 1980s and early 1990s, electronic records began to be developed commercially for both hospital and outpatient use. By the mid-1990s they had become big business to companies such as Cerner, GE, and Epic, which sold large centralized systems to hospitals and health systems.

These large organizations have spent a great deal of money on trial and error. The U.S. military has spent many billions of dollars on developing multiple electronic record systems—most of which have been costly failures. Its latest iteration, known as "Armed Forces Longitudinal Technology Application," or AHLTA, is widely seen as performing poorly and has already cost more than $5 billion. The price tag on a suitable replacement is now expected to cost an additional $15 billion.[7] The private sector has seen its share of challenges as well. Kaiser Permanente spent nearly $2 billion on various electronic record systems that have been scrapped, and is now $4 billion into a troubled rollout of a system from Epic Systems Corporation.[8] The introduction of EMRs into smaller offices and clinics is a more recent phenomenon that has only become of practical importance within the past decade.

Electronic medical records are far more heterogeneous in terms of design and functionality than their paper counterparts. A really simple EMR can consist of a program that simply organizes text documents. Complex EMRs can not only aggregate many different types of medical information (such as text, images, formularies and drug databases, video, radiographs, sounds, labs, and pathology), but also provide modules intended to assist providers with their prescriptions, diagnoses, clinical trials, and medical references.

The advantages of computers and electronic medical records are most pronounced in exactly the same areas in which paper records fail. Good, well-designed electronic medical records:

- Take up little or no physical space.
- Can be shared easily.
- Can be rapidly searched to locate specific pieces of information, or to identify all cases meeting specific criteria.
- Can easily be transmitted over long distances should the need arise.
- Readily handle information that is created and/or reported digitally, such as computerized tomography scans or automated laboratory results.
- Allow orders and other transactions initiated by clinicians to be automatically routed to the recipient.

All these functions are valuable for someone in the healthcare system—and most particularly for large organizations. Managing a wall of charts is easy for a small medical office. The same person who greets each patient can reach back to pull a chart or file away a note. Fighting over charts in small offices is an uncommon occurrence. But in large healthcare and vendors organizations, the time that computers can save is money. Electronic records can reduce internal filing and transportation expenses, speed delivery of patient information to multiple departments, and feed production data automatically to wholly-owned production profit centers such as the pharmacy, lab, or radiology departments. They can pass critical billing data directly to billing office computers, and allow management to keep tabs on the relative practice patterns, cost, and profitability of individual healthcare providers. Computerized physician order entry systems can be programmed to enforce specific drug formularies, or even change formularies in real time based upon the changing price of drugs. Computerizing medical records makes it possible to really *control* what goes on in an otherwise fragmented healthcare system for the first time—both for better and for worse.

Given the benefits, why aren't these things ubiquitous?

As it happens, electronic medical records have their share of disadvantages. Many of these are the opposite of advantages presented by paper-based systems. Electronic systems are often more time-consuming than their paper counterparts, far more complex and prone to defects, more expensive to buy and maintain, generally have poor connectivity, and in many cases do not work nearly as well. Given the importance attached to "going digital" in 21st century America, we should examine these problems in more detail.

Healthcare IT, Provider Time, and Workflow

Probably the most fundamental drawback of electronic medical records lies in the nature of computers themselves. When compared to paper, computers are a rotten input device for the average physician. If you've ever been in the close confines of a clinic or emergency department exam room as a patient, it's possible to appreciate how difficult it can be to conduct an interactive history and physical exam in the presence of a computer screen, keyboard, and mouse. The vast majority of clinicians find it difficult to type, click, look at the patient, listen to them, and speak all at the same time. In contrast to the open format of paper, the vast majority of computer programs in healthcare are highly structured—forcing providers to accommodate the software rather than the other way around.

The result is usually a substantial loss in provider productivity. For those who make their living by providing care to lots of patients, this is a serious problem. In 2001, Makoul, Curry, and Tang did a study directly comparing the time use and behaviors of a group of three physicians who were experienced in using EMRs in the course of office visits with a group of three physicians using paper-based records. Although the sample of 204 patient encounters was not large enough to show a statistical difference in the length of time required for all visits, the standard EMR visit took 26.7 minutes, compared with 23.6 minutes for a paper-based visit—a 13% increase. The difference in time required for initial patient visits was statistically significant: 35.2 minutes for EMR visits versus 25.6 minutes for paper-based encounters—a 37.5% increase in visit length.[9] A summary of all the available studies regarding the impact of computerized systems on physician time was done by Poissant et al.[10] Disregarding one study which looked at just a single doctor and another in which the number of doctors and exact methodology are unknown, all but one found that the amount of time required to document clinical information was substantially higher when computers were used than for paper.[†]

The bottom line is that, for the vast majority of clinicians, EMRs take more time and operate less efficiently than their paper counterparts. Because time is the only inventory a clinician has, the net effect on most small practices is to either reduce income or increase the

---

[†] The most stunning part of these results had to do with the impact of "computerized physician order entry (CPOE)." In the case of CPOE, the increase in physician time required compared with paper-based order entry averages well over 100%, and required more than three times the amount of time in a large recent study.

amount of physician time required to see the same number of patients. Either outcome is a bad one from the perspective of the average, nonsalaried provider.[§]

Complexity

In his *Wall Street Journal* column on computer technology, Walter Mossberg once wrote, "Just remember: you're not a 'dummy,' no matter what those computer books claim. The real dummies are the people who—though technically expert—couldn't design hardware and software that's usable by normal consumers if their lives depended upon it." Nowhere is this more pronounced than in the case of healthcare information technology (HIT).

In the clinical world, the difficulties and frustrations associated with implementing and learning how to use medical information technologies are legendary. As one well-known HIT pioneer and former EMR booster recently put it: "When you put an EMR into a primary care practice, your life is hell for the next year."[11]

The vast majority of healthcare providers would probably agree with this assessment. It's generally accepted that EMRs dramatically reduce provider efficiency and productivity for an extended period of time. Dr. Kishore Tipimeni has described the typical experience:[12]

> During the implementation phase, three distinct groups of physicians emerged. The more tech-savvy physicians, through much effort, were able to be fully implemented in

---

[§] The distinction between salaried and nonsalaried providers is extremely important in this case. There is an enormous differential between the deployment of these systems in small independent practices as compared to large healthcare organizations such as the VA, the military, and Kaiser Permanente. Although virtually all clinicians in these organizations are required to use EMRs, fewer than 20% of clinicians in smaller private practices have elected to do so. The reason is simple: Salaried clinicians are the only ones who can afford to ignore the acquisition costs, time costs, and productivity losses. Large institutions are willing to ignore these losses because electronic systems produce compensating gains when used to process lab, pharmacy, and billing transactions. The majority of independent providers are only acting rationally when they decline to "go digital."

6–9 months. Another group of physicians who were very frustrated with the data entry required by the EMR decided to hire an additional employee to do the data entry for them. The third group of physicians could not tolerate the training and implementation and refused to use the EMR altogether. At the end of the 1-1/2 years, the practice had directly spent $350,000, had 6 out of 10 physicians using the EMR, and had increased the number of employees in the practice. None of the physicians using the EMR were seeing the same number of patients that they were under the paper chart system. On average, each physician was seeing only 35 patients for a full day in the clinic. This resulted in a lost revenue of $432,000 per year ($100 × 5 patients × 3 days × 4 weeks × 12 months × 6 physicians). As one can see, the total cost of the EMR for the practice including acquisition, implementation, increased overhead, and lost revenue was approaching $1,000,000 for what seemed like a $200,000 EMR. Although the practice did decrease their cost of transcription and had more accurate billing of office visit charges, these improvements did not come close to making up for the loss of productivity and increased overhead.

We can find similar descriptions almost anywhere that "conventional" electronic medical information systems have been installed. A loss of practice efficiency and productivity—at least for a period ranging from six months to two years—is typical. The reasons are very consistent:

1. People in all aspects of clinical practice have a limited ability to learn and use the systems. Medical assistants, clerical staff, and clinicians are busy, generally nontechnical people with limited time and attention available for learning complex systems on top of their hectic day jobs. Most medical software is considerably more complex than standard office applications such as word processors and spreadsheets, and many (if not most) healthcare staff are not college educated. A few hourly training sessions are hardly adequate to provide familiarity, much less proficiency.

   Even where electronic systems are deployed, this complexity means that the vast majority of their features and capabilities go unused. A study of how doctors used electronic hospital records in Norway found that, in practice, they used only 2 to 7 of the 23 clinical functions that the records were designed to perform.[13]

2. Hospitals, clinics, and practice patterns vary considerably. There is no such thing as a "one size fits all" medical software application, and considerable customization and configuration is often needed to make even the best software workable.

3. The vast majority of EMR software (and, in fact, clinical software in general) is poorly conceived and executed. This is especially true with regard to medical practice as it takes place in the private sector.

This last point might seem harsh, but it is amply supported by the evidence. Indeed, some experts would say that it does not go far enough—medical software applications in large organizations such as the military and health maintenance organizations are not just poorly written, but often defective as well. Here are just a few recent examples:

- In the United Kingdom, the chief executive of London's Royal Free Hospital berated a new National Health System EMR for "causing heartache and hard work." The hospital IT project is part of a £12 billion effort to put 50 million patient records online by 2014. Problems with the system cost the hospital trust £10 million, caused outpatient booking to take four times longer than normal, and forced the hospital to hire an additional 40 employees to help handle the extra workload.[14]

- "An electronic health records management system being rolled out by Kaiser Foundation Health Plan/Hospitals has been nothing short of an IT project gone awry, according to sources at the company and an internal report detailing problems..." The project in question is a $4 billion system from Epic Systems Corporation that has been plagued with persistent problems, and was meant to replace several other multibillion dollar Kaiser EMR systems that are being scrapped. "The 780-page internal report... detailed hundreds of technical problems with the system—some affecting patient care—that appear to bear out the concerns of [a Kaiser employee] and others in the organization that the system is a failure." One example was a power outage at Kaiser's data center that lasted for 55 hours and 7 minutes, affecting the ability of numerous health facilities to access the system.[15]

The military's AHLTA medical record system has cost $5 billion thus far, and is expected to cost an additional $15 billion to upgrade to a usable form that can share data with VA medical record systems. Here's a sample of what dozens of different military healthcare providers had to say about the AHLTA in a 2008 online discussion:[16]

"AHLTA tries to do too much. We would be much better off with a program which allows you to just write a simple note. It would take fewer screens and would be more amenable to a transcriptionist typing a simple dictated note. It makes no sense to pay a physician salary (GS-14, -15) to be a typist (GS-4, -5). A coder can then code each note separately. The time it takes to type and flip through screens for me is as much time as it is to see the patient, clearly impacting productivity, and decreasing job satisfaction. This program would never make it in the civilian market because doctors would never use it. We use it because we are forced to."

"We have a system (AHLTA) that slows providers by 20%. The cost of this across DOD must be astounding! The system only "works" because providers spend two hours a day tediously doing 'data entry.'"

"Prior to AHLTA, I was able to provide over 5000 visits a year with excellent notes. Now I am lucky to reach 3600/yr with a note that is cryptic in nature and difficult for the follow-on provider to specifically visualize where I took the 1mm melanoma skin cancer off of the forehead due to lack of a user friendly and efficient way to illustrate the location of that biopsy on a figure, or quickly attach a Polaroid picture to the note as we did in the past. Now we are encouraged NOT to attach digital photos that are difficult to load and consume large amounts of bandwidth."

"I am very concerned about the many patient safety issues that are prevalent in AHLTA. We have thousands of duplicate patients, significant allergy synchronization issues, labs not writing back to AHLTA, and our providers have to check both AHLTA and CHCS, encounters that are NOT in AHLTA, from services such as emergency departments who don't use AHLTA at all due to the known performance and other issues, note text that frequently doesn't state what was truly intended, and discovered this week are notes that appear to stay on our LCS and not get posted to the CDR where they are visible by other sites. Yes, we hope that patient care is enhanced by our electronic health record, but in the process we've created a quagmire of risks...."

Despite scattered and well-publicized success stories offered by individual hospitals and EMR manufacturers, there is still little evidence that the benefits of many electronic systems outweigh their risks and disadvantages for the vast majority of practices. Some excellent discussions on this topic have been written by Dr. Scot Silverstein, a physician and director of medical informatics at a large hospital.[17]

> While clinical IT is now potentially capable of achieving many of the benefits long claimed for it...there is a major caveat and essential precondition: The benefits will be realized only if clinical IT is done well. For if clinical IT is not done well, as often occurs in today's environment of medical quick fixes and seemingly unquestioning exuberance about IT, the technology can be injurious to medical practice and biomedical R&D, and highly wasteful of scarce healthcare capital and resources.
>
> Those two short words "done well" mask an underlying, profound, and, as yet, largely unrecognized (or ignored) complexity... Unfortunately, even well-designed clinical IT applications often lack the sustained agility in critical functions such as charting, information retrieval, and decision support to keep up with the pace of the hospital and clinic, and with the pace of change in medical science and practice. These applications can distract clinicians and make their work harder and more stressful. Worse, much of the technology now available comes nowhere near the optimal design possible."

Poor design is rampant in healthcare IT, and is not restricted to EMRs by any means. As one researcher who has studied the use of computexrized physician order entry (CPOE) observed:

> "Many information systems simply don't reflect the health care professional's hectic work environment, with its all too frequent interruptions from phone calls, pages, colleagues,

and patients. Instead, these are designed for people who work in calm and solitary environments. This design disconnect is the source of both types of silent errors. The screen itself can cause errors. Choices that appear too close together result in ordering the wrong tests or sending orders for the wrong person. If a system is rigidly structured, it causes users to focus closely on entering details and switching from screen to screen to enter information. Some patient care information systems require data entry that is so elaborate that time spent recording patient data is significantly greater than it was with its paper predecessors. What is worse, on several occasions during our studies, overly structured data entry led to a loss of cognitive focus by the clinician."[18]

It has even been necessary to add a new medical term to the dictionary: "e-iatrogenesis."

E-iatrogenesis is defined as patient harm caused at least in part by the application of health information technology.[19] This "new" harm has always been a part of introducing computers as a potentially important and helpful new medical tool, but it has largely been overlooked. This is partly as a result of unbridled enthusiasm over new computer technologies, but also because researchers have been slow (or possibly even reluctant) to look for it. A comprehensive study by Koppel and colleagues found that a widely used CPOE system actually *facilitated* 22 types of medication error risks, with many of these potential errors occurring frequently.[20] Nor are these problems limited to computerized medical systems in the United States:

In mid-December 2006, the *London Times* reported on the inadvertent prescription of Viagra to a set of patients in the United Kingdom. This error occurred when general practitioners using the UK's National Health Service "e-Formulary" attempted to prescribe "Zyban" (a medication commonly used to assist patients in smoking cessation). The system mistakenly selected "sildenafil" (the generic name for Viagra) instead. A spokesperson for the NHS denied that any untoward effects had resulted, and that immediate steps had been taken to rectify the error, including notifying over 900 practitioners at more than 300 clinics warning them of the potential problem for their patients.[21]

Still more problems with the design of CPOE were uncovered by a study published in early 2009, when it was observed that doctors override roughly 90% of the medication alerts prompted by the system.[22] The problem is not that the alerts are being ignored inappropriately, but instead that too many of the electronic alerts were irrelevant to the clinical circumstances. As one author of the study commented, "The systems and the computers that are supposed to make [physicians'] lives better are actually torturing them."[23]

Hospitals and health systems often have the financial wherewithal to "tough it out" when they make poor IT decisions—pouring good money after bad in the hope that things will eventually work themselves out. Most independent clinicians don't have that luxury. The best estimates seem to be that 20% to 30% of private practices who buy EMRs end up scrapping them—with many of those reverting back to paper.[24,25] There is perhaps no other industry in which about a quarter of all purchases are quickly discarded as defective or unworkable. It is virtually inconceivable that one out of every four cars, copiers, pieces of accounting software, or cell phones would be scrapped so readily.

With word-of-mouth advertising like this, one has to agree with the person who said: "Given these many economic obstacles, it is noteworthy not that so few practices computerize their clinical activities, but that so many actually do."[26]

High Cost, Poor Connectivity

All of this might not be so bad if all these healthcare information technologies were cheap, but they're not. As we can see in Table 9.1, conventional electronic medical record systems are quite expensive, costing about as much to buy for each doctor as a luxury automobile. Recurring annual maintenance costs for this type of software are typically 18%–20% percent of the acquisition cost.

Of course, to place these costs in context we also need to look at the financial benefits that the systems can provide. The best estimates of these are provided in Table 9.2, from the same government report on EMRs.

TABLE 9.1   Cost Components Associated with EMR Deployment in Small Clinics[27]

Type of Costs	Wang, 2003 Financial Costs per Physician (6-Yr Cum)	Miller, 2004 Financial Costs per FTE Provider (1-Yr)	AAFP Vendor Survey Financial Cost over 3-Year Period (EHR Stand-Alone System, Average Total Cost for Three-Physician Practice)	Gans, 2005 Financial Costs per Physician Estimated by Survey (no timeframe noted)
Acquisition Costs	**$42,900**	**$43,405**	**$49,837**	**$33,000**
·Hardware	$12,301	$12,749	$20,590	
·Software	$8,527		$15,794	
·Software training and installation		$22,038	$3,020	
·Workflow redesign, training, and paper-electronic chart conversion	$3,400			
·Productivity loss during implementation	$10,667	$7,473		
·Other implementation costs		$1,145	$1,998	
·Technical/network system support	$7,994		$3,151	
Annual Costs [3] (recurring)		**$8,412**	**$2,642**	**$18,000 ($1,500/mo.)**
·Software maintenance and support		$2,439		
·Hardware replacement		$3,187		
·Internal IS/external IS contractors		$2,047		
·Other ongoing costs		$739		

TABLE 9.2   Reported Financial Benefits of EMRs in Smaller Practices[28]

Benefit Category	Benefit	Wang, et al., 2003 Financial Benefits per Physician for EMRs (6-year cumulative)	Miller, et al., 2005 Financial Benefits per FTE Provider for EMRs per Year (estimated after year 1)
Clinical Utilization	Drug savings	$55,384	
	Reduced radiology use	$13,332	
	Reduced laboratory use	$3,855	
	Drug utilization		
Patient Safety	Reduction in ADEs	$7,430	
Workflow Efficiency	Chart pull savings	$12,988	
	Transcription savings	$11,690	$5,334
	Personnel savings (excl. transcription savings)		$6,759
	Paper supply savings		$1,051
Revenue Cycle	Reduction in billing errors	$12,207	
	Improved charge capture	$12,368	
	Increased revenue from increase visits		$2,664
	Increased coding levels		$16,929

On the surface, the benefits seem considerable. However, a closer inspection reveals some problems. None of the financial savings in drug use, radiology, laboratory tests, or adverse drug events (ADEs) accrue to the physicians who are supposed to buy these systems. Instead, the benefits accrue to public and private insurers and healthcare administrators. Savings in chart pulls and transcription costs could benefit providers, but only if they employ personnel dedicated to these tasks. This will not be the case for most small practices. A reduction in billing errors and improved charge capture might well improve clinician revenue, but only because the government has made billing so complex that only a computer can keep track of the minutiae required to submit a clean claim. There are less expensive billing applications that can perform these same tasks.

The net result is that providers have little or no financial benefit to show for a large and ongoing expenditure of their gradually dwindling incomes. The American Medical Association claims that the average physician will receive only about 11 cents of every dollar potentially saved by using healthcare IT, while shouldering all the acquisition and maintenance costs, as well as the loss in productivity.[29] A review of the studies and analyses surrounding the net financial impact of EMRs on clinicians is pretty depressing:[30]

- A 2008 Congressional Budget Office study was unable to find any convincing evidence that the financial benefits to providers of electronic health records would outweigh their costs, even as "...the average drop in revenue from...loss of productivity was about $7,500 per physician. That amount might understate the actual loss in productivity...because in some practices, physicians worked longer hours to keep the practice's income the same as it was before adoption."[31]

- A cost-benefit analysis of the use of EMRs in primary care was able to show a net benefit to physicians at five years, but only as a result of achieving savings in drug expenditures, radiology costs, and laboratory utilization. These benefits only occurred if a high percentage of patients were capitated—placing the burden of these costs directly on the physician.[32]

- A survey of the financial impact of the use of EMRs in hospitals was likewise unable to turn up any reliable evidence of benefit. "Other researchers have found the same results. For example, a 2005 review of 256 published studies attempted to quantify an EMR's economic value. Although 82 of these studies considered the hospital inpatient setting, *not one rigorous study was found that quantified the economic benefits of a full-functioned, vendor-supplied system.*"[33]

By this point, we have to hope that all this additional cost and loss of productivity in the clinic can be offset by a dramatic increase in connectivity. After all, one of the big drawbacks of paper is that it has to be transferred—either physically or by imaging—and the data re-entered into computers at the destination. But at least once the data is in paper form, it can be sent anywhere and be easily used by anybody.

By now it should be no surprise that the news here is grim as well. To directly quote the Office of the National Coordinator for Health Information Technology in its listing of *Current Market Barriers and Challenges to Widespread Adoption of Health Information Technology:*[34]

- Limited capacity for interoperability
- Few health information technology products include standards
- Standards are not rigorous and lag behind commercialization
- There is no viable health information exchange infrastructure

There is really not much need to elaborate on this point. The vast majority of digital medical data currently resides in proprietary, monolithic software and database systems that have little or no ability to share information with the other 380 commercial medical record systems currently in use in the United States alone. A variety of data sharing models have been tried, most notably the "regional health information organization" model, but none have met with a great deal of success. This is certainly not for lack of trying. Billions of dollars have been spent in the attempt.

Paper Versus Computers—The Evidence to Date

All this leaves us in an awkward place. We know that electronic healthcare information technologies (HIT) have potential value, and that the federal government is strongly encouraging (and even mandating) their adoption. However, we also know that these systems can, under certain circumstances, add to the workload of healthcare providers and even disrupt the process of clinical care. We also know that many of these systems are highly complex, expensive, and often unreliable. Can we at least say that—in contrast to the paper systems they're to replace—the wholesale adoption of these technologies will generate substantial healthcare benefits?

Here, too, the answer is no, but it's not for lack of trying. People have been trying to empirically prove the medical benefits of electronic medical records and other healthcare information technologies for at least a decade. The results have been equivocal at best.

As we saw previously, the 2005 RAND Corporation study predicts both great health and financial benefits if health information technologies are broadly deployed in the United States.** These included potential benefits from improvements in safety and economic efficiency. The key word here is "potential." Most of these benefits—including the medical ones—have been hard to find in practice.

Several studies have made a concerted effort to measure the benefits of EMRs and other IT measures empirically.

- In 2007, Linder and his colleagues looked at the association between the deployment of EMRs and 17 ambulatory indicators related to quality of care. To do this, they reviewed data from more than 25,000 patients seen by almost 1,500 clinicians, and compared the presence and absence of quality care indicators for doctors using EMRs to those who did not.

** Many politicians, including President Obama, have repeatedly cited the results of this study as a justification for government programs that will eventually force all U.S. healthcare providers to purchase and use EMRs, e-prescription systems, and other healthcare information technologies—often against their will.

There was no statistically significant difference in the performance of EMR versus non-EMR clinicians in 14 of the 17 indicators. In two cases, the EMR group performed better (not giving benzodiazepine drugs to patients with depression, and in doing routine urinalysis tests). However, the EMR group was *not* as good as the paper-based group when it came to using statin drugs in patients with high cholesterol.

- A 2008 study specifically looked the value of EMRs in the management of heart failure in more than 15,000 patients. In this case, EMRs and paper were no different in six out of seven quality measures, with EMRs having an advantage only when it came to providing educational materials.[35]

- A substantial amount of work has been done to look at whether EMRs can improve the care of patients with diabetes, as shown in Table 9.3.

TABLE 9.3   Studies Comparing Diabetic Care in Practices Using Healthcare Information Technology as Compared to Practices Using Paper-Based Systems

Study and Year	Technology	Result
Meigs[36] (2002)	Web-based decision support tool	Technology increased the use of testing, but resulted in no clinical improvement in patients.
Montori[37] (2002)	Diabetes Electronic Management System	Technology increased testing, but did not result in better clinical results in patients.
O'Connor[38] (2005)	EMR	"In this controlled study, EMR led to an increased number of HbA1c and LDL tests but not to better metabolic control [over a four year period]."
Jones[39] (2006)	PDA-based diabetes electronic management system	PDA improved the annual number of eye and foot exams, but did not have any significant impact on outcomes of diabetes care.
Orzano[40] (2007)	Simple clinical information systems (both paper and computer-based), and EMR	Use of simple clinical information systems generally improved diabetes care, whether paper- or computer-based. Use of EMRs did not have a positive impact.

continues

TABLE 9.3   Continued

Study and Year	Technology	Result
Crosson[41] (2007)	EMR	”...After adjustment, patient care in the 37 practices not using an EMR was more likely to meet guidelines for process, confidence, treatment, and intermediate outcomes than the 13 practices using an EMR.”
O'Connor[42] (2007)	EMR	"EMR use not associated with better glucose, blood pressure, or lipid control in patients with diabetes."

What is remarkable about these studies is that they all lead to similar conclusions.

- Even the most recent and positively optimistic study on the impact of clinical information systems on patient outcomes is disappointing. In 2009, a multiple hospital study done in Texas cheerfully reported that:

  > Hospitals with automated notes and records, order entry, and clinical decision support had fewer complications, lower mortality rates, and lower costs.[43]

Unfortunately, after we take technology scores and the study design into account, the results of using healthcare IT don't look nearly as promising as originally advertised. The most widely deployed technologies—electronic notes, records, and test result systems—had absolutely no significant beneficial effect on patient mortality, complications, or length of hospital stay. In fact, the only result that reached statistical significance among these parameters was a *higher* complication rate for patients with heart failure. Because electronic notes, records, and lab results make up the vast majority of the functionality provided by current EMRs, these results suggest that even under the most favorable possible circumstances (that is, hospitals where the technology is both present and is enthusiastically accepted and used by providers), EMRs are still providing little or no clinical benefit.

These studies—and especially the apparent finding that some technologies are actually associated with increases in complications—raise still another question: Is it possible that some healthcare information technologies are actually *increasing* healthcare costs while *reducing* the quality of care?

It shouldn't be a surprising idea. We know that technologies produce unintended consequences. We also know that computer software has a rich history of confusing and unintuitive user interfaces, bugs, and flawed logic. Most of us have also had the experience of being overwhelmed by features and options that seem like great ideas to marketers and programmers, but simply make life harder for the average user. And there is even a more potentially sinister side. Far more than for paper, the logic programmed into software can be used to introduce outside bias into healthcare transactions. What if this bias benefits some businesses to the potential detriment of other businesses *and* the patient?[††] Almost any clinician who has used a complex EMR or CPOE system will have stories about defects that

---

[††] As a simple example, let's imagine that providers are required to use e-prescribing software and that there are two major suppliers. The first supplier is a software firm underwritten by pharmaceutical manufacturers. Their software is specifically designed to prompt physicians to use the safest and most effective drug based on what is known about a given patient, with the cost of that drug being the least important factor. The second supplier is underwritten by a capitated health maintenance organization and drug benefit management firms. Their software takes price into consideration first, with the expectation that even if a low-cost drug works for very few people, it should be tried as first-line therapy. Only failure of the drug will allow more expensive options to be given serious consideration. Which option is the "better" one? It depends on your perspective. As a patient and clinician, the first program will give you the best chance of being successfully treated in the shortest period of time. From the perspective of the insurer, the second program is more likely to cost you the least amount of money. One might easily argue that one system improves quality but raises costs, while the other saves money but sacrifices quality. Both of them bias the provider. This scenario is hardly far-fetched. Indeed, a 2009 *Wall Street Journal* article suggests that it's already here: "A software program offered free to doctors, from Allscripts and a bunch of tech companies and health plans, puts a green smiley face next to generics and other preferred drugs, and a red frowning face next to more expensive ones." (Rubenstein S. "E-prescribing: Green Means Generic; Red Means Pricey Brand." http://blogs.wsj.com/health/2009/01/21/e-prescribing-green-means-generics-red-means-pricey-brandn/.

can adversely affect both workflow and care. There is no current method for ensuring that healthcare software is inherently safe or effective. In early 2010, the Director of the FDA's Center for Devices and Radiological Health testified that several categories of health IT-induced adverse consequences were known to the FDA:[44]

> ...In the past two years, we have received 260 reports of HIT-related malfunctions with the potential for patient harm—including 44 reported injuries and 6 reported deaths. Because these reports are purely voluntary, they might represent only the tip of the iceberg in terms of the HIT-related problems that exist.
>
> Even within this limited sample, several serious safety concerns have come to light. The reported adverse events have largely fallen into four major categories: (1) errors of commission, such as accessing the wrong patient's record or overwriting one patient's information with another's; (2) errors of omission or transmission, such as the loss or corruption of vital patient data; (3) errors in data analysis, including medication dosing errors of several orders of magnitude; and (4) incompatibility between multivendor software applications and systems, which can lead to any of the above.

Dr. Silverstein has observed that in many respects, HIT is really an experimental technology that providers are being forced to deploy under penalty even before its potential safety consequences are known.[45]

Of course, none of this necessarily means that all health information technologies are worthless. Far from it. There is clearly a great deal of benefit that be derived from being able to share the right information at the right time with the right people. A small subset of doctors who have chosen to deploy EMRs in their own practices love them and would never want to go back to paper. But the evidence clearly does not support the popular view that paper systems are so inherently bad, and computerized systems are so inherently good, that we must rush headlong to replace one with the other. Given the enormous cost of HIT—both in human and financial terms—a more rational approach is needed.

Electronic Healthcare Information Technology: Friction or Grit?

The United States is poised on the brink of what is almost certainly a great mistake. We are in the process of converting the gathering and dissemination of healthcare information from a source of friction, to an outright wrench in the works. Bill Gates once wrote: "The first rule of any technology used in a business is that automation applied to an efficient operation will magnify the efficiency. The second is that automation applied to an inefficient operation will magnify the inefficiency." By federal law, we are now in the process of magnifying inefficiency in healthcare on a massive scale.

In recent years, both Republican and Democratic administrations have bought into the idea that we can fix what ails healthcare by spending tens of billions on HIT, and then forcing our providers to use it whether they want to or not. This is being done in the name of "efficiency"; as if using paper and simple, unsophisticated electronic information systems is the only thing holding back a flood of economies and cost savings. Any doubt that both political parties have "drunk the HIT Kool-Aid" has been effectively removed by the actions and appointees of Presidents Bush and Obama.

Soon after lauding the use of EMRs in his 2004 State of the Union address, then-President Bush issued an executive order creating the Office of the National Coordinator for Health Information Technology (ONCHIT). The function of the office was to "provide leadership for the development and nationwide implementation of an interoperable health information technology infrastructure to improve the quality and efficiency of healthcare." This leadership was intended to "...reduce medical errors, improve quality, and produce greater value for health care expenditures..." It was clearly intended that this new bureaucracy aggressively promote a pro-HIT agenda. An important part of this new organization was the new Office of Health Information Technology Adoption (OHITA). One of the OHITA's stated duties is to:

> Develop and coordinate strategies to incentivize adoption of health information technology, to reduce the risk of health information technology investment, and to promote health information technology diffusion...[46]

At the same time, Bush made it a stated goal to have every patient's medical record be electronic by 2014.

What this actually meant in practice for then Department of Health and Human Services (HHS) Secretary Michael Leavitt was that healthcare providers should be financially punished by the federal government—regardless of the actual quality of care that they provide and any other qualifications—if they did *not* immediately purchase and implement any and all computer software and other technologies the government might want to mandate. This policy was explicitly spelled out in a press release issued by HHS in December of 2007:

Statement by Mike Leavitt, Secretary of Health and Human Services, Regarding Medicare Physician Payment Legislation and Health Information Technology

The benefits of utilizing health information technology for keeping electronic health records and other purposes are clear. This technology will produce a higher quality of care, while reducing medical costs and errors, which kill more Americans each year than highway accidents, breast cancer, or AIDS.

Congressional leaders are working on legislation to address Medicare's physician payment system, staving off a reduction in reimbursement rates that is set to take effect in January and is required by law.

In my view, any new bill should require physicians to implement health information technology that meets department standards in order to be eligible for higher payments from Medicare.

Such a requirement would accelerate adoption of this technology considerably, and help to drive improvements in health care quality as well as reductions in medical costs and errors. I'm confident that many members of Congress are of a like mind on this issue and I will actively work with them in the near future.[47]

While disagreeing with the previous Bush administration on many points, President Obama made it clear that he and his administration had similar views. In a speech just prior to his inauguration, Obama was reported as saying: "[Healthcare IT] will cut waste, eliminate red tape, and reduce the need to repeat expensive medical tests." He added that the switch also would save lives by reducing the number of errors in medicine.[48]

Almost $20 billion in HIT funding was immediately included in an emergency stimulus package intended to bring the U.S. economy out of the worst recession since the 1920s. The program is structured as a "play-or-punish" proposition for healthcare providers. The basic provisions are these:

1. Healthcare providers have until 2011 to purchase a "certified" EMR to qualify for extra payments from Medicare that will not be received by providers who do not implement an EMR by that time. All certified EMRs must include e-prescribing functionality.

2. Beginning in 2011, the federal government will pay providers who are "meaningful" EMR users supplementary amounts based on their Medicare and Medicaid charges. These payments begin at a maximum of approximately $18,000 in 2011, and decrease rapidly to zero by 2015.

3. If providers are not using EMRs by 2015, Medicare will reduce their allowed payment for services by 1% each year thereafter until at least 75% of providers are "meaningful" EMR users.

4. Medicare providers using EMRs are required to submit whatever data Medicare desires with respect to "quality of care."

5. Only "certified" EMRs can be used by government agencies or those using federal dollars to purchase EMRs.

6. An HIT Policy Committee is given the task of recommending a policy and framework for adopting HIT nationwide. The HIT Policy Committee has 18 members, *of whom only one is designated to represent the healthcare providers who would actually use the technology*. Three members represent patients and consumers, one represents healthcare labor unions, one represents private insurers, and one represents healthcare IT vendors. Only one member is required to know *anything* about privacy and security matters.

We have seen that many of the claims made for HIT have yet to be substantiated either scientifically or economically for most healthcare information technologies. Yet if anything, the movement toward the rapid deployment of HIT (forcibly if necessary), is accelerating. How can we explain this apparent discrepancy between evidence and the actions of the federal government?

If we follow the tried-and-true course of following the money, the only clear winners in this "emergency" federal program are large, established manufacturers of very large, expensive, and highly proprietary pieces of EMR software. This software will require constant provider expenditures for maintenance and upgrades long after federal subsidies expire. Their mandatory deployment practically guarantees a few large vendors an enormous windfall. The entire EMR industry had estimated sales of only $1.2 billion in 2007. President Obama's "economic stimulus" law virtually guarantees that more than $20 billion will be spent on certified EMRs over the next five years alone.

The "HIT-Industrial Complex" has finally come of age.

In a healthcare system that needs efficiency and innovation more than anything, none of this bodes well for patients, providers, taxpayers, or those who might not be interested in having the federal government dictating the details of how doctors will practice medicine. Dr. Silverstein has nicely summarized the situation:[49]

> **All is unfortunately not well in the world of clinical information technology.** In medicine, a field characterized by significant risk and unpredictability, a somewhat remarkable and unexpected atmosphere of "technologic determinism" (a belief that computer-based automation is almost magically beneficial) seems common. The appropriate levels of critical thinking and skepticism essential in a demanding area such as introduction of computer automation in medicine appear largely absent, on a worldwide basis, to the point that those who've led IT projects to automate traditional business activities (such as accounting, finance, manufacturing) are deemed the appropriate leaders to *automate clinical medicine.*

The road leading to the current stimulus bill—one taken by both political parties—is the logical result of technological determinism. The political policy itself might best be characterized as the principle of "technological manifest destiny" in healthcare. This is the idea that all providers must use specific EMRs and other HIT because politicians and regulators say that it is their destiny to do so—regardless of the true impact on costs or the provision of care.

These issues are international in scope. Richard Granger, former head of the UK's "Connecting for Health" national clinical IT program, had this to say about a program described by some UK members of Parliament as "the largest government IT debacle ever":[50]

> Sometimes we put in stuff that I'm just ashamed of...Some of the stuff that [our large American clinical IT vendor] has put in recently is appalling... [vendor] and [prime contractor] had not listened to end users... Failed marriages and co-dependency with subcontractors... A string of problems ranging from missing appointment records, to inability to report on wait times... Almost a dozen cancelled go-live dates... Stupid or evil people... Stockholm syndrome-identifying with suppliers' interests rather than your own... A little coterie of people out there who are "alleged experts" who were dismissed for reasons of non-performance.

Australia too, is having serious problems with its own national EHR.[51,52]

If we hope to fix our own healthcare machine, we have to start by not making it worse. So let's turn to science as the rightful arbiter of any conflict of opinion about healthcare policy.

The day after President Obama gave a speech announcing his intention to implement EMRs throughout the country by 2015, the National Academies of Science (NAS) issued its report on a study titled "Computational Technology for Effective Health Care: Immediate Steps and Strategic Directions."[53,††] The goal of the study was to objectively examine the capabilities of current and future technologies and derive principles for success in the evolution from paper- to computer-based information technologies. The researchers

---

†† The study was chartered by the National Library of Medicine, performed by the National Research Council of the NAS, and funded by the Department of Health and Human Services, the National Science Foundation, Vanderbilt University Medical Center, Partners HealthCare System, the Robert Wood Johnson Foundation, and The Commonwealth Fund. This is as qualified and unbiased a group of healthcare-specific organizations as one will ever find.

gathered evidence and data from many sources. The primary observational evidence was derived from committee site visits to eight medical centers around the country—for the most part acknowledged leaders in applying IT to healthcare—on the theory that many of the important innovations and achievements for healthcare IT would be found in such institutions thought to be leaders in the field.

The entire report is well worth reading. Based upon extensive research, observations and analysis, the committee produced six crucial recommendations for actions by the federal government:

1. Incentivize clinical performance gains rather than acquisition of IT per se.

2. Encourage initiatives to empower iterative process improvement and small-scale optimization.

3. Encourage development of standards and measures of healthcare IT performance related to cognitive support for health professionals and patients, adaptability to support iterative process improvement, and effective use to improve quality.

4. Encourage interdisciplinary research in three critical areas: (a) organizational systems-level research into the design of health care systems, processes, and workflow; (b) computable knowledge structures and models for medicine needed to make sense of available patient data including preferences, health behaviors, and so on; and (c) human-computer interaction in a clinical context.

5. Encourage (or at least do not impede) efforts by health care organizations and communities to aggregate data about healthcare people, processes, and outcomes from all sources subject to appropriate protection of privacy and confidentiality.

6. Support additional education and training efforts at the intersection of healthcare, computer science, and health/biomedical informatics.

It is hard to imagine a greater contrast than that between these evidence-based and scientifically derived HIT recommendations, and the 2009 HIT "stimulus" policies that were enacted by Congress without the benefit of a single public hearing.

Now, how do we fix this mess?

Part III

How to Fix It

"Americans can always be counted on to do the right thing...after they have exhausted all other possibilities."

—*Winston Churchill*

10

Defining the Desired Outcome

"Common sense is in medicine the master workman."
—*Peter Latham*

As we've learned, our American healthcare machine was never actually planned in advance. Instead it evolved over time through a combination of tradition, politics, regulation, and rational response to (sometimes perverse) economic incentives. One drawback to this type of evolution is that the resulting system was never actually designed with a specific end result in mind. One can generalize by saying that our healthcare system is supposed to provide medical and preventive health services, but this says nothing about the expected cost, quality, level of accessibility, or a host of other factors. It's as if we've built a vehicle with the general idea of being able to transport people, but without specifying how much we're willing to pay, how many people it should transport, how fast it needs to go, or how safe it should be in a crash. It should be no surprise that, when a vehicle like this is built over a long period of time and by many competing interests, no one wants to buy it.

One result is that if we're going to "reform" healthcare and rebuild the machine, we'd better have a good idea of exactly what we'd like it to do ahead of time. There are many such lists originating from many different interest groups. Rather than argue the relative merits and defects of each of these, we will start with a relatively short list of goals that seem reasonable based upon common sense and the public good.

Presumptive Goals: An Efficient, Effective, Fair, and Sustainable Healthcare System

We'll start by assuming that everyone—regardless of political persuasion or economic status—would like American healthcare to be efficient, effective, fair, and sustainable.

We need to be *efficient* because resources are inherently limited. Efficiency in this case means that we're able to derive the maximum health benefit from a given expenditure of financial, time, and human resources.

Being *effective* means that the system should do a good job of preventing and treating medical problems within the limits of the nation's available science and resources.

Fairness is needed because there is a general sense that, within the resources available both to the healthcare system and individuals, respectively, the healthcare system ought to treat everyone in a known, uniform, and predictable way.

Finally, the system needs to be *sustainable* because if it is too cumbersome to operate, use, or maintain, it will collapse of its own weight. We already have a system like that, and no one is happy. If the programs, policies, and economics we use to fix it aren't sustainable, we'll just need to rebuild it all over again.

Removing the important sources of inefficiency and accomplishing our presumptive goals has certain structural requirements that can't be ignored.

Structural Requirement #1—Universal Healthcare Coverage

Proponents of universal healthcare coverage have long argued for its adoption on the basis of fairness. Although fairness is a worthy goal, efficiency is an equally valid reason for wanting everyone to have insurance. Universal coverage is mandatory if the system is to be efficient and transparent.*

- Universal coverage solves the problem of risk-splitting—at least on a national level. Risk-splitting (that is, excluding high-risk individuals from the insurance pool), might maximize profits for individual insurance companies, but it is an inefficient way to insure the health of the population as a whole. Larger insurance pools are inherently more efficient at spreading risk.

- Universal coverage provides predictability for healthcare providers and patients. This allows them to behave in ways that are consistent and rational in the long-term.

- Universal coverage makes it possible to standardize business processes such as billing, referrals, forms, and registration across all patients and providers. Standardizing these processes reduces friction.

- Universal coverage generates economies of scale. What was previously a market of just more than 250 million Americans immediately becomes a market of 305 million. This corresponding increase in market size makes it possible to spread the cost of research and innovation over a larger economic base. This should allow us to reduce costs and improve the quality of drugs and other medical tools over time at a faster rate than would otherwise be possible.

Structural Requirement #2—Retention of a Private Market for Additional Healthcare Services

Simply put, this means that patients must to be allowed to use their own money to purchase more or better healthcare services than may be provided by universal coverage.

---

* We need to add one proviso to this claim. *Universal coverage can contribute to healthcare efficiency if and only if it is not also associated with a system that essentially places medical decisions in the hands of government regulators.* It is perfectly possible for government and healthcare administrators to undo every efficiency and healthcare benefit by simply substituting their own medical judgment in place of the judgment of providers and their patients. Standardized treatment "guidelines" that essentially become mandatory based upon regulatory incentives and disincentives are a prime example of this behavior.

Why is this necessary? First, the presence of a private market means that we can use "invisible hand" market mechanisms to allow patients to ration their own care. Healthcare is like any other good, in that some people will prefer more and some will prefer less based upon quality and price. Utilizing personal preferences is a far more efficient way to allocate scarce resources than centralized decision-making. Second, if we don't allow purchasing healthcare services within our own market, people will go elsewhere to purchase them, taking their dollars with them. When Canadians were restricted from privately purchasing healthcare services in Canada, they simply crossed the border into the United States to do so. "Medical tourism" is already becoming routine for cosmetic surgery, heart surgery, and other procedures that can be obtained more cheaply overseas. Finally, the presence of a private market can be use to subsidize the public market for healthcare. Allowing some individuals to pay higher prices based upon amenities such as more convenient hours, nicer offices, and shorter waiting times can subsidize the infrastructure used for providing services to the general population.

Structural Requirement #3—Providers Must Be Able to Price Their Services Freely

Using market forces as a efficient regulatory mechanism can only work if the price of supply is allowed to vary with demand. This is not the currently the case for the majority of healthcare providers. The federal government currently demands that the vast majority of providers seeing Medicare patients accept whatever Medicare pays as payment in full, regardless of what their costs or usual fee might be.[†] This is the case even if these same patients might be willing and able to pay extra for these services. Moreover, Medicare pays the same professional fee for the same procedure to every provider, regardless

---

[†] This practice of agreeing to accept whatever Medicare reimburses as payment in full is called "accepting assignment." Under assignment, providers cannot bill patients for anything for services that Medicare covers, no matter how little Medicare might pay. Providers may elect not to accept assignment, but this usually results in delayed Medicare payments and a host of other administrative headaches. As a result, most providers either accept assignment or (increasingly) drop out of Medicare entirely.

of their relative experience, qualifications, bedside manner, or personal skill.

These practices would be strange in any other field. It would, for example, be hard to imagine paying a skilled attorney or accountant with 30 years' worth of experience at the same rate as someone fresh out of school. Instead, every other profession uses the marketplace to balance the tradeoff between supply and demand based upon price. Expert attorneys charge high fees as a way of limiting demand for their services, while lawyers right out of school charge low fees as a means of generating the business they will use to gain experience. Using market forces effectively means that healthcare providers must be able to use these same pricing mechanisms whenever they interact with patients.

Structural Requirement #4—The Price of All Healthcare Goods and Services Must Be Transparent, Fully Disclosed, and Easily Available

Markets simply don't work unless producers and consumers have adequate, accurate, and readily available pricing information. One of the major defects of our current healthcare system is that both patients and providers know practically nothing about the cost of almost everything. It's hardly their fault. The price of a given medication will vary dramatically depending upon where it's filled, and with any discounts that a given health plan might have negotiated. The effective price to patients will vary even more based upon their own deductibles and co-pays. "Usual and customary" fees established by clinicians mean little because they too are subject to dozens (or even hundreds) of negotiated contracts and Medicare assignment.

All this variation makes it virtually impossible to compare prices for the vast majority of healthcare goods and services, or for market forces to function. How can one make effective purchasing decisions if no one knows what anything costs? How can providers adjust their prices to be competitive if it's impossible to know what your competitors are charging? Most of all, the lack of pricing information makes it difficult to produce meaningful comparisons of the true cost and effectiveness of competing treatments.

Structural Requirement #5—The System Must Ration Healthcare Overtly, Rather Than Covertly

In our discussion of health insurers we touched briefly on the topic of overt versus covert rationing of healthcare. Rationing healthcare is inevitable in every society because our ability to consume these goods and services far outstrips our ability to produce and pay for them. Overt rationing is a process by which the mechanism of rationing is clear and obvious for everyone to see. Methods of overt rationing include rationing by price (that is, you can have elective cosmetic surgery only if you can afford to pay for it), by time ("it will be three months before we can get you in for that heart bypass surgery"), and setting limits on the types of conditions and treatments that insurance will and will not cover (treatment of psoriasis might be covered, while the treatment of warts is not). Covert rationing is a process in which limits on care aren't stated explicitly. Instead, various administrative and bureaucratic barriers are implemented that make it hard for providers to deliver certain types of care. It is designed to avoid explicitly saying "no," but to make the process of delivering certain types of care so miserable, expensive, and time-consuming for patients and providers that they simply give up.

Fogoros and others have written persuasively and at length about the corrosive effects of covert rationing on the doctor-patient relationship and the appropriate delivery of care. From our perspective, it is at least as important that covert rationing is terribly inefficient. In the long run, it will cost us less and produce better care to "bite the political bullet" and ration healthcare goods and services overtly and explicitly.

With these structural requirements defined, we can start the process of crafting solutions in earnest. In doing so, there are three rules that will help both the process and the result:

1. **Simplify, simplify, simplify.** Complex machines are always more expensive, less reliable and harder to maintain than

simple ones. When given a choice, we should take the simpler approach wherever possible.[†]

2. **Make use of free market forces.** If there is one thing that history has made clear, it is that markets usually provide the most efficient and most sustainable way to distribute resources within any given industry. The nice thing about markets is that they automatically take many factors into account simultaneously, and with very little administrative overhead. Factors such as personal taste, travel costs, convenience, and family considerations are difficult or impossible to consider with any other scheme of resource allocation. They are impossible to consider in a healthcare system that is centrally planned and administered.

   Markets aren't perfect, of course. Free markets simply allocate resources efficiently—they don't necessarily accomplish a number of important socially or medically desirable goals. Nor, as we have recently learned in the financial sector, can completely unregulated markets always be trusted. Regulatory agencies such as the FDA will never go out of style.

3. **Within the confines of overt and transparent rationing, medical decision-making must be the exclusive province of patients and their providers.** Historically, the supremacy of science, logic, and personalized care in the delivery of healthcare services has been fleeting. At various times in the past, medical care has been overruled by religion, tradition, politics, and bureaucracy.

   At some point, we are all patients. As patients, there is considerable danger in giving nonmedical personnel a place at the bedside. Insurers, governments, churches, vendors, and technologies all have agendas that can easily conflict with our own.

[†] Like any rule, this one has its limits. As H.L. Mencken once observed, "There is always an easy solution to every human problem—neat, plausible, and wrong." The only way to know whether a simple solution is really a good one is to have enough experience and expertise in the field to know the difference.

Much of American medicine has become a contest between outside organizations trying to push or limit certain types of care, and providers trying to trying to serve as advocates for their patients. Under the current system, these outside special interests have many ways to tip the balance in their favor.

Many of the decisions that lead to good medicine and healthcare practices are not black and white, and never will be. There are simply too many variables. These range from incomplete knowledge, to the fact that many patients have many different medical problems simultaneously, to the social and emotional circumstances surrounding a given patient. The role of physicians is to weigh whatever is known about the disease and available treatment and present the options to their patients.

One of the greatest mistakes we can make in restructuring healthcare is to allow outside forces—whatever their origin—to come between patients and the providers seeking to care for them. Government poses an especially serious threat in this regard; not because it means to do harm, but because its involvement is both a blunt instrument and a slippery slope.

It's a blunt instrument because any government or insurer can only implement blanket policies that are poorly tailored to individual circumstances. It's a slippery slope because once bureaucrats and regulators are involved in dictating the terms of care, it is nearly impossible to get them out or set limits on what they can and can't do.

Armed with these rules and our insight about where the most important problems in healthcare occur and why, we can begin to describe solutions that will give us the most bang for the long-term buck. Some of them will create short-term political disruptions. However, even these disruptions are likely to be relatively painless and inexpensive compared to our current approach to healthcare "reform."

11

Overhauling Payment for Healthcare Goods and Services

"Let us not seek the Republican answer or the Democratic answer but the right answer."
—*John F. Kennedy*

The process of funding, buying, and selling healthcare goods and services serves as the foundation of the entire healthcare system. How we handle these activities govern whether, when, and under what terms medical care will be available. If the underlying financial system is flawed and unsustainable, the rest of the healthcare system is guaranteed to be as well.

If we're going to eliminate the defects of the current system while avoiding the wholesale creation of new problems, we need to do far more than tweak the current machine. What's required is a complete overhaul. While inherently disruptive and challenging, the prospects are not as hopeless as one might think. One advantage that we have is that the system we'll be building will be much simpler to understand and operate than the current one for virtually everyone involved. Another advantage is that the current system is so broken that simply tweaking it around the edges won't make things better. The social and financial pressure to take definitive action will simply continue to grow.

So where do we begin? Because the healthcare machine ultimately runs on money and self-interest, the logical place to begin is the source of that money. In his 1993 healthcare reform proposal, economist Uwe Reinhardt observed that every single healthcare dollar ultimately originates from American households. All the terms that we normally use to describe healthcare finance, such as employer-based purchasing, government insurance, and self-pay really refer to how those dollars are *channeled* rather than where they *originate*. This is illustrated in Figure 11.1.

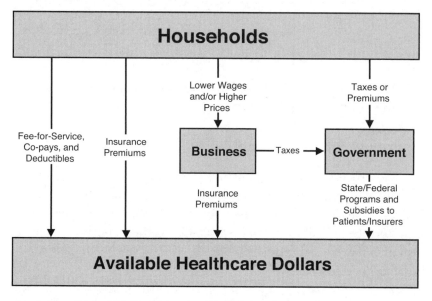

Adapted from Reinhardt, U. "An 'All-American' Health Reform Proposal." *Journal of American Health Policy* (May/June 1993): 11-17.[1]

Figure 11.1   Sources of Healthcare Funding

As this figure illustrates, the popular concept of health insurance as being "employer-based" or "government-sponsored" is somewhat misplaced. The healthcare dollars originating in households are diverted toward healthcare by one of three methods: (1) premiums paid directly by the family; (2) premiums that are extracted from households by employers in the form of lower real wages; and (3) premiums that are extracted from family income in the form of taxes. Because all dollars come from the same place, the real question is how we structure this collection to minimize the number of parts and amount of friction generated within the healthcare machine. Logic would suggest that one or even two mechanisms for collecting insurance premiums would be far more efficient than three, but which method is most practical?

We've already determined that the problems posed by risk-splitting can only be solved by requiring universal healthcare coverage. Universal coverage means that premiums must be collected paid on behalf of all individuals regardless of age, health, employment, or tax status. As it happens, the number of employees and the number of individual tax returns filed every year are fairly similar, totaling about 140,000,000. However, the number of tax returns actually represents a far larger percentage of *households*. This is because each employee in a single household will be counted separately in the employment statistics, while many people who are retired or not currently employed do file individual tax returns. On this basis alone, it makes more sense to rely on the mechanisms used for federal taxation to collect premiums rather than employers. There is another reason to avoid involving businesses in the process of collecting premiums, however. Every financial and administrative burden added to business reduces the financial resources available for businesses to use in their primary function: employing people. Any mechanism we can create that takes employers out of the loop wherever possible will maximize employment and personal income.* Taking employers off

---

* It is useful to note that the few states that have mandated universal healthcare coverage have generally added to the societal burden of providing and tracking healthcare coverage. They have done so by increasing the number of entities involved rather than removing the burden from anyone. Employers who were already providing and administering health insurance programs derived no efficiencies from the program. In the case of Massachusetts, the total administrative burden of employers increased substantially. Employers with more than ten employees were, for the first time, required to provide a "fair and reasonable contribution" to the premium of health insurance for their employees. Many of these organizations are small businesses that have only three alternatives in the face of this mandate: (1) increase expenses and take the premiums out of profits; (2) reduce wages to employees to make up the cost of the premium; and/or (3) minimize the number of employees covered under the law.

the hook leaves only two alternatives: self-payment and government-mediated collection of premiums.[†] Because the federal government would ultimately be responsible for monitoring and enforcing universal self-payment into the insurance pool, there is nothing to be gained by a system of enforced self-payment. That leaves us with using the current taxation infrastructure as the most logical collection mechanism. All premiums collected would be placed into separate, dedicated, individual or family accounts that may only be used to fund health savings accounts (HSAs) and purchase universal basic health insurance.

Essential Elements of an Efficient Health Insurance Plan

A great deal has been written about universal health insurance. Books and articles seem to cover the topic from every possible perspective. Here we will focus only on what is needed to make a universal health plan efficient, rational, and sustainable.[†] We're already determined that the system created should reduce the number of parts in the machine, ration overtly rather than covertly, and make use of

---

[†] As Reinhardt points out, state and/or federal collection and stewardship of healthcare insurance premiums should not be considered or called a tax. Instead, individuals are simply channeling payments they would have made one way or another in any mandated universal health insurance program through the administrative functions of the government. *These funds cannot and should not be used for any purpose other than providing a specified and uniform health insurance benefit*—regardless of whether the insurer itself is the government or some other entity.

That said, there is no reason that the centralized funneling of premiums through the government could not be facilitated through a modification of the same mechanism used to collect payroll taxes. Payroll taxes are already used to collect funds for a variety of programs including Medicare. A modest modification to add another category would have relatively little impact on businesses.

[†] Much of this discussion borrows heavily from the works of Drs. Fogoros and Reinhardt previously cited, as well as other work that will be referenced in turn. The author is grateful for the obvious amount of time and effort that they have put into their observations and written works.

market forces wherever possible. What do these requirements imply with respect to our universal insurance plan?

Figure 11.2 illustrates the elements of a universal healthcare system that meets our basic requirements.

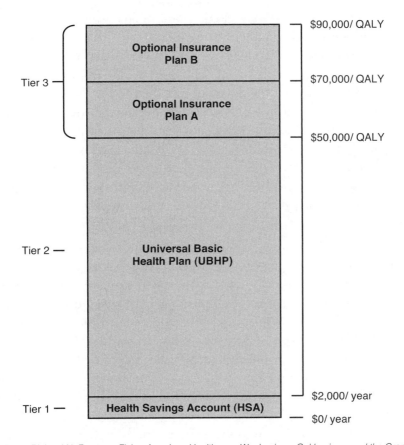

From: Richard N. Fogoros, *Fixing American Healthcare: Wonkonians, Gekkonians, and the Grand Unification Theory of Healthcare.*

Figure 11.2   General Design of an Ideal Universal Healthcare Insurance System

What do all the terms in this figure mean and how does it work?

As shown in the figure, the sources of spending for healthcare goods and services are divided into various layers, or "tiers." The first source of financing comes from the patient in the form of a health savings account (HSA). To fund the HSA, households with incomes above a given threshold are required to deposit a specified amount (in this example, $2,000 per adult or $1,000 for each child) into their healthcare account each year. These amounts and any interest that they earn would be nontaxable in a manner similar to Individual Retirement Accounts (IRAs). "For households whose incomes fall below a certain lower threshold, these funds would be directly deposited into individual HSAs by the federal government. For households whose income falls between the lower and upper income thresholds, a sliding scale [would] be used to determine how much tax-deductible money they must contribute, and how much the federal government will contribute annually toward the individual HSAs.... Any money in the HSA that is not spent on healthcare during the course of the year remains in the HSA and earns tax-free interest. The money that accumulates in this fund is the property of the individual owner—the government has no claim on it and cannot tax it."[2] Except, as we shall discuss later, HSA funds can only be spent on healthcare.

If a family is relatively healthy over time, the amount of money in an HSA can grow considerably. These funds can be utilized in one of three ways. First, they can be rolled over into an IRA and used for retirement when an individual reaches retirement age. Second, excess funds can be used at any time to buy Tier 3 care services. Finally, there is a strong argument for allowing at least a portion of the accrued interest to be used for immediate personal spending. Most people have a financial time horizon that is quite short. It is important that they be able to realize some selfish near-term benefit to having funds remain in their HSA rather than spending it as quickly as possible—especially if these funds are coming from the federal government rather than from their own paychecks.

Regardless of how much they might have personally contributed to their HSA, it is very important that every American feel that the money in their HSA is *theirs*, and just as real and as valuable as any funds that they might have in their wallet, checking account, or retirement fund. From our previous observations, we have learned that incentives work, and that financial incentives in particular are extremely effective in producing specific behaviors. In our particular case, the behavior that we would like to produce in all Americans is a desire to consciously balance spending money on healthcare goods and services with the desire to keep their HSA account intact so that the accumulated wealth can ultimately be spent on nonmedical goods and services if at all possible. We'll discuss exactly how HSA money is spent on healthcare services shortly.

The second tier of healthcare financing comes in the form of a Universal Basic Health Plan (UBHP) that covers every legal resident of the United States. The UBHP provides healthcare coverage under a system of open rationing.

In broad outline, all medical services that achieve a target level of cost-effectiveness are covered. In the example used in Figure 11.2, the UBHP covers all healthcare services that can be provided for up to $50,000 per quality-adjusted life year (QALY). Services that consume more than $50,000 per QALY are not covered."[§]

A brief introduction to the concept of quality-adjusted life years will be helpful for readers who might not be familiar with the term. A QALY is an attempt to gauge how much good a particular medical intervention might generate with respect to two factors: its ability to extend life and the likely quality of the added life that will be obtained. One year of perfect health equals 1.0 QALY. One year of life with some degree of disability will reduce the QALY score by an amount proportional to the perceived reduction in the quality of life. For example, being unable to engage in normal activities for two weeks out of each month, but feeling fine the rest of the time, would be judged to reduce the quality of life for a patient by 50% over the course of one year, yielding a QALY of only 0.5. If a treatment were then made available that guaranteed complete recovery for a period of one year, it would result in a gain of 0.5 QALY. If that treatment

---

[§] Fogoros notes that "Using QALY as a cost-effectiveness measure is fraught with problems and is extremely controversial. The standard method of calculating QALY is not adequate for the rationing scheme we are proposing here." The reader is referred to his book for a more detailed discussion of how ethical precepts can be used to guide rationing decisions, QALY calculations, and its use in explicit rationing. A detailed discussion on how to calculate QALY can be found by referring to: Sassi F, "Calculating QALYs, Comparing QALY, and DALY Calculations." *Health Policy and Planning Advance Access* published on September 1, 2006, DOI 10.1093/heapol/czl018. Health Policy Plan. 21: 402-408.

happens to cost $1,000, the cost is $1,000/0.5 QALY = $2,000 for each QALY gained. If the same treatment is likely to work only half the time, the cost per QALY increases. In this case, it would increase to $1,000/(50% effectiveness × 0.5 QALY) = $4,000 for each QALY gained.

The point of trying to measure and use QALYs is that if health-care resources are limited (as they inevitably are), we would like to have some means of deciding which tests and treatments give us the most total medical benefit for those scarce dollars. In the case of the proposed Universal Basic Health Plan, we can decide to cover any treatment that has a cost/benefit of some threshold level (for exam-ple, $50,000/QALY). At least theoretically, this approach will generate the most years of useful life for the country as a whole. This is in con-trast to the current situation, in which Americans might be spending enormous amounts of money on expensive end-of-life treatments for some people, while failing to allocate enough money for relatively inexpensive therapies that would greatly benefit others for a long period of time. Another advantage to this approach is that the thresh-old of coverage can be easily moved up or down depending upon the funds that are available for use in purchasing basic healthcare goods and services. This is a far easier, fairer, and more rational approach to adjusting benefit levels than arbitrarily excluding specific goods and services or mounting administrative obstacles to care.

Although this approach is eminently logical, it's not necessarily easy. One recurring concern with the use of QALY-mediated rationing has to do with the ethics of applying a raw value scale to individual cases. For example, a given treatment for cancer might have a very high QALY score in a 30-year-old, but a much lower score in a 75-year-old simply because of their age difference. This creates a situa-tion in which the same treatment might be given to one person but is denied to the next on efficiency grounds—a situation that is problem-atic for many Americans. This conflict between "distributive justice" and "social benefit" has given rise to a balanced approach that has been dubbed the "Equal Opportunity Standard" (EOS). This approach goes a considerable way toward adjusting the QALY approach to meet mainstream standards for both ethics and economic rationality.** A second and more functional problem is that there is no complete "master list" of QALY scores for the vast majority of medical interventions. Because it is impossible to rank treatments without actual knowledge of their relative effectiveness, this is work that has to be done under any scheme for rationally allocating healthcare resources.

Comparing treatments is a substantial amount of work—work that has been largely neglected by most (if not all) healthcare systems around the world. Clinical trials and comparative analyses involved require substantial amounts of time, effort, and money. However, they represent money well spent, and represent a true capital investment that will lower overall costs over time, and not a consumptive expense. One approach is a four-step process:

1. **Establish a health standards commission.** Composed of doctors, nurses, representative patients, and an advisory panel of economists, statisticians, and ethicists, the main job of the commission is to establish a system for determining appropriate values to use in cost-effectiveness calculations as described in subsequent steps.

2. **Establish one or more usable quality-of-life scale(s) for a range of health states.** The purpose of the scale(s) is to assign a quality-of-life index to various physical disease states. This is an assessment of what fraction of full functionality is lost by virtue of different types of disease-induced disability. For example, it might be the case that living in a bed-ridden state is judged to result in a life that is only 25% of full functionality,

---

** In brief, the EOS approach modifies the standard QALY approach by incorporating a relatively small number of ethics rules. These rules specify whether and how adjustments will be made in the calculation of the quality-of-life index, the probability of treatment success, the duration of benefit, and post-therapy quality of life when coming up with QALY scores. The net result is an implementation of the QALY approach that balances the strict societal beneficence and strict distributive justice methods of allocating resources. For our purposes here, the important concept is that these tools exist and can be used to effectively and efficiently ration healthcare resources in a way that can be readily seen, calculated, verified, and understood by everyone involved in the healthcare system. Readers are referred to Fogoros' *Fixing American Healthcare* for details of the EOS approach.

whereas being in a wheelchair results in a quality of life that is 60% of full health.

Given the potential differences of opinion and the inherent subjectivity associated with this process, this task might be one of the most difficult and controversial that the commission must face. At one extreme, some might claim that the slightest disability dramatically reduces livability, while others might believe that quite severe disabilities leave one mostly intact. Nevertheless, it is doable. There should be no question in anyone's mind that illness-induced disability does reduce the quality of life. The issue to be negotiated and resolved by the commission is by how much.

3. **Develop an exhaustive list of condition-treatment pairs.** A treatment pair consists of a condition (for example, strep throat) for which a specific treatment is recognized to be useful (for example, penicillin). Fogoros lists 11 elements to be determined in the course of this process. These include factors such as the probability that the treatment will achieve the desired effect on the condition being treated, a list of underlying medical conditions that affect the probability of benefit (for example, allergy to penicillin), the predicted duration of benefit (permanently if the strep throat is cured), expected impact of the benefit on quality of life, the influence of side effects, and the cost of the treatment. The total amount of information to be compiled is considerable, but manageable over time.

Although daunting, every possible treatment and condition does not have to be completely evaluated before a QALY-based system is implemented. Even if just half of the various medical conditions and treatments are reviewed and the comparative cost/benefit ratios on QALY calculated, a considerable amount of benefit can be derived by implementing the system around them—particularly if these are among the most important conditions financially.

4. **The last step is to calculate the expected benefit and cost-effectiveness of each treatment considered.** These calculations can be done automatically after determinations of the various parameters are known, and a specific patient is matched against a specific proposed treatment. Some estimates of

benefit will be more accurate than others. For example, the probability of success of a given drug in a given patient really depends upon a number of variables (for example, the metabolism rate of the drug in the liver) that might be difficult or impossible to know with any certainty ahead of time. Nevertheless, the system proposed is still far fairer, more rational, and more efficient than any aspect of the current system.

A QALY-based system like the one proposed has many potential benefits, not the least of which is rationalizing our country's healthcare research and development efforts. Current research emphasizes the development of medications and other treatments without respect to their cost. The result is often treatments that might be useful, but are so expensive that they will either result in bankruptcy of the healthcare system, or "crowd out" other healthcare services. The new system proposed will change manufacturer incentives from creating expensive therapies to creating therapies that have a relatively high cost-to-benefit ratio. A high cost-to-benefit ratio can be obtained in three ways: by improving effectiveness, by lowering cost, or by reducing side effects.

With the development of a practical QALY-based rationing system by use of the Equal Opportunity Standard, the third tier of healthcare financing now comes into play. No country can possibly pay for unlimited access to healthcare. By explicitly setting limits on the basic level of care that the country as a whole is willing to afford, a gap now remains for services that are still desired by patients but are too expensive relative to the benefits they provide. This gap can be filled by individuals purchasing additional private insurance that covers these services.[††]

[††] Although some might argue that this creates a "two-tiered" healthcare system filled with "haves" and "have-nots," the fact is that any system that does not provide every conceivable benefit to all citizens upon demand (a financially unsustainable proposition) will *always* be two-tiered. Nothing can stop patients from simply leaving the country to receive healthcare elsewhere if their medical desires are not satisfied at home. However, forcing them to receive their healthcare elsewhere simply deprives the healthcare system at home of dollars that could have been used to support universal care. From an socio-economic perspective, this is irrational and counterproductive.

Using Universal Coverage to Generate Efficiencies in Financing

Contrary to the expectations behind the Massachusetts and 2010 PPACA health reform laws, ensuring that everyone has access to health insurance does little to fix the system. Everything depends upon simplification.

Too Many Gears

The design of the Universal Basic Health Plan (UBHP) helps in a number of ways:

- **Variances in state-mandated benefits are eliminated, as they are superseded by the terms of the UBHP.** After the UBHP is implemented, federal laws must be passed that prevent the re-creation of nonuniform coverage requirements. The elimination of state-to-state insurance requirements will immediately reduce the administrative overhead associated with universal coverage.

- **Standardization of benefits for the UBHP eliminates variability in deductibles and co-payments.** Under the UBHP all deductibles and co-pays should become uniform nationwide. This step alone will obviate the need for millions of inquiries and transaction exceptions each day.

- **It is easy to determine whether a given patient is covered for a specific condition under terms of the UBHP.** An enormous amount of time and resources are currently consumed in determining whether a given healthcare visit or treatment is covered under the terms of each patient's specific insurance plan and obtaining approvals and pre-authorizations. With knowledge of cost, effectiveness, side effects, and expected impact on quality of life, the new universal healthcare system will allow coverage determinations to be made instantly by use of universally accessible "coverage calculators" available to everyone on the World Wide Web. Relevant data regarding the patient, disease, treatment, and price are entered, and the cost per QALY is automatically calculated. Treatments exceeding the cost/QALY threshold of the UBHP are not covered universally, but can be purchased with funds from the patient's HSA, Tier 3 insurance coverage, or personal savings.

This process is likely to result in new system efficiencies totaling many billions of dollars each year, and completely eliminate the paperwork and frustration associated with healthcare insurance pre-approvals, referrals, and denials. But these benefits are still going to be severely limited unless we can reduce the variability that patients and providers face in dealing with large numbers of disparate insurers and payment methodologies.

One way of addressing this problem is to go straight to a government-operated single-payer system of basic insurance. A great deal has been written about this approach, and there are even entire organizations devoted to its development and implementation.[3] A common argument made by these groups is the need to reduce the administrative overhead expense incurred by insurers. After all, Medicare's administrative costs are a small fraction of those insured by private companies.[††] Private insurers have to include the costs of advertising, commissions, taxes, and profits in their overhead, while government-run programs do not. And none of these costs include the administrative and financial burdens imposed on patients, providers, and businesses by public and private insurance plans alike. A recent study pegs this cost as being between $23.2 billion and $31 billion annually for providers alone, or nearly $70,000 per healthcare provider per year.[4]

In a December 2008 study, McKinsey Global Institute estimated that the United States spent $91 billion more than expected on health insurance administration when compared to other countries and adjusting for GDP.[5] This number grew to at least $108 billion in 2009. Of the 2009 expenditures, almost $40 billion consisted of sales, marketing, and general administrative expenses that are

---

[††] Depending upon the source, it is claimed that Medicare's administrative expenses average somewhere between 2% to 5.2% of claims costs, while those of private insurers are somewhere between 8.9% to 25%. (Matthews M. "Medicare's Hidden Administrative Costs: A Comparison of Medicare and the Private Sector." The Council for Affordable Health Insurance. January 10, 2006. http://www.cahi.org/cahi_contents/resources/pdf/ CAHI_Medicare_Admin_Final_Publication.pdf.

above and beyond that spent by other countries with an equivalent per-capita GDP. However, another $33 billion represents the excess administrative cost of running our *public* insurance systems such as Medicare and Medicaid. This might seem odd until one realizes that Medicare administrative costs have grown almost 30% *annually* since 2003. The increase is a direct result of two factors. The first is using private insurers to administer Medicare Advantage and Medicare Part D benefits. The second is the rapidly escalating levels of regulation imposed by Medicare and Medicaid themselves.

What single-payer proponents miss is that it is unnecessary to move to a completely government-run healthcare system just to garner administrative efficiency. There is no reason why we cannot continue to have and utilize insurance from many different private companies. *The trick is that the administrative components of the health plans that they offer under the UBHP must all be the same.* If all private insurers are required to provide identical UBHP offerings with identical forms, processes, and procedures, administrative costs will fall close to the levels incurred under a single payer. The most efficient administrators of these plans would still be free to make a profit from doing so.[§§] Regardless of who administers the UBHP, a role for private insurers will remain in the provision of Tier 3 coverage. Tier 3 insurance allows Americans to buy coverage above and beyond the level that our society can universally afford to provide for

---

[§§] This approach would largely defuse the current controversy over the potential addition of a publicly operated healthcare plan. As long as the public plan and all privately insured plans under the UBHP have the same simple benefit terms, administrative forms, and requirements, prohibitions on covert rationing and premiums, there should be no reason that private plans could not compete based upon superior customer service. Private insurers would also have an opportunity to compete for customers wanting Tier 3 coverage. While some might argue that the terms of UBHP coverage removes the ability of insurers to "negotiate better pricing" from providers, there is absolutely no evidence that this currently happens in an economically sustainable or beneficial way. Instead, "negotiated benefits" simply end up being cost-shifted to others. For example, all of Medicare's discounted fee "savings" are not savings at all, but simply costs being borne by patients in the form of provider rationing (providers close their offices to Medicare patients because they cannot afford to see them), or private insurers who must pay higher rates to providers to offset the Medicare cuts and allow those providers to remain in business.

everyone. While insurers should be free to write these policies as they wish, it is in the best interests of the public, payers, and the healthcare system that certain elements of the UBHP be consistently applied to Tier 3 policies as well. In particular, Tier 3 policies should utilize exactly the same identifiers, applications, claims submission procedures, rules for payment, and paperwork as UBHP policies. The only difference should be the QALY limits covered by the policies. This requirement is critical for ensuring that the same fragmented and inefficient system of billing and administration we have currently is not resurrected in the future. We already *know* that this approach is wasteful and dysfunctional. It would be unconscionable to reproduce it.

Simplifying and Retooling Payment for Medical Services

The way we finance healthcare is important, but the entire purpose of financing is to compensate providers fairly and efficiently. If we want a healthcare system that delivers services efficiently and without wasting money, there is simply no substitute for simplicity in payment.

Physician payment in the United States is now based upon the performance of "procedures." Compensation for each procedure is determined by the Rube Goldberg-esque RBRVS process. This has produced completely predictable results:

- Because the services of specialists are valued far more highly than the services of generalists, there is a relative shortage of primary care providers.

- Because they are rational, providers seek to maximize the number of high-value procedures performed and minimize the time required to perform them. When there is a choice between two equally efficacious treatments (for example, a medication versus a procedure), any economically rational clinician will be biased toward providing the procedure.

- Healthcare providers spend hours each week on billing and charting duties that have little or nothing to do with actual patient care. This effectively reduces the quantity of medical resources available to the nation. Some 40% of physician work time is now spent outside of the exam room.

- Because of its political nature, the existing payment system gives government bureaucrats and lobbyists disproportionate and unwarranted power to interject themselves into provider practices and the physician-patient relationship.

In redesigning and rebuilding a more efficient healthcare system, our task should be to craft a payment mechanism with five key characteristics. It must be:

1. **Simple, understandable, and easy to implement in any type of medical practice.** Documentation requirements for payment purposes should be minimized.

2. **Consistent and reliable.** It should make it easy to quantify and predict how much healthcare goods and services will cost.

3. **Subject to market forces.** Prices should have the ability to rise and fall in response to levels of supply, demand, business expenses, and local conditions. Other things equal, this will have the effect of guiding patients and providers toward more cost-effective healthcare purchases.

4. **Free of clinical bias.** In practical terms, this means that the system should give providers as little incentive as possible to recommend one course of action over another for financial (as opposed to clinical) reasons.

5. **Free of political bias, regulation, loopholes, and other intricacies designed to slow or minimize payments, or dictate the means by which healthcare services should be delivered.**

All these requirements are in direct response to what we've learned about the complexity, inadequacies, and pitfalls of the current U.S. payment system. But what kind of system could possibly produce results like this? Oddly enough, the answer is the most obvious and common that one can imagine when buying professional services: Simply pay healthcare providers by the hour.

Simplifying Provider Payment Based Upon Well-Established Market Principles

A rational payment plan must take into account the economic incentives faced by patients and insurers as well as providers. There is an economic "balance of power" among these three parties that must be carefully maintained. If too much power accrues to patients, spending and the demand for services will grow out of control. If insurers grow too powerful, providers are easily victimized. Insurance benefit levels can rise or fall unsustainably depending upon whether the insurer is a government plying constituents with benefits for political reasons, or a private insurer seeking to maximize profits. If providers become too powerful, the price of care may climb to inappropriate and unsustainable levels. Healthcare is a three-legged stool. If any one of the legs is too long or too short, it's nearly impossible to maintain a useful and usable equilibrium.

Taking advantage of market forces requires that: (1) prices are always publicly available and transparent to producers and consumers; (2) prices must be allowed to vary with supply and demand; and (3) regulation and obstacles to care have to be kept to the minimum required to protect the public and allow for orderly markets. The first two requirements can be accomplished quite easily by simply allowing clinicians to charge whatever they wish for their time, just like lawyers, accountants, and other professionals. A single hourly rate would cover their services, overhead, and other routine operating expenses.

When compared to the surreal complexity of RBRVS, it seems astonishing that a simple, reliable, and understandable approach like this has never been seriously proposed. How would hourly billing for healthcare services work? The approach is illustrated in Figure 11.3. For the sake of this example, let's assume that the average hourly rate charged by a particular type of clinician (for example, endocrinologists), in a given geographic area (for example, metropolitan Denver, Colorado) is $100 per hour ("Line A" in the figure).

Although $100 per hour is the average, it is important to understand that all clinicians are free to charge whatever they wish. In our example, Clinician #1 chooses to charge the mean, or $100 per hour, Clinician #2 charges 30% more, or $130 per hour, and Clinician #3

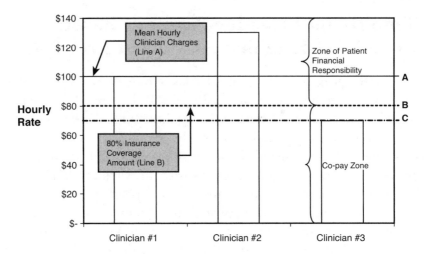

Figure 11.3   Using Hourly Compensation to Balance Supply and Demand for Healthcare Services

charges just $70 per hour. Every clinician is free to raise or lower her hourly rate at any time, but *all* current rate information (not only for clinician's hourly rates, but also for these and other healthcare goods and services) must be posted and easily available to consumers at all times. The best place to post these rates is on a national website dedicated to this purpose. There, patients would be able to search for providers by price, specialty, geographic location, waiting times, and a host of other factors. This information would be entered directly into the site and kept current by each provider's business office.

There are many reasons why providers might choose to vary and set their fees at different levels. Clinicians with a great deal of expertise and experience in a given field might believe that their services are worth more than average. Presumably they will charge relatively higher prices for this added value. New providers just out of medical training will have little experience and empty appointment slots to fill. They might want to charge lower rates in their quest to build their patient base and gain experience and revenue as quickly as possible. Still other providers will choose to offer plush offices, luxurious surroundings, 24-hour email access or other amenities, and will increase their rates to cover these costs. Clinicians wanting to serve poorer populations will minimize their rates to maximize patient access. Most importantly, providers who want to track and publicize their excellent clinical results will now have a clear incentive to do so, because those results will help justify higher charges. Patients should be willing to pay more for care that is demonstrably better than that provided by competing providers whose results are either unpublicized or not as good.

Where does insurance fit into all of this? With clinicians free to charge whatever they want, how much can we expect insurers to pay?

A reasonable answer, and the one that is most consistent with a free-market approach, is that the UBHP will pay for a substantial fraction of the average cost of healthcare goods and services within each geographic region. For the example, in Figure 11.4, we've set this level to be 80% of the average hourly rate for local providers.

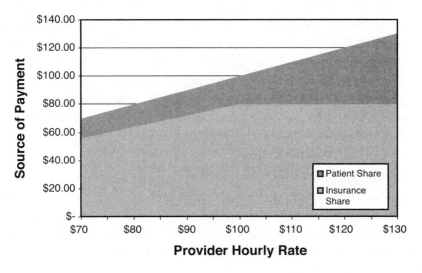

Note: Assumes that basic universal insurance will contribute to a mean hourly clinician rate of up to $100 per hour, and a 20% patient co-pay for amounts up to $100. The patient pays for all hourly costs incurred in excess of the $100 per hour.

Figure 11.4   Example of the Relative Contributions of Patient and Insurer Financial Responsibility at Various Provider Hourly Rates

If the clinician's hourly rate is higher than the 80% level established, the patient is responsible for 100% of the balance.*** In most cases this difference will be paid with funds from the patient's health savings account. If the hourly fee is less than or equal to the 80% level, however, the patient is only liable for a co-pay for the charges covered by insurance. For example, if the provider charges exactly the allowable insurance rate of $80 for an hour of time and the co-pay level is 20%, the insurer will pay a total of $64 and the patient will pay $16 from their HSA. At an hourly rate of $100, the patient will pay $20 per hour, and the insurer will pay $80. Regardless of the amount charged for the visit, it is critical that the patient bear some financial responsibility to limit truly unnecessary care.

In the longer term, the average hourly rate will have an effect on insurance payments because it serves as a proxy for measuring the supply and demand of local provider services. If clinician-set charges consistently rise over time in a given locality, the supply of services is inadequate and the dollar value of 80% insurance coverage should be increased. On the other hand, if clinician-set charges decline over time, there is too much supply and the dollar value of 80% insurance coverage should be reduced accordingly. To accomplish this, a moving average of posted rates is maintained for each clinical specialty in each geographic area. Using the average of these rates as a benchmark, the dollar value of the 80% coverage level is adjusted up or down on a regular basis.

Many might scoff at the notion that provider charges might ever go down as well as up. Few of us have ever known a time when the price of anything associated with healthcare has gone down. But likewise, we have never known a time when the prices of most healthcare services were actually simple, clear, and readily known ahead of the time

---

*** The fact that each American will have an HSA with a known balance at the beginning of each year will dramatically reduce the administrative overhead associated with billing and collecting patient balances. Financial institutions can be asked to issue HSA debit cards. Because the hourly rates charged by the provider and the hourly reimbursement paid by insurers under the UBHP are both known, the difference between the two can easily be charged to the HSA debit card at the time of service. This function alone will measurably reduce practitioner costs and allow them to reduce their hourly rates while preserving net income.

when the services are actually performed. When the price of health-care goods and services is known, amazing things begin to happen.

Almost 30 years ago, Tierney, Miller, and McDonald published an article titled "The Effect On Test Ordering of Informing Physicians of the Charges for Outpatient Diagnostic Tests."[6] They performed a study that was remarkable in its simplicity. One hundred and twenty-one physicians were divided into two groups: a control group and an intervention group. Both groups displayed similar behavior when it came to ordering outpatient tests, both in terms of the numbers of tests ordered and the cost of testing per patient visit. Then, for a 26-week intervention period, both groups used a computer order entry system to request lab tests. The only difference was that physicians in the intervention group were shown the *price* of each test as it was ordered, and the *total cost* of all testing ordered on that day for the patient being seen. The result: Doctors in the intervention group ordered 14% fewer tests than those in the control group, and the charges for the tests that they did order was 13% less. Yet there was *no measureable change in the clinical outcomes* of the patients in the intervention group. And when the pricing information disappeared, so did the savings. After pricing information was removed in the 19-week period at the end of the study, the intervention group of providers immediately began ordering more tests, and the cost savings disappeared.

The amazing thing about this study is that neither group of physicians had any incentives whatever to reduce the number of tests ordered or the cost of doing so. There were no financial incentives or penalties. No government regulations. No capitation payment schemes in which doctors were rewarded for withholding care and punished for ordering more tests. They simply behaved naturally in the presence of information about pricing that is almost uniformly missing within our current heavily regulated, mind-numbingly complex, and price-opaque healthcare system. Imagine the impact if patients and providers both were to have ready access to pricing information about every medical expense and any alternatives.

If incentives are clear, prices are known, and payment is linked to the patient's own perceived benefit, there is absolutely no reason that the price of healthcare goods and services cannot reflect market conditions. The cost of Lasik surgery—a procedure not generally covered by insurance—has declined dramatically over the past ten years while quality has improved. The cost of cosmetic procedures such as Botox injections and plastic surgery differs dramatically from place to place based upon market conditions. The real key to efficiency is a hitherto unused tool: rational patient choice.

Just as providers have the right to charge whatever they want, patients must have the right to use the services of any clinician, anywhere in the country, without having it affect the insurance benefits that they receive. Combined with ready access to pricing information, patients can then make rational decisions about which provider to use based upon many factors, including price. Just as providers might have any number of reasons for increasing or decreasing their hourly charges, patients will have many reasons for choosing one provider over another. Local providers will often be preferred over more distant providers on the basis of convenience. Providers with more experience in treating a specific condition may be chosen over providers with less experience. But price will be a factor common to every decision. Every patient knows that some or all of the charges will come straight from their HSA balance. Because HSA balances are "real money" (in that a percentage of the unspent balance can be used for discretionary spending each year, or rolled over to accrue interest that can be spent later), patients will have clear incentives to think twice before choosing a more expensive provider.

Although traditional HSAs are spent down completely before any insurance coverage is available, the long-term importance of cost sharing makes it worth reconsidering this approach. After a given HSA is used up, there is relatively little financial leverage that can be applied to patient care decisions (unless there is also a provision for continued spending from the patient's own personal non-HSA funds). A better approach might be to ask patient HSAs to cover 100% of the cost of each new medical expense up to a lesser amount (for example, $150) before insurance cost-sharing kicks in. Other things being equal, this would preserve shared responsibility for a longer period of time. The free market system of time-based provider compensation has many other advantages over the current artificially complex system. The amount spent on billing and administrative overhead would plummet. While clinicians would still report the diagnoses, treatments, and procedures performed, actual billing would be based solely upon time spent—a very easy metric to measure and report. Because time is so easily tracked and documented, many of the opportunities for fraud and abuse that exist in the current system would disappear. Because providers are paid the same amount for their time regardless of interventions chosen for a given patient, they will have no incentive to perform more expensive procedures as opposed to using medical or educational interventions. And where government regulators are currently preoccupied with asking providers to measure and demonstrate their clinical effectiveness, a market-driven system will generate an immediate incentive to do so. Clinicians who are able to prove that they are clinically better will be able to attract more patients and charge higher hourly rates than their regional competitors—an incentive that most doctors currently lack.

Perhaps most importantly, the combination of QALY-based overt rationing and hourly compensation would go a long way toward restoring the integrity of the physician-patient relationship. Freed of conflicts of interest and CPT constraints on patient education, doctors can once again become honest advocates for whatever course of action is in the best interest of each patient, and take the time to fully explain the available options.

What are the potential drawbacks to this approach? There are two important changes that we can expect:

- **Increases in waiting times.** With less incentive to "crank out" patients and procedures as if they were widgets, fewer visits and procedures will be performed per unit of time. Many of visits that do take place will take longer. Combined with universal access to care, this will almost certainly lead to longer waiting times.

  Whether this is a bad thing depends upon one's perspective. On one hand, it is clear that trying to jam 30 minutes of care into the 7–10 minutes that primary care providers are currently allotted is inefficient and ineffective. Most of the education and counseling that would allow patients to understand and care for their medical conditions cannot possibly be provided in that period of time. In medicine as elsewhere, haste makes waste. On the other hand, in the short term, our supply of providers is essentially fixed. The net effect will therefore be better and more appropriate care, but with the appearance of waiting lists and lines we have not previously seen.

- **Short-term changes in provider compensation.** After market forces are allowed to take effect for the first time, some provider incomes will rise even as others fall. Longer waiting times in some specialties—especially primary care—will allow high-demand providers to increase their hourly rates. In most cases, compensation for these providers will rise significantly after being held artificially low by the politically determined RBRVS system. Reductions will gradually occur in the average hourly compensation of other groups of providers, but these will probably take more time to filter through. Most of these reductions will accrue to certain specialties that have been relatively overcompensated by performing large numbers of quick, but profitable procedures.

Having transferred the basis of compensation from procedures to time, it is reasonable to ask about checks and balances. What's to keep clinicians from simply padding their hours? Could we expect expect routine checkups to take hours, as providers linger over every little detail? Although any compensation system carries the potential for abuse, there are several reasons to believe that healthcare is much less subject to time padding than many other professions, such as law and accounting. First, compared to attorneys and accountants, physicians and other healthcare providers are relatively scarce. There are only about 820,000 clinically active physicians in the United States, compared with more than 1,200,000 active attorneys. In practice, this means that the majority of clinicians are already booked to capacity. With full practices and waiting lists of patients to be seen, there is little or no reason for healthcare providers to dwell any longer than necessary on a given case. For most clinicians, heavy patient loads and waiting lists are a far greater concern than trying to fill idle hours. Second, unlike many other professions, most clinical services are delivered face-to-face. This allows budget-conscious patients to act as a restraining influence on visit times. Instead of looking for reasons to prolong their visit, patients will be looking for opportunities to speed it up. Third, truly transparent pricing will allow patients to screen providers based on price even before making their first appointment.

High-priced providers will be under pressure to better meet the financial constraints of their patients.

Minimizing Insurance and Regulatory Overhead

The third requirement for freeing the healthcare markets—minimizing regulation and obstacles to care—is undoubtedly the most challenging to achieve and maintain over time. In the absence of any sort of free market in healthcare, the existing system has assembled an inexhaustible supply of administrative obstacles to care. These include referrals that are needed before patients can see specialists, pre-authorizations for treatments and tests that will inevitably be needed to properly manage care, provider panels that restrict who a patient can see without incurring financial penalties, and a wide variety of "passive aggressive" insurance behaviors.

Removing these administrative and bureaucratic limitations on care is going to be difficult for several reasons. First, it has traditionally been claimed that these limitations are needed to prevent patients and providers from over-utilizing healthcare resources. (It's not clear whether this theory has ever been tested scientifically. If so, it would be even more useful to determine in what percentage of cases the test or treatment was *appropriately* denied, delayed, or canceled as opposed to being *inappropriately* denied, delayed or canceled.) Insurers will be loath to give up any measures that delay or discourage expenditures from their reserves. Second, as any parent knows, passive aggressive behavior can be hard to define. If the insurance company office in charge of billing questions is slow to respond to queries or answer its phones, is it intentional or simply inadvertent understaffing? Third, no matter how many of these questionable rules and hurdles might be identified and banned, it's always cheap and easy to come up with new ones to replace them.

No matter how daunting the task, eliminating these obstacles once and for all is the only way to implement a system that is less expensive, more efficient and responsive to market forces. The alternative is the status quo: a public-private insurance system whose first allegiance is inevitably going to be protecting politicians and reserves rather than

patients. Protecting patients, our pocketbooks and posterity is going to
require a completely new way of thinking. With patients and physicians properly motivated, the burden of covert rationing must be
placed on insurers. If an insurer wants to require physicians to obtain
referrals or pre-authorizations, then it will need to justify its requests
on a case-by-case basis. If valid claims are denied arbitrarily they may
be appealed to a system of independent "claims courts" with the power
to levy penalties on any party showing bad faith. Insurers who abuse
their power must be punished, regardless of whether they are public
or private. A national regulatory and investigative panel must keep
careful and continuous watch over rules and policies that threaten to
supplant market-based limitations on care with administrative ones.

Application of Market Principles to Other Healthcare Goods and Services

It is relatively easy to see how these same principles could be
applied to pricing and providing many types of medical goods and
services. In fact, an accepted precedent for this approach already
exists in the form of "reference pricing" for drugs. In reference pricing programs, a baseline level of payment is set for the prototypical
(and usually generic) drug within a given class of medications. In
2003, the German healthcare system chose the generic drug simvastatin (sold by Merck under the brand name of Zocor) to be the prototypical statin—a class of drugs used to reduce the amount of
cholesterol in the blood. After the prototype was selected, the maximum amount that the German healthcare system would reimburse
for any statin drug was set to be the full amount that the system
would pay for simvastatin. Other drugs could certainly be prescribed
and used, but the full difference between the cost of other statins
such as Crestor and Lipitor and the cost of simvastatin would be
borne by the patient. (In our case, this difference could come from
the patient's HSA.)

There are some legitimate criticisms of reference pricing. For
one thing, it places a centralized bureaucracy in the position of determining which drugs are truly equivalent, even though they might
not really be equivalent within the personal chemistry of an individual patient. Second, it has been persuasively argued that this
approach stifles incremental innovation on the part of pharmaceutical

manufacturers. If the baseline statin reduces cholesterol by 29%, and a drug company could create a new drug within the same class that would reduce cholesterol by 48%, why should they bother doing so if the insurance industry's reimbursement policy forces most patients to make do with the inferior drug?

Many of these concerns have merit, but most of them can be addressed by modifications to the system. For example, a superior approach for long-term drug pricing would be to establish a reference based upon cost per QALY for an "average patient," rather than simply choosing the cheapest drug in the class. This would largely remove bureaucratic and political concerns from the reference equation by providing and objective and verifiable alternative. The QALY approach would also have the benefit of encouraging the development of drugs that provide incremental improvements in performance, as long as their cost/QALY is less than or equal to comparable medications. The current system simply rewards the cheapest drug available with little or no regard for comparative efficacy.

Applying market-based pricing to non-emergency inpatient services is slightly more complex because so many different types of products and services are used in the course of a typical hospitalization. However, the same principles of transparent pricing, basic, uniform, universal insurance coverage, and market-based price adjustments can be applied. The optimum approach to hospital pricing might depend upon the purpose of the hospitalization. Hospitalizations for elective procedures (including foreseeable events such as childbirth) are probably best covered by a single, global, and well-publicized fee, much as they are now. This would give patients the ability to comparison shop, weigh data on experience, expertise, and historical results, and consider options such as traveling to different cities or states in an attempt to secure the best possible combination of price and outcome. Insurance coverage would follow a similar model to that for clinician services, paying a large fraction of the average procedure price for a given region. Patients choosing less expensive facilities—either within or outside their local region—would have the opportunity to minimize their own expenses. For proof, we can look at what happens when patients are fully responsible for virtually all their own healthcare expenses, and providers and institutions are free to operate on a free-market basis. Ironically, one of our best role models in this regard is India.

As shown in Figure 11.5, India spends very little of its GDP on healthcare relative to developed countries, and 80% of what it does spend is funded by patients, private firms, and charities. As a result, Indian healthcare providers have had to become both creative and price-conscious when offering services. Government has recently helped the innovation process by liberalizing restrictions on the industry, offering tax breaks for health investments in smaller cities and rural areas, easing restrictions on lending and foreign investment in healthcare, and encouraging public-private partnerships.[7]

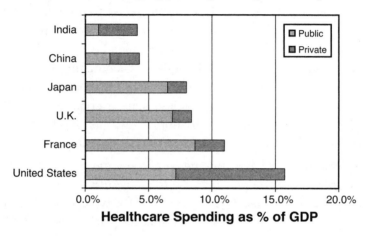

Data from: World Bank Development Indicators, 2010.

Figure 11.5   Ratio of Public to Private Spending in Selected Countries, 2007

The result has been "a happy collusion of need and greed [that] has produced a cauldron of innovation, as Indian entrepreneurs have devised new business models." Some notable examples:

- For years India's private-health providers, such as Apollo Hospitals, focused on the affluent upper classes, but they are now racing down the pyramid. [One company]... plans to take advantage of tax breaks to build hospitals in small and medium-sized cities (which, in India, means those with up to 3 million inhabitants)... Apollo's founder plans to do the same. He thinks he can cut costs in half for patients: a quarter saved through lower overheads, and another quarter by eliminating travel to bigger cities.

- Columbia Asia, a privately held American firm with more than a dozen hospitals across Asia, is also making a big push into

India. Rick Evans, its boss, says his investors left America to escape over-regulation and the political power of the medical lobby. His model involves building no-frills hospitals using standardised designs, connected like spokes to a hub that can handle more complex ailments. His firm offers modestly priced services to those earning $10,000–20,000 a year within wealthy cities, thereby going after customers overlooked by fancier chains.

- LifeSpring Hospitals is a chain of small maternity hospitals around Hyderabad. "This for-profit outfit offers normal deliveries attended by private doctors for just $40 in its general ward, and Caesarean sections for about $140—as little as one-fifth of the price at the big private hospitals. It has cut costs with a basic approach: it has no canteens and outsources laboratory tests and pharmacy services. It also achieves economies of scale by attracting large numbers of patients using marketing. LifeSpring's doctors perform four times as many operations a month as their counterparts do elsewhere—and, crucially, get better results as a result of high volumes and specialisation."

- Nearly 60% of Indian hospitals use healthcare IT, but not in the same way as it's typically implemented in the United States. "Instead of grafting technology onto existing, inefficient processes, as often happens in America, Indian providers build their model around it."[8]

One has to wonder, if Indians can use market forces to innovate in healthcare, why can't Americans?

Pricing healthcare services for emergency and nonelective services is more difficult, because by definition such circumstances do not lend themselves to data collection, deliberation, and consumer choice. The current approach uses a fixed-fee "prospective payment system" (PPS). The PPS uses about 500 so-called "diagnosis-related groups" (DRGs) to come up with a lump sum payment for given types of hospitalization services. If a hospital's expenses for a given case are less than the amount set for the DRG, it makes money. If they are greater, the hospital loses money. There are two problems with this approach. First, hospitals do not necessarily have complete control over all their costs. Second, Medicare and Medicaid payments are often so low that it's virtually impossible for hospitals to recover their costs. This combination can cause considerable trouble when profitable elective admissions are moved to more efficient and economical specialty hospitals or technology turns them into outpatient procedures. In their capacity as providers of emergency and nonelective services, hospitals are really functioning as public utilities. They cannot refuse emergency cases, discharge patients for nonpayment, or even decide whether and where to build new facilities without government oversight. Given these conditions, it is unreasonable for anyone to expect free markets to finance essential hospital services any more than they are used to finance police, fire, road, or sanitation services.

With these limitations in mind, there is really only one practical way to price nonelective hospital services appropriately: Continue the current prospective payment system based upon DRGs, but modify it to exclude elective procedures and minimize administrative overhead wherever possible. Elective procedures would be handled by using competitive pricing for elective services as described previously. If this approach is to work, we must ask hospitals to keep two sets of books for the services they provide—one for elective and one for nonelective services. Elective revenues derived through market forces should not be asked to subsidize nonelective admission expenses, or vice versa.[†††] A second requirement is that insurance payments for

---

[†††] Experience has now shown that mixing elective and nonelective care gives us the worst of both worlds: inefficient elective care and underfunded nonelective care services. For evidence, we need look no further than the growth of ambulatory surgery centers. Often built, owned, and operated by physicians, ambulatory surgery centers (ASCs) are typically efficient, innovative, and profitable operations. As such, they are capable of providing excellent care faster and cheaper than conventional hospitals. Because they are not saddled with the high cost of providing emergency and nonelective care services, they represent a less expensive and more attractive option for patients who might have a bad knee but are otherwise well. In contrast, the conventional hospitals have high overhead and a burden of low-reimbursement emergency services that makes them uncompetitive in comparison. The resulting flight of elective procedures to ambulatory centers leads to a vicious cycle of declining hospital revenue and less experienced, less efficient surgical teams. The usual hospital response is to demand regulatory changes to reduce the attractiveness and increase the financial burden of ASCs. Unless elective and nonelective admissions are financially separated, there is really no way to achieve medical and economic efficiencies in either one.

nonelective admissions cover the full cost of hospitalization. Current underpayments by Medicare and Medicaid are not sustainable over time, especially after elective-procedure revenue is segregated from nonelective expenses. Finally, patient cost-sharing for nonelective care must be structured differently from other medical expenses. Even the most conscientious patients can do little or nothing to influence the cost of true medical emergencies, and co-payments are of no real benefit for minimizing related expenses after the appropriate QALY measures are in place. On the other hand, this system does require that true emergencies be separated from emergency room and hospital abuse. Patients attempting to use emergency rooms as after-hour clinics should either be referred directly to 24-hour clinics set up to handle such patients, or charged twice the "normal" HSA co-pay for abusing the emergency care system.

Putting It All Together: Streamlined Healthcare Financing and Payment

The net result of the changes we've described is to both reduce the number of parts in the healthcare machine and eliminate the majority of grit thrown into the system by the RBRVS-based payment system. A reasonable estimate of cost savings generated by these measures alone will total almost $500 billion annually, as shown in Table 11.1.

TABLE 11.1   Estimated Source of Annual Cost Savings As a Result of Described Changes to the U.S. Healthcare Financing and Payment System*

Source	Annual Savings
Administrative Savings	
Excess administration expenses of public and private insurers	$138 billion
One-half of excess Inpatient nonclinical labor	$21 billion
One-half of outpatient nonclinical labor	$8.5 billion
Reduced billing, collection, and related expense[†]	$44 billion

continues

TABLE 11.1 Continued

Source	Annual Savings
Clinical Savings[‡]	
More cost-efficient use of drug therapy	$45 billion
More cost-efficient use of outpatient clinical services	$103 billion
More efficient use of hospital clinical services	$118.5 billion
Total Estimated Annual Savings (Based on 2008 spending levels)	**$478 billion**

[*] Unless otherwise noted, figures are from McKinsey Global Institute report "Accounting for the Cost of Health Care in the United States." January 2007. McKinsey numbers based upon 2003 statistics have been increased to reflect a 41% increase in healthcare spending between 2003 (total U.S. healthcare spending of $1.7 trillion) to 2008 (total U.S. healthcare spending of $2.4 trillion).

[†] Based upon average provider billing costs of 7% of gross collections, and a 50% savings in billing expense upon adoption of the changes and simplifications described in the text.

[‡] Calculated based upon a 15% increase in the efficiency of drug use, inpatient and outpatient goods and services based upon price transparency, improved physician counseling and patients choice in the presence of free-market incentives.

Where do these savings come from? Many of these estimates draw from McKinsey's study of where excess spending occurs in the U.S. healthcare system, relative to what would be expected for the relative size of our GDP.

- **Insurer administrative expense.** According to McKinsey and others, in 2003 the United States spent about $98 billion more than expected for the administrative expenses of public and private insurance entities alone. This is the equivalent of $138 billion in 2008. Virtually all these excess expenses can be eliminated with claims and policy standardization and the simplification of impossibly complex RBRVS payment system. This estimate does not assume any reduction in insurance company profits.

- **Nonclinical labor costs.** These include estimates of cost in excess of "estimated spending according to wealth" (ESAW) for both inpatient and outpatient nonclinical labor costs. Nonclinical labor costs generally represent administrative overhead associated with regulatory compliance, billing, and sales and

marketing, but excludes outside contract services, maintenance, professional fees, and utilities. Virtually all these excess
expenses are attributable to the proliferation of insurers, rules,
regulations, and exceptions caused by fragmented insurance
coverage, differences between state laws, and problems caused
by the complexity of the current payment system that are
addressed by use of in-house billing staff. Virtually all these
excess expenses (a total of about $30 billion) can be eliminated
by a combination of de facto carrier defragmentation and
reductions in regulatory burden. For the purposes of this calculation, we will attribute half of the savings to simplified payment mechanisms and half to reductions in regulatory burden.

- **Reduced billing, collection, and related expenses.** While
some of the excess billing costs attributable to the current system will be accounted for under nonclinical labor costs, a large
portion of the savings will come from a different accounting category: other operational costs and expenses. Many providers and
hospitals outsource their billing and administrative support
functions, and an entire industry does nothing but battle health
insurer complexity, covert rationing, and counterproductive government regulation. The number and diversity of these companies is staggering. They include medical billers who gather data
and prepare and submit the medical claims, couriers who transport the data, and thousands of software vendors. Computer
software is used to enter and compile claims and insurance data,
check it for errors and omissions, and configure it for submission
to insurers. Software is also used by both insurers and providers
in an attempt to game the system—denying or minimizing the
dollar value of claims on one hand, and trying to maximize them
on the other. Tens of thousands of people are required to create,
sell, service, and maintain this software at an enormous cost.
Other companies build their businesses around government
regulations. These include state and federal requirements concerning continuing medical education, record keeping, credentialing, privacy, laboratory operations, and more.

The average clinical operation spends approximately 7% of its
gross income annually on medical billing alone. With gross hospital and outpatient care costing a total of $886 billion in 2003,

billing functions accounted for about $62 billion. This had increased to $88 billion by 2008. Insurance defragmentation (brought about by standardization of policies and administration), billing simplification, and use of self-guiding market forces should allow us to cut these billing costs by at least half, saving $44 billion annually.

- **More efficient use of pharmaceuticals, outpatient, and hospital care services.** The tragedy of covert rationing is that measures intended to reduce healthcare costs almost always end up having the opposite effect. Intentional complexity (no matter how well intended), cost opacity, deception, obfuscation, and regulation all create confusion and perverse incentives, producing ill-informed and/or irrational decisions on the part of patients and providers alike. Without a QALY-type approach, resources are wasted on what is payable, rather than what is effective and the best value for the money.

One very visible example is our current spending on end-of-life care. An astonishing 30% of annual Medicare spending goes to the care of the 5% of Medicare patients in their last year of life, and 78% of this amount—or almost *one-quarter of all Medicare costs*—are incurred in the last 30 days of life. A QALY approach to making healthcare purchasing decisions would reduce this spending dramatically, as many expensive and minimally effective treatments would fall outside of the cost/QALY coverage range of the Universal Basic Health Plan. Although some may bluntly object to the overt rationing involved in this process, there is considerable evidence that reducing the invasiveness and severity of end-of-life interventions is more humane as well as less costly to patients and society alike.

As shown in Figure 11.6, there is an inverse relationship between healthcare spending in the last week of life and the quality of death for cancer patients. The same study showed that having patients with advanced cancer and their physicians simply *discuss* end-of-life care wishes reduces the cost of care in the final week of life by 35.7%, or an average of $1,041.[9]

Knowing this, it's worthwhile to compare the financial incentives inherent within the current system with those in the QALY and market-based system we've discussed. In the current system,

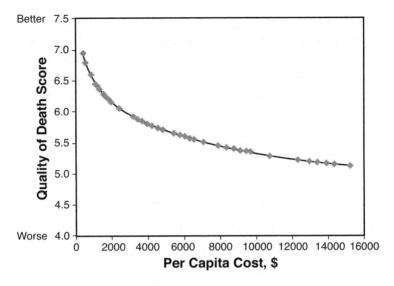

From: Zhang B, Alexi A, Wright AA, Huskamp HA, et al. "Health Care Costs in the Last Week of Life: Associations With End-of-Life Conversations." *Archives of Internal Medicine* 2009; 169(5):480-488.[10]

Figure 11.6 The Relationship Between the Cost and Quality of Life in the Final Week of Life

providers aren't paid to talk to patients, they're paid to perform procedures—the kind of expensive procedures that will drastically increase the cost of end-of-life care. There's an excellent chance that simply talking to a patient about care and end-of-life options would be considered a nonbillable event by insurers. The incentives inherent in the RBRVS system maximize both medical spending and the likelihood of a harsh and lingering death. When combined with cost/QALY-based insurance coverage, paying providers for their time will have the exact opposite result.

With savings like those resulting from smarter, less expensive, and more humane end-of-life care, it seems certain that the revised healthcare funding and payment systems proposed will generate at least a 15% reduction in the overall cost of providing any given level of healthcare benefits. Applied to the healthcare spending levels of 2008, these savings would total about $250 billion annually.

Altogether, the savings accrued by reducing the effective number of wheels in the healthcare financing system and reducing the complexity of payment will provide a considerable financial windfall even as they allow for a substantial increase in the quality of care provided. This windfall will almost certainly exceed the new cost of providing care to all Americans who are newly insured under the UBHP. Although the percentage of newly uninsured in the U.S. population will be roughly 16%, the healthcare spending reductions generated by our changes in insurance financing and payment alone total 20% of 2008 healthcare spending. We can spend the resulting financial windfall in one of two ways. The first is to take these savings and spend them on nonhealthcare goods such as debt reduction, tax reductions, or investments in our country's nonhealthcare infrastructure. The alternative is to keep this money within the healthcare system and provide an even higher level of overall benefits. But we needn't stop at these savings. There is still more we can do.

12

Dumping Redundancy

"The Department of Education and another ministry were worried about duplication of effort, so what did they do? They set up two committees to look into duplication and neither knew what the other was up to. It really is a world beyond parody."

—*Rory Bremner*

Although faulty insurance funding and payment mechanisms are the single biggest source of extra parts in our healthcare machine, there are others that are even easier to address. Medical licensure is the most obvious place to start. Because diseases, anatomy, and treatments are the same everywhere, it makes no sense to license physicians on a state-by-state basis. Fortunately, moving to a unified licensure and regulation need not be difficult or expensive.

The simplest fix is to simply declare that all state medical licensure is reciprocal, much in the same way that all drivers licenses are reciprocal. If you can legally practice medicine in one state, you can practice in all of them. All that is necessary is for the federal government to mandate that, as a function of interstate commerce, all states shall automatically honor each other's medical licenses. Any provider would be free to practice in any state as long as he notifies the local state board of his presence. Of course, just as with driver's licensure, each state is also free to discipline or limit any provider as necessary to protect the public. Creating a national database of physician licensure, malfeasance, and disciplinary actions would be relatively simple. Each physician would be identified by a single unique license number that would follow her from state to state, just as DEA numbers (used to track physicians with respect to their prescription of narcotics) do currently.

Steps to reduce duplication and create uniformity in healthcare licensure requirements should follow quickly. A single set of medical licensure application materials should be adopted for nationwide use, as would any continuing medical education requirements and conditions for license renewal. Any ethical guidelines, penalties, disciplinary, and rehabilitation programs should be also be promulgated uniformly. One of the most important benefits of reciprocal licensure will accrue to patients and their families. By having physicians use a single license no matter where they practice, all licensee information—including provider training, license status, specialties, practice addresses, and so on—can be made readily available to prospective patients by use of a single public website. This would be a vast improvement over the current patchwork of state websites and provider tracking mechanisms. The consolidation of provider licensing and identification will save billions of dollars in license fees, processing errors, and unnecessary paperwork each year. Saving many billions more and reducing medical error rates would be easy with the introduction of a parallel unique patient identifier. The creation and use of unique patient identifiers has historically been the subject of great controversy in the United States. The most frequent concern is that universal healthcare identifiers would somehow have an adverse impact on patient privacy. For those who work with patients on a regular basis, this objection is hard to appreciate. The fact is that all patients are already uniquely identified somehow. If the government or anyone else wants to violate medical confidentiality, they don't need a special number to do so. A name, address, date of birth, and statistical matching algorithm will serve just as well. *The key to privacy lies not in the identifiers used, nor in who assigns them, but in how that information is controlled.* Much of the public's concern stems from the ease with which *any* identifier—in conjunction with a universal electronic medical record—could be used to pry into anyone's personal healthcare history. What the public really wants is for patients themselves to retain control over access to their medical information.

Creating and using personal patient identifiers would create instant cost savings and improvements in patient safety. Concerns over privacy could be relatively easily addressed through two measures.

The first is the passage of laws making it a felony for government employees or others to intentionally use or release medical information about any person for nonmedical purposes without that patient's consent. Upon passage of this law, a unique patient identifier would immediately be created and issued for everyone in the U.S. The second measure is to set up a relatively simple, secure Internet-based mechanism that patients would use to approve the release of medical information from one provider or institution to another. With an interface no more complex than an ATM, this application would be financed by the government and administered by an independent nonprofit agency. Any time that any electronic medical record system was asked to transfer information to another, a permission request would be sent to the patient's permission account. The patient would then be notified by email and/or telephone, and permission could be instantly granted or denied by use of a PIN. Provisions could easily be made for record access in emergency situations, when the patient might be unavailable or unresponsive. This type of simple, effective personal privacy system is exactly the type of technology that has been overlooked or ignored by a "medical-industrial complex" that is intent on regulation, protecting market share by creating proprietary, nonstandard technology, and controlling of the practice of medicine and use of medical information.

Credentialing Made Easy

As discussed previously, credentialing is the process by which institutions compile and verify the professional qualifications of their providers. This process is currently undertaken separately by each institution. The duplication and redundancy involved cost providers, hospitals, and clinics billions of dollars annually, adding to the cost of medicine and providing little or no benefit to the vast majority of patients. The current situation is roughly equivalent to every business in America being responsible for maintaining current driver's license information for everyone who picks up or delivers packages to their business locations. They might indeed find and eliminate some unqualified drivers, but only at a ridiculously high aggregate cost.

The insanity of this process is that virtually all these institutions require the exact same information. Like the process of granting and verifying medical license status, this function is tailor-made for centralized collection and dissemination over the Internet. A far simpler, easier, cheaper, and more reliable credentialing system could easily be created:

1. Use federal money to fund a nonprofit, centralized credentials information center. The credentials center need not consist of much more than an Internet-connected computer server with a robust database behind it for collecting and aggregating the information submitted.

2. Standardized, web-based data submission forms would be created for completion by professionals nationwide. Hard-copy credentials such as degrees, certificates, scores, and so on would be scanned and uploaded as image files. Each set of information would have to be entered once, and only once, per professional.

3. Institutions wishing to review and document the credentials of their professional employees and associates need only create a webpage of their own linking to selected information contained in the national credentialing website.

4. Professionals would be asked to review the information within the central database annually, and only update it as necessary.

There are private for-profit services that currently provide some of the functionality just described for providers, but they do not necessarily offload the responsibility for data collection and storage from the many thousands of healthcare institutions around the country. A national system would produce substantial economies of scale and create much-needed uniformity in data collection and reporting.

The Financial Benefits of Eliminating Redundancy

The modifications that we've discussed in this chapter are fairly modest, and their visible impact will be subtle to the casual observer.

The vast majority of citizens never see the cost and chaos caused by redundancy in licensure, credentialing, and patient identification. These costs are typically rolled into the administrative costs of healthcare. The result is that everyone pays, but without realizing it. Rather than appearing as a line item in any invoice, these costs are included in the cost of every visit, hospitalization, procedure, and prescription.

Let's look at each cost and the resulting saving individually.

Medical Licensure and Credentialing

Conover and colleagues estimated the annual total regulatory cost of professional accreditation and licensure to be $6.5 billion in 2004. They further estimated the net cost (that is, financial costs less financial benefits) to be $1.8 billion annually.[1] If we can streamline the credentialing process and eliminate redundant licensing the net benefit will, of course, be higher. According to the Federation of State Medical Boards (FSMB), approximately 54% of all physicians who have held an active license from 1998 to 2008 obtain multiple licenses at some point. If we assume that the typical healthcare provider maintains an average of 1.25 licenses at any one time, it should be possible to reduce the cost of the existing system by an additional 20% by eliminating the costs attributable to that fractional license. This would provide an additional saving of $1.3 billion, for an annual total savings of $3.1 billion per year.

Unique Patient Identifiers

The RAND Corporation has calculated a one-time cost of about $11 billion to implement a national patient identifier.[2] The ongoing annual costs of maintaining such a system would be minimal, unlike the existing system of detailed data collection and cross-checking. But what does the current patchwork system cost? If we assume that the annual maintenance costs of the two systems will be identical, the best estimate of current expense might be the costs related to exception handling—that is, handling cases in which the lack of a UPI makes it necessary to incur additional administrative expense to sort out which patient one is dealing with.

According to the RAND study, the existing statistical approach to retrieving patient data using the best available matching technology results in an error at least 8% of the time. Americans make an average of 3.8 outpatient visits per year, or almost 1.2 billion visits annually. In addition, there were about 38 million hospitalizations in the U.S. in 2002. If we assume that at least three patient identification matches are needed per outpatient visit (a conservative number when we consider that each visit generates a substantial number of corresponding tests, prescriptions, and referrals—all of which require identity tracking), and ten patient identity matches are required over the course of each hospital visit, the total number of identification matches would be approximately 4 billion each year. (This is almost certainly a gross underestimate.) Nevertheless, the number of initially faulty or ambiguous matches that need to be more carefully examined will total at least 8% of this figure, or 320 million matches per year.

In clinical practice, patient identity problems are typically resolved in a variety of ways. Patients, providers, or medical information systems might be called, faxed, or queried for additional information. Records will be double-checked, and processes might be put on hold. In worst-case scenarios, the error will go undetected, potentially costing lives or thousands of dollars in misdirected resources. However, if we merely assume a simple average time cost of 15 minutes being required to resolve each error or ambiguity at a fully burdened hourly wage rate of $15 per hour, the total excess administration personnel burden of the current system would be approximately $1.2 billion per year. This number does not take into account any savings that might result from a reduction in medical errors or health consequences resulting from mistaken patient identities.

The result of combining the savings from streamlined medical licensure and credentialing and instituting unique patient identifiers are summarized in Table 12.1.

TABLE 12.1 Estimated Source of Annual Cost Savings As a Result of Eliminating Redundancy in Medical Licensure and Credentialing, and Instituting UPIs

Source	Annual Savings
Administrative Savings	
Excess annual expense for multi-state medical licensure and redundant credentialing	$3.1 billion
Administrative savings as a result of implementing unique patient identifiers	$1.2 billion
Total Estimated Annual Savings	**$4.3 billion**

13

Blowing Sand Out of the System

"Simplicity is prerequisite for reliability."
—*Edsger Dijkstra*

The process by which providers are paid for their services is the most important single source of grit in the gears of the healthcare machine, but there are plenty of others. Having addressed the question of financing and paying for healthcare previously, it's time to tackle two other system ills: well-intentioned but dysfunctional government regulation, and medical malpractice.

The Role of Government in Healthcare

It's relatively easy to see where the actions of government have gone wrong in healthcare—from aiding and abetting in the fragmentation of healthcare payment and services to promulgating regulations and payment systems that are too complex and ambiguous to be followed. What's more difficult is clearly establishing a set of guidelines for government itself to follow when dealing with the delivery of healthcare services. Even with the very best of intentions, it's very easy—and almost inevitable—for government to overreach in its attempts to ensure that healthcare is widely available, affordable, and of good quality. What should the role of government be in our overhauled system, and how does this translate into concrete actions?

Rather than speculating based upon philosophy, historical precedents, or politics, we should ground ourselves in the two true bases of healthcare: the natural laws of medical science and economics. These two fields ultimately govern all healthcare-related cost, behavior, and outcomes. Regulatory efforts that ignore these laws are doomed to eventually fail. Based upon what we know about the inherent limitations of clinical medicine and economics, it is possible to come up with some concrete limitations when it comes to governing the healthcare system. Together these rules should be the basis of a dedicated "Healthcare Constitution" for the United States.

Good Governing Rule #1: First of all, do not harm. *Primun non nocere* (Latin for "first, do no harm") is a fundamental precept of the Hippocratic Oath, and should be one of the fundamental rules governing lawmakers and regulators. In practice, rules should never be made without complete consideration of the adverse consequences that they are likely to have. Unfortunately, violations of this rule abound in our current system. Most financial managers could have predicted that a complex and difficult payment system would generate enormous administrative overhead for the healthcare system as a whole—even as it creates opportunities for confusion, "gaming the system," and even outright fraud. It should be equally obvious that paying for procedures will result in lots of procedures being performed, while mandating pain management courses for physicians who will never treat a chronic pain patient will result in lost provider resources for no clinical gain.

Good Governing Rule #2: No matter how well-intentioned, never create regulations, programs, or policies that interject themselves into the actual provision of medical care. However wise they might be, legislators and healthcare regulators are not the providers at the site of care. Aside from banning specific treatments or procedures that it finds to be generally unsafe or unethical, it is both unscientific and unwise for government to set policies that dictate, encourage, or discourage specific clinical actions. For example, even though the vast majority of patients with elevated cholesterol levels might benefit from having it treated, there will always be exceptions. In these cases, legislation or guidelines that reward or punish patients or providers for failing to treat high cholesterol will create inappropriate incentives, and would be both medically and economically incorrect.

The vast majority of Americans are rightfully scared and intimidated by the prospect that government bureaucrats will be the third decision maker in the room when they and their providers are making medical treatment decisions. As we've seen, there are many ways in which bureaucrats (and insurers in general) can and do insert themselves into the physician-patient relationship, ranging from arbitrary denials of appropriate referrals, tests, and treatments, to financial incentives, to guidelines of care. Like the potential for government abuse of power that caused the Founding Fathers to install specific prohibitions and checks and balances into the Constitution, these and other interventions will inevitably occur unless they are actively guarded against. It is no trivial issue. Whoever decides what "best practices" are and enforces compliance with them (regardless of how valid those criteria might be), effectively controls the clinical decision-making process.

Good Governing Rule #3: Never mandate the use of any healthcare technology, whether it's the use of a gamma knife, an imaging modality, or an electronic medical record. Healthcare is an enormous field with many niches and subtleties. Mandating the use of any specific technology is inefficient and bad business practice. In most cases, technology mandates are political pay-offs to specific companies or industry lobbies. Just as military vendors will force the Pentagon to purchase fighters, bombers, and ships it neither wants nor needs by lobbying Congress, the medical-industrial complex will gladly legislate bad healthcare decisions. The most recent case of this is in the electronic medical record mandate passed into law with the 2009 economic stimulus bill. Crafted by the largest players in the healthcare information systems industry, this Congressional mandate will cost the healthcare economy billions of dollars and untold thousands of man-hours that can and should be spent elsewhere. In healthcare as in the military, the lure of technology is strong. Any technology can find plenty of advocates who will promise the world if it is adopted. In this as in many areas, the best judge of technology is the market itself. If the technology is truly useful and cost-effective, providers will buy it without prodding.

Good Governing Rule #4: Reconsider the collection of data for its own sake. Part of the justification for the rush to implement electronic medical records is that the data gathered in the course of clinical encounters can and should be "mined." We seem to have an almost preternatural desire to gather and publish healthcare data, regardless of its value. Anyone not convinced of this merely needs to take a look at the medical literature. Virtually every week there are research papers published that confirm once again what we already know: Smoking is bad for you.[1] Obesity is caused by excessive calorie intake.[2] Exercise is good. The reasoning seems to be that the more data we have, the more benefit we will derive. The federal government is particularly obsessive in this regard. Doctors are continually having data about their patients collected, tabulated, and reported back to them in an attempt to "boost quality." The major problem with this approach is that, no matter what system is used, much of the data collected in today's complex clinical setting is either wrong, worthless, or both. In medical research as elsewhere, "garbage in, garbage out."

The point of all this is not to say that medical history is uniformly useless, inaccurate, or even costly. The point is that data collection for its own sake is a slippery slope, and is a potentially important cause of inefficiency and cost in both the existing and future healthcare systems. In the 1980s it was fashionable to talk about "government paperwork" and "paperwork reduction." Much of that urgency seems to have been lost as computers databases ask for the same or greater amounts of information, but in a "clutter-free" format. Especially in healthcare, it is important that government return to the wording and spirit of the Paperwork Reduction Act of 1980:

> Before approving a proposed collection of information, the Director shall determine whether the collection of information by the agency is necessary for the proper performance of the functions of the agency, including whether the information shall have practical utility. Before making a determination the Director might give the agency and other interested persons an opportunity to be heard or to submit statements in writing. To the extent, if any, that the Director determines that the collection of information by an agency is unnecessary for any reason, the agency might not engage in the collection of information.

Good Governing Rule #5: Emphasize simplicity and clarity, and enforce its use in healthcare-oriented laws and regulations. Based upon everything that we've learned about the workings of the healthcare machine, this rule speaks for itself.

Government Regulation: The Quest for Quality

"Virtue is more to be feared than vice, because its excesses are not subject to the regulation of conscience."
—*Adam Smith*

"There is no such thing as free regulation."
—*John Hutton*

Government regulations are almost always created and promulgated with the best of intentions. Regulations intended to encourage "quality" in the delivery of healthcare services are typical in this regard. Unfortunately, we've seen that even well-intentioned efforts such as quality-of-care guidelines, "never" events, and pay-for-performance often create substantial costs and administrative overhead in exchange for little, if any, measureable benefit. Pay-for-performance (P4P) is just the most recent example. Following the Institute of Medicine's report titled "Crossing the Quality Chasm," an enormous amount of time, attention, thought, and money have been poured into P4P programs and regulatory thinking. Yet even the most recent report and analyses of these programs have failed to find any of the promised benefits, but plenty of unintended consequences and adverse side effects.[3,4,5]

Much of medicine is simply too complex to reduce to simplistic rules and complex incentives. Given the inherent limitations that we've identified in current programs, how can we retool government actions to foster quality, but without the harm?

Probably the most constructive thing that can be done in the short term is to immediately rescind, abolish, and otherwise eliminate the vast majority of the government "healthcare quality improvement" programs, rules, and regulations than have been contrived and placed into effect thus far. (This would, of course, exclude traditional safety programs such as the approval of drugs and medical devices by the FDA.) As shocking as this might seem, a complete regulatory reboot is needed if we're going to meld rational regulation and the new healthcare financing and payment strategies that we've outlined. Introducing universal coverage, patient responsibility, and free markets into the healthcare system will produce a complete re-evaluation of incentives and behaviors on the part of patients and providers alike. Government and regulatory agencies simply must re-evaluate and overhaul their programs and behaviors as well.

The Universal Basic Health Plan and market-based incentives for patients and providers promise to dramatically change the most important functions of government. The current healthcare system rewards procedures and allocates provider payment dollars through political rather than economic processes. It is effectively anti-competitive, and actively shields patients from the financial consequences of their treatment options. Under these conditions, programs and behaviors that foster high-quality and cost-effective care have to be artificially created, because it's impossible for the market to create them. With the UBHP and market forces, continuing these artificial initiatives would simply foster continued inefficiency, and they should be discontinued. There are far better ways for the government to spend its time and money.

Quantifying Cost and Benefit

When it comes to quality, the first and most important activity of government in healthcare has to be funding, compiling, and disseminating research into the comparative effectiveness of medical treatments and technologies. Despite all the lip service paid to fostering "best practices," without extensive, comprehensive, and current data into the cost per QALY of each and every important medical, surgical, and technological intervention, everyone—including patients, providers, families, and the government—is simply stumbling around in the dark when trying to determine the best course of action for any particular case at any particular time.

Assembling complete, accurate, and current QALY data might be more challenging than landing on the moon. It will require a total investment of hundreds of billions of dollars and years to complete. Ongoing funding will be needed to continually update and disseminate the information gathered.* In most cases, the federal government is the only organization with the ability to finance this work, and it is proper and appropriate that it should do so. The best roles of government are those in which it performs functions that the private sector is ill-equipped to tackle, and QALY research is certainly one of them. Small companies and makers of low-cost interventions will not have the capital to document the cost-effectiveness of their products, and makers of more expensive alternatives will typically have no incentive to see the clinical and financial comparison performed. Once performed, the research will only be useful if the data is readily and widely distributed. Because the data is constantly changing, the only realistic means of distribution would be through a publicly accessible application running on the World Wide Web. One can readily imagine a government-hosted service in which any healthcare provider and any

---

* The fact that this research will take some time to build a critical mass of data should not be a barrier to the implementation of the UBHP, especially if our initial efforts concentrate on those conditions and treatments that are financially most important. There is already ample data to ensure insurance coverage for most of the most common and important tests and treatments. There is no question about covering basic laboratory tests, basic medication standards such as pain relievers, blood pressure, cholesterol, asthma and diabetes medications, and fixing broken bones. Where research will be needed is in sorting out the roles of expensive imaging studies, new medications and treatments, and the ultimate outcomes of old medications and treatments over time. As a recent article in Slate observed, although it's the initial results of drug trials that are used to decide whether a medication or treatment will be approved for use as "safe and effective," it's the long-term results largely ignored by current research efforts that really matter. In his 2004 book *Powerful Medicines*, Jerry Avorn proposed a two-phased drug evaluation approach in which "the initial FDA approval of a drug should be seen as the beginning of an intensive period of assessment, not the end." "No doctor," he writes, "would ever start a patient on a new medicine without scheduling any kind of follow-up, but that's exactly what the U.S. healthcare system now does." (Sanghavi D. "When the Lights Go Out—What Can Reality TV Teach Us About Clinical Drug Trials?" Slate, May 13, 2009. http://slate.msn.com/id/2218280/?from=rss.)

By definition, determining the cost/QALY is a dynamic, permanent, ongoing process. The resulting cost/QALY comparisons (which are the purpose of the entire exercise), will change as prices change and new tests, treatments, and technologies become available.

patient in the country would be able to enter in the relevant details of a case: the patient's age, sex, diagnosis, co-morbidities, and so on (with as much detail as the application will eventually allow based upon the available research), and the program would return a typical cost per QALY score for each treatment alternative within whatever geographic region the user might designate. Changing the parameters to reflect the costs of different treatments, locations, or providers would allow various permutations to be rapidly calculated and compared.[†]

Depending upon circumstances and the level of effort put into this research, it might even be possible to calculate risk-adjusted cost/ QALY scores for individual treatments provided by individual institutions. This is not a trivial or simple exercise, and whether it is truly practical depends upon the number of risk-adjusted cases performed and the degree to which the results are statistically valid. It might not be possible to generate useful results for individual providers or smaller institutions. However, facilities that specialize in specific treatments or procedures may well build up enough cases and expertise to show that their results are better and more cost effective than those of the general provider population. Documenting the differential effectiveness of such bona fide, proven "centers of excellence" would have many beneficial effects, ranging from serving as a model and benchmark for other providers, to serving as a national magnet facility for the management of patients requiring these specific treatments.

For all practical purposes, nothing like this exists today—largely because our efforts at securing quality and reducing costs have been misdirected into complex, guideline-mediated cost and quality dead ends instead of investing in systematic comparative clinical research. Imagine the remarkable cost and quality impact of this single software tool based upon intensive QALY research compared to what we have now:

[†] The author already knows of at least one piece of software technology that is perfectly suited to integrate these types of data and generate evidence-based options and recommendations. It is currently sitting around unused because the existing healthcare system does not place any particular economic value on these capabilities.

- Because of the research sponsored and made public by the federal government, we would have the *actual facts* regarding what treatments work under what particular set of circumstances, and what their expected impact is likely to be on a single understandable and reasonably quantitative measurement that attempts to combine the critical factors of lifespan and disability.

- Based upon those facts, it would immediately be clear and unambiguous as to what services would be covered by the UBHP and Tier 3 insurance coverage. No delays, appeals, arguing, or arbitrary interpretations of rules or policies would be required. Patients and providers could immediately get down to talking about which course of action would be best for each particular case. They would know exactly what resources were available, and how much the patient's own contribution could be expected to be.

- Based upon published and widely available risk-adjusted QALY assessment scores and the free-market pricing offered by different facilities nationwide, patients requiring nonemergency care would be able to gauge for themselves which facilities and providers offer the best mix of geography, cost, and quality for their own personal circumstances. With the nationwide insurance portability offered by the UBHP, they can be secure in the knowledge that their care will be covered wherever they might choose to go. This ability to compare and choose might seem like little to ask, but is virtually impossible given the existing system.

- Because QALY research and results dissemination will be ongoing, new diagnostic modalities and treatments will be objectively evaluated, priced, and placed into use or "put out to pasture" quite quickly. As our experience and medical research and information infrastructures grow, this process will become far faster and less expensive than it is today. More importantly, these tools will unquestionably produce better informed, more aware, and higher-quality providers. Each time a clinician sees a patient, these clinical information tools will present them with information about the range of case-specific treatment options currently available, their comparative effectiveness in QALY terms, and the range of prices under which these therapeutic and treatment modalities are available across the country. This

approach makes current methods of continuing medical education (enforced by government regulation and carried out only
as provider time permits) seem primitive in comparison.

None of these improvements in quality, timeliness, convenience,
provider education, or minimizing the cost of care requires any sort of
government regulation, clinical guidelines, or "pay-for-performance"
incentives to achieve. Nor are the heavy hands of insurance company
test or treatment requests, pre-approvals, or appeals needed to
reduce improper utilization of medical resources. In fact, the only elements that are needed to achieve these results are our nation's commitment to investing in clinical research, the widespread
dissemination of information about diagnostic and therapeutic
options, and pricing transparency. This has got to be a permanent
effort. If we really want to have an efficient and effective healthcare
system, clinical QALY research will need to become a permanent part
of the services that government provides, just like the Centers for
Disease Control, the Postal Service, and national defense.

Government Regulation: Forestalling "Fraud and Abuse"

Much is made of saving money through elimination of "fraud and
abuse" that exists within the current healthcare system. Depending
upon the context and who you ask, this term can mean many things.
To a government regulator, it might mean genuinely criminal charla-
tans who invent patients, enroll them in Medicare, and bill their
insurance for healthcare goods and services that were never delivered. For providers who have been abused by "the system," it can
mean ambiguous and maliciously interpreted government rulings
that create "regulatory speed traps" in which well-intentioned
providers billed for services that were allowable at the time, but were
retroactively ruled to be fraudulent. Still others might use this term to
signify care that might be provided and billed for legitimately, but
might not have been "necessary." Another example might be the billions of dollars in excess funds paid to private insurance companies
who "cherry pick" the healthiest Medicare patients, and then place
them in plans that are more expensive than traditional Medicare.

The astute observer will notice a common element to all these
forms of fraud: complexity. Complexity (along with the lack of a

unique patient identifier), makes it relatively easy for true criminals to hide and operate within the patchwork of clearinghouses, health plans, identifiers, and billing codes that exist today. Complexity in the Medicare laws, rules, regulations, and billing practices give government prosecutors the leeway needed to reinterpret billing practices retroactively and abuse the enforcement power that has been entrusted to them. Complexity makes it possible for private insurance companies to engage in a continuous sleight-of-hand in which it's impossible for the patients or businesses selecting health insurance to meaningfully compare Plan A with Plans B through Z with respect to cost, benefits, and ease of use.

The greatest reduction in fraud and abuse will come in the form of prevention rather than enforcement. Just as a penny saved is a penny earned, reducing opportunities for fraud by making the system simpler and more transparent is more cost effective than trying to recover the money after it's been taken.

In March 2009 testimony before Congress, the Office of the Inspector General (OIG) reported on many different types of fraud and abuse afflicting Medicare and Medicaid fraud. These included payments for unallowable services, improper coding, fraudulent claims submissions, overcharging, manipulated billing, gaming the system, and much more. Clearly not all these problems will be solved by any changes to the system, but some can be curbed considerably. One example is OIG's discovery of "reimbursement rates for certain items and services that are too high, resulting in waste and opportunities for fraud and abuse. For example, in 2006, OIG reported that Medicare had allowed, on average, $7,215 for the rental of an oxygen concentrator that costs about $600 to purchase new. Additionally, beneficiaries incurred, on average, $1,443 in co-insurance charges."[6]

These sorts of overcharges are possible *only* because it's virtually impossible for most people to know what anything in the healthcare system is *supposed* to cost. By the same token, billions of dollars were paid for services that were not properly documented or medically necessary. Many of these payments probably could have been avoided if QALY data for these same treatments were widely available and readily consulted by patients and providers alike.

Based upon its experience and investigations, OIG has recommended a five-principle strategy to combat medical waste, fraud, and abuse:

1. Scrutinize individuals and entities that want to participate as providers and suppliers prior to their enrollment in healthcare programs.

2. Establish payment methodologies that are reasonable and responsive to changes in the marketplace.

3. Assist healthcare providers and suppliers in adopting practices that promote compliance with program requirements, including quality and safety standards.

4. Vigilantly monitor the programs for evidence of fraud, waste, and abuse.

5. Respond swiftly to detected frauds, impose sufficient punishment to deter others, and promptly remedy program vulnerabilities.

Although principles #1, #4, and #5 clearly speak to vigilance in participant screening and law enforcement, principles #2 and #3 speak directly to the basic payment methodologies and administrative requirements of the existing system. These two principles will be well served by the new and vastly simplified system we've described. These savings would be realized without the need for additional enforcement resources. The National Health Care Anti-Fraud Association estimates that about $60 billion worth of healthcare spending is lost to fraud each year. Improving transparency and simplicity while boosting the application of clinical research to healthcare interventions should easily reduce this amount by at least 20%, saving more than $12 billion annually.

Addressing Medical Malpractice and Defensive Medicine

We've previously documented the damage caused by our current handling of claims, incidents, liability, and compensation medical malpractice claims. The current system serves no one well, with the possible exception of plaintiff and defense attorneys. It spends more money on administrative expenses than payments to patients, leaves many legitimately injured patients uncompensated, punishes many doctors that have done no wrong, and generates an enormous burden on society in the form of defensive medicine. Our best estimates of the financial impact in 2009 are about $40 billion in direct costs, and more than $80 billion in unnecessary expenses for defensive medicine. *This is more than the total amount of U.S. spending on public health and home healthcare combined.* There are two important ways that we can and should approach fixing these related problems. The first is preventing the factors that lead to malpractice claims to begin with. The second is in rapidly, fairly, and consistently resolving claims after they've arisen.

Reducing Errors Versus Reducing Harm Versus Reducing Claims

Preventing medical malpractice errors is not the same thing as preventing medical malpractice claims. Not all claims are the result of true medical errors, not all errors result in harm, and not all harm results in claims.

Medical Errors

Broadly defined, medical errors are fairly common. In their review of the literature, Sandars and Esmail found that physician consultations seem to have an error rate of between 0.5% and 8%. Prescribing and prescription errors might occur in up to 11% of all prescriptions, mainly due to errors in dose. In the hospital setting, we actually know very little about the frequency of errors, as opposed to the frequency of adverse events that are caused by errors. The 1991 Harvard Medical Practice Study found that about 2–3% of hospital admissions were associated with adverse events attributable to medical errors. This number has been supported by several subsequent studies.

Like most things in medicine, there is not even complete agreement over what constitutes a true medical error. Elder, Pallerla, and Regan found more than 25 different definitions for "error" in the medical literature, and subsequently showed that there were significant differences in physician opinion on whether certain undesirable events were really "errors". For example, 100% of physicians felt that overlooking an abnormal result was an error, but is it really a "medical error" if a test result is simply unavailable during a patient visit, or if a blood tube is broken by a courier?[7]

Despite this variation, we do know a substantial amount about the types of errors that do occur. In the hospital setting, the Institute of Medicine's highly publicized report "To Err Is Human" found that the vast majority of errors are "systems related," and not attributable to individual negligence or misconduct.[8] Systems failures are cases in which one or more of the many transactions required for the proper diagnosis and treatment of a patient fails. Using medication as an example, the correct medication needs to be ordered for the correct patient, communicated to the pharmacy, dosed properly by the pharmacy, and then delivered to the correct patient at the correct time and in the correct manner, and only if it is not contraindicated for some reason. An error of omission or commission at any stage—whether by a person, a machine, or an act of God will result in an error. It should be obvious that the more complex the process and the greater the number of people and parts involved, the greater the potential for error.

As in the hospital setting, most errors in outpatient clinics are also caused by system failures. Phillips et al recently characterized 935 outpatient medical errors reported by more than 400 clinicians and medical staff. For the purpose of this study, an error was defined as things that happened in the practice "that should not have happened and that you don't want to happen again."[9]

What one immediately notices about their data is how frequently administrative and "process" errors occur (96% of the cases), compared to errors of knowledge and skill (4%). This largely agrees with the results found in hospitals; the vast majority of errors occur as the result of communication problems or failures of the healthcare system rather than the personal failings of healthcare providers themselves. An international survey of medical errors (shown in Table 13.1) found a higher rate of clinician error, but the same pattern of administrative and communications errors.[10]

Before moving on to proposing a solution, at least one more set of evidence is worth examining, concerning ordering and handling medical tests.

TABLE 13.1 Primary Care Errors Reported in Canada and Five Other Countries

TYPE OF ERROR	CANADA (N=95) N(%)	OTHER COUNTRIES (N = 413) N(%)
Office processes (eg, office administration, filing systems, charts, scheduling appointments)	28 (29)	132 (39)
External investigations (eg, laboratory tests, diagnostic imaging)	17 (18)	56 (16)
Treatment (eg, medication)	24 (26)	85 (24)
Communication (with patients, with other physicians)	9 (9)	53 (15)
Financial accounting (eg, processing insurance claims wrongly charged for care not received)	2 (2)	3 (1)
Work force management (eg, errors in scheduling after-hours coverage	3 (3)	7 (2)
Clinical knowledge (eg, failure to follow standard practice	12 (13)	77 (22)

From: Rosser W, Dovey S, Bordman R, White D, Crighton E, Drummond N. "Medical Errors in Primary Care." *Canadian Family Physician* (2005); 51: 386-387.

In 2005, Dr. Nancy Elder and colleagues launched a study to characterize the problems and errors associated with obtaining outside tests on patients in primary care office practices. Ordering, obtaining, and distributing the results of lab and radiology tests is interesting for two reasons. First, testing is an exceedingly common practice in the United States, and is a major source of cost, errors, and potential patient hazard if the process is mismanaged. Elder and her colleagues found that, "...the average family physician sees about 100 outpatients per week and orders diagnostic tests on 39% of them. Thus, a four-physician family practice center manages about 30 diagnostic test reports per day, and each test report might contain 1 to 20 individual test results."[11] Simply ordering these tests is more complex than one might imagine. A single doctor might order tests from multiple locations (offices, hospitals, nursing homes, and clinics) and

from many different entities—all with different paperwork requirements. Gathering and tabulating the results from all these sources is
equally challenging. Studies suggest that somewhere between 15 and
54 percent of the medical errors reported in the primary care setting
are related to the testing process.[12]

Second, testing is prototypical of many common clinical tasks that
are subject to systematic errors. For example, the process of ordering
and collecting test results is quite similar to the processes involved
with ordering, filling, and administrating medications, arranging for
and delivering chronic care services, and even referring patients to
specialists.[13] Let's look at some of the problems that Elder et al found
in the primary care setting (see Table 13.2).

TABLE 13.2   Common Problems Encountered in Medical Testing

Offices Affected	Problem Type	Examples
All	Errors in charting and filing systems	Filing and chart problems
	Errors in ordering or implementation	Problems with getting test implemented Problems with order forms Orders not transmitted fully Wrong test ordered Specific x-ray problems
	Not following procedures	Protocols and procedures not followed
>75%	Errors in tracking and return	Delayed or no return of laboratories Results to wrong provider Unclear results
	Errors notifying patients	Delayed patient notification Not all patients notified Wrong results to patient
	Inadequate systems	No tracking system Partial or flawed tracking system
	Lack of standardization	Clinician choice on notification Lack of standardization
	Communication	Communication Transition from laboratory to office

continues

TABLE 13.2   Continued

Offices Affected	Problem Type	Examples
	Duplication of Effort	Multiple handoffs
		Duplication of effort
>50%	Errors in response and documentation	Provider response problems
		Results, but no clinical context
	Insufficient staff	Insufficient staff
<50%	Errors in follow-up	No follow-up system
	Insurance problems	Insurance confusion

Data adapted from: Elder NC, Graham D, Brandt E, Dovey S, Phillips R, Ledwith J, Hickner J. "The Testing Process in Family Medicine: Problems, Solutions, and Barriers as Seen by Physicians and Their Staff." *Journal of Patient Safety* (2006); 2(1): 25-32.

As we can see in Table 13.2, there are many places for a simple lab or radiology study to go wrong. There are hazards associated with virtually every step of the process. Dr. Elder and her colleagues then went on to document the most common reported barriers to changing the status quo. These results are shown in Table 13.3.

TABLE 13.3   Barriers to Changing the Testing Process

Offices Affected	Problem Type	Examples
	Leadership or staff involvement and support	No buy-in from staff or providers
		People do not follow protocols
>75%		Must do things own way
		Powerlessness
	Costs	Cost of Technology
	Tension associated with change	Expectations of mediocrity
		Personal resistance to change
		No perceived consequences
>50%	Staff changes required	Additional labor needed
	External support	Problems with outside systems
	Work environment	Too busy, too many patients

continues

TABLE 13.3   Continued

Offices Affected	Problem Type	Examples
	Patient-related	Patient expectations
<50%	Monitoring and feedback	Lack of feedback and communication
	Skepticism regarding ideas	Lack of evidence regarding changes proposed

Data adapted from: Elder NC, Graham D, Brandt E, Dovey S, Phillips R, Ledwith J, Hickner J. "The Testing Process in Family Medicine: Problems, Solutions, and Barriers as Seen by Physicians and Their Staff." *Journal of Patient Safety* (2006); 2(1): 25-32.

What can we learn from all these data points?

The first thing we can observe is that the complexity associated with ordering and obtaining lab results is a microcosm of the machine that describes the healthcare system as a whole. The number of moving parts is daunting. Not only do we have institutional "gears" in the form of clinics, laboratories, and insurance plans, but individual people, including providers, patients, clinic staff, billing staff, and laboratory staff as well. Passing the samples and information to each of these individuals constitutes a separate transaction, and each transaction has a small but finite chance of an error occuring. Given that many billions of test, medication, medical visit, and other transactions occur each year, the surprise is not that errors occur, but that there are so few. Processes with large numbers of moving parts are inherently subject to breakdown. Some of the variables that complicate matters—such as insurers requiring that tests for one patient be sent to a different laboratory than tests for a different patient—are strictly artifacts of our current payment system.

A second lesson has to do with the interplay between people and technology.

There is no question that the *appropriate* use of health information technology could substantially reduce the number of errors associated with healthcare transactions. One reason why so many people are needed for processing these transactions is that, although paper is an excellent medium for manual data entry, it's a very poor medium for the transmission and recall of information. After an order for a test or medication is written, many of the steps required specifically involve repetitive recall and transmission. These are exactly the roles in which computers and electronic networks such as the Internet are most efficient. By themselves (and with well-written and debugged software), computers rarely (if ever) transpose numbers, lose results, forget to file them, or file them in the wrong place. These facts argue strongly in favor of a much greater role for the use of computers and electronic networks in the management of information-intensive healthcare processes. However, the results of the research done by Elder and others point to at least one additional complication—these technologies must get along well with the people who have to use them, or they can be the source of error rather than the solution.

Providers in the testing process study made three observations that simply cannot be ignored. The first and most important is the need for simplicity. As one clinician correctly observed, "Systems have to be simple or people don't do it." Any new system has to be easier, simpler, and more trouble-free than the one it replaces, or people will resist its adoption. In fact, fundamental market forces actually *require* that they resist adopting and using complex and user-hostile tools. This is the primary reason underlying the poor adoption rate of "conventional" electronic health records—especially the "feature-laden," rigid, complex, and expensive types of EHRs mandated by the new federal certification process. Complexity in healthcare transactions is equivalent to dumping sand in the gears. What should be smooth and fast revolutions become halting. In many cases, more time is spent learning software, recalling passwords, typing, clicking, and trying to circumvent poor design than actually providing care-related services.

The second observation is that any electronic healthcare system is only as good as its connectivity. More than 90% of the utility of electronic information systems is the result of the right person being able to access the data they require wherever and whenever it's needed. After all, the whole purpose of the technology is to allow providers to complete healthcare transactions quickly and easily. It doesn't matter whether that transaction is ordering a lab test, prescribing a medication, reviewing a history, or viewing an image. If the electronic systems don't connect quickly, easily, and simply, it might be easier and faster to rely on paper-based data and a fax machine.

To anyone who has ever worked with a typical legacy healthcare IT system, one study subject's remark that "It would literally take an act of God to get those computers to talk to each other" is hauntingly familiar. Just as no one actually planned the patchwork of hospitals, clinics, offices, insurers, government offices, and intermediaries that make up the healthcare system as a whole, our current HIT infrastructure has built on proprietary systems that are often specifically built with no thought given to connecting to rival proprietary systems. Forcing providers to purchase more of the same will have little or no beneficial impact on error rates.

The third and final observation is that cost matters. Healthcare is an industry like any other, in which providers cannot simply invest in technology because it might reduce costs for others. Eighty-eight percent of the providers surveyed listed cost as a major barrier to implementing technology in their own practice setting. *If we want to improve efficiency and reduce errors, cheap and simple is going to get us much further, much faster than complex and expensive.* As we'll see in the next chapter, this is quite doable.

Thus, there are several mutually consistent keys to reducing the vast majority of medical errors: those caused by communication errors and "system failures." Many of these are analogous to solutions that we already know are needed to increase the efficiency and reduce the cost of the healthcare system as a whole.

- **Reduce the number of "parts" needed to complete healthcare transactions wherever possible.** In this case, the "parts" consist of the number of institutions and staff who are directly involved in completing healthcare transactions. This involves minimizing the number of different labs or pharmacies that providers are required to use strictly for insurance (that is, administrative) reasons, standardizing and simplifying laboratory and pharmacy paperwork, and replacing manual labor with linked electronic data processing systems.

- **Emphasize the development and deployment of cheap, easy-to-use data capture and transaction processing software, and ensure that software has a high degree of connectivity.** Features are far less important than the being able to deploy quickly and painlessly to the majority of healthcare delivery sites in the United States.

- **Implement unique and universal patient identifiers.** These will reduce the amount of time and effort required to uniquely identify patients and the potential number of errors involved in processing them—especially when combined with electronic transaction processing.
- **Simply allow more time for communication.** Fatigue or rushing appears to be a cause in 10% of self-reported physician errors.[14] This is hardly surprising when the workload and pressures inherent within the current payment system allow an average of about 7.5 minutes for an average follow-up visit. In addition to its other efficiency benefits, compensating providers at an hourly rate is a simple, but potentially effective, means of reducing error rates.

Patient-Mediated Errors

There is one other participant that must be accounted for if we truly want to reduce errors: the patient himself. Patients are hardly immune to making their own errors, many of which can seriously and adversely affect healthcare costs and outcomes. Like provider errors, the majority of these fall into two categories: communication errors and process errors.

It should be no surprise that communications errors on the patient's side are extremely common. Providers can say and write whatever they want, but unless the patient both *hears* and *internalizes* the message, no actual communication has taken place. Patients need to understand that both of these tasks are their responsibility; there is literally no substitute for them.

Patient process errors are equally common. The current insurance system often requires patients to obtain referrals before they can be seen by the proper specialist, or to utilize specific providers and vendors of everything from medications to imaging studies. Paperwork abounds, making it extremely easy to make mistakes that will delay care, or result in not being able to obtain care at all.

One extremely common process error is failing to follow medical instructions. Failure to take medications properly was labeled "America's other drug problem" in 1989, when the National Council on Patient Information and Education coined the phrase.

It's expected that Americans will be given 4.5 billion prescriptions in 2010, and a prescription is written in the course of 65% of all physician visits. Despite accounting for just 13% of the population, the elderly account for one-third of all medications dispensed and 42% of all retail drug expenditures. One large home healthcare company reports that its clients are each on an average of 12 medications. Unfortunately, repeated studies have now shown that a great deal of our investment in medication is probably being wasted because patients are unwilling or unable to comply with their prescribed drug regimens.

In a 2000 study, Bedell and colleagues looked at the correlation between what doctors prescribed and what was taken in actual practice.[15] More than 75% of the cases showed discrepancies between the medical record and the medications that patients were actually taking. Fifty-one percent of these patients were taking medications that were not recorded, 29% failed to take a recorded medication, and 20% were taking medications at a different dose than prescribed. Elderly patients are generally less adherent to their prescribed medications than younger patients. This is hardly surprising, given that they are frequently sicker, less mentally alert, and take large numbers of different medications.

All these patient medication errors and misunderstandings are expensive. Medication noncompliance is the number one reason that elders are forced out of independent living and into far more expensive supervised care institutions. Medication dollars are wasted, and hospital care is ultimately required when noncompliance allows medical conditions to spiral out of control.

Petrilla and colleagues reviewed 30 years' worth of medical studies on medication compliance interventions and found 12 that significantly improved medication compliance.[16] These included fixed-dose combination drugs, once-daily or once-weekly dosing schedules, unit-dose packaging, educational counseling by telephone, case management by pharmacists, treatment in pharmacist- or nurse-operated disease management clinics, mailed refill reminders, self-monitoring, dose-tailoring, rewards, and various combination strategies. They observed that "personalized, patient-focused programs that involved frequent contact with health professionals or a combination of interventions were the most effective at improving compliance. Less-intensive strategies, such as prescribing products that simplify the medication regimen or sending refill reminders, achieved smaller improvements in compliance but might be cost effective due to their low cost."

There is no question that combined interventions can be extremely effective. In the 2006 Federal Study of Adherence to Medications in the Elderly (FAME) study, a combination of educational visits with a pharmacist and administering medications in prepackaged form according to individualized daily regimens increased medication adherence by more than 35%, from an initial baseline of 62% adherence to 96% adherence, after just eight months.

Despite being effective in getting people to take the proper medications, person-based interventions are expensive and their cost-effectiveness over time has not yet been studied. Fortunately, there are relatively simple, inexpensive, and eminently useful technologies that can and should be routinely employed, especially for older patients who are living alone and on multiple medications. Automated medication dispensers are one example.

An automated medication dispenser might sound ridiculous to many, but they can plug the portion of the adherence gap between pillboxes and relatively expensive human monitoring. Some of the most common causes of patient-mediated medication errors are caused by confusion over when to take pills, how many to take, patients not remembering whether they took them, names of medications, incorrect use of medicine boxes, and cognitive or visual problems.[17] A new generation of less expensive digital medication dispensers can correct many of these problems at a reasonable cost. For example, a new machine from easyMEDS, LLC, stores an entire week of a patient's medication in an easy-to-load canister containing medication cups that can be prefilled by a pharmacy, the patient, a friend, family member, or caregiver. Once the canister is inserted, it automatically aligns itself for dispensing according to the correct date and time. When a dose is due, the machine alerts the patient with audio and visual cues. To silence the machine and obtain the correct medications, the patient simply presses a large button. If the button is not pressed, the machine begins calling a series of numbers to let friends, family members, or caregivers know that something is wrong. They can then check on the patient to find out what's wrong. Other monitoring capabilities (such as fall alerts, door sensors, and so on) can potentially be added to the basic setup. The real keys to this machine are its simplicity of operation and low price—about one-third that of comparable devices.

These types of common sense innovations can substantially reduce many of the errors and much of the waste currently associated with medication use. Coverage could be provided under a patient's HSA, the UBHP, or a combination of both. The existing patchwork of state and federal regulations actively works against simple solutions such as these. Medication dispensers are currently reimbursed by Medicaid in 28 states, but not in the remaining 22 states. Medicare does not pay for them anywhere.

Reducing Unwarranted Medical Malpractice Claims

A substantial number of medical malpractice claims don't actually involve actual medical errors or malpractice, yet they incur substantial costs to the healthcare system and society as a whole. Why are they filed, and what can we do about it?

Several studies have looked at patients' perception of medical errors. The High Plains research network looked at 180 events that were perceived by patients as being medical mistakes.[18] Of these, 30% really were mistakes (although they did not have any adverse impact on health status in about 40% of the cases), 41% were clearly not mistakes, and there was not enough information available to properly classify the remainder. After looking at the cases where no mistake occurred, the investigators found that (as in other studies), patients and their families confused true mistakes with a broad range of issues, including unanticipated outcomes, communications difficulties, and perceived violations of trust in the physician-patient relationship. Given what we've learned about covert rationing's erosive effect on honest communication and the physician-patient relationship, it is highly likely that the payment system itself sows the seeds of this distrust.

Resolving the Malpractice Claims That Do Occur

Malpractice claims will always be with us. We still need to find a better and more efficient way of handling and resolving the claims that do occur.

What clearly does not work is the system we have. Administrative costs are high, resolution is slow, attorney fees absorb much of any award, and juries who are unfamiliar with healthcare are asked to learn about medicine and judge the merits of the case in "crash course" fashion. The results are consistently inconsistent. Many cases with no underlying medical error or harm result in awards being made, while other valid cases result in no award at all. From a societal view, the greatest cost of the existing system is what it does to the efficiency of utilizing healthcare resources. Defensive medicine exacts a massive toll on everyone. From a provider perspective, every patient they see is treated as a potential lawsuit. Not only does this adversely affect mutual trust and the physician-patient relationship, but it results in massive expenditures for tests with little or no probable utility. Thus, our goals for any reform of malpractice claims management should include the following:

1. Handling of malpractice cases should be *consistent*, both from case to case and from geographic region to geographic region. If the resulting system is fair and just, consistency breeds confidence and dependability.

2. The system should produce results that are both *medically and socially appropriate*. Medically appropriate means that there is a realization that healthcare is not an exact science, and that providers cannot expect to be held responsible for unfortunate results not of their making. Socially appropriate means that awards consistently and fairly match the losses suffered by the victim.

3. Only those directly involved should be dragged into the legal system, and compensation should be proportional to each defendant's involvement. This is an indictment of "joint and several liability," in which whoever has the deepest pockets suffers the most, regardless of their culpability for any harm done. Joint and several liability completely distorts true relationships between the parties involved, and acts as a tax on society as a whole.

4. The system should minimize administrative expenses. As we've seen, administrative expenses are one of the major contributors to the dysfunction pervading the entire healthcare system. (In the existing system, costs consume about 40% of all judgments or settlements involved.[19])

5. Justice (and the resolution of cases) should be swift. (The typical medical malpractice case currently takes three to four years to be resolved.)

6. Finally, the results should boost the confidence that all of us have in our healthcare system.

So called "tort reform" efforts are typically one-sided affairs promoted by hospitals and medical associations. They typically try to make it harder to sue for malpractice or seek to place financial caps on punitive or other damages. As a result, they offer few, if any, efficiency improvements. In contrast, there are two real alternatives to the current system: no-fault compensation and specialized healthcare courts.

No-fault medical error compensation is an idea very similar to worker's compensation. Anyone injured as the result of a medical error would receive financial compensation according to a fixed schedule. Although this sounds like a good idea in the abstract, it's unworkable in the context of modern healthcare. "No-fault" implies that any patient harmed in the course of medical care would be compensated, just as any employee harmed in the workplace might be compensated, regardless of whether the employee or employer is at fault. But while it's reasonable to expect that no one should become sick in the course of performing a job, healthcare presents a different situation. Being sick is an inherently dangerous business, and virtually every treatment comes with its own raft of potential complications and side effects. "No-fault" implies that patients would be compensated anytime a complication is encountered—a concept that blurs the line between the respective roles of injury compensation and health insurance. Would insurance pay for cancer treatment, but leave the no-fault compensation plan to pay for its side effects? On the other hand, if compensation is strictly contingent on the existence of a medical error, how is the system "no-fault"? If a medical error is required, the system becomes little more than a dedicated medical malpractice court system.

A federal system of specialized healthcare courts is a much better alternative; one that provides the balance of consistency, justice, and expertise needed. Specialized courts are hardly unique. There are many dedicated specialty courts in the United States today, including patent courts, tax courts, bankruptcy courts, and a wide range of administrative courts, including those for worker's compensation, Social Security, and vaccine liability.[20]

One of the most consistent proponents of this approach has been Common Good, a bipartisan not-for-profit organization that advocates reforms intended to make the American legal system fairer, more sensible, and more reliable. Common Good's approach to health courts meets all the requirements we've identified as being critical to improving efficiency and lowering costs. As presented in Congressional hearings, the basic features of their proposed health court system are as follows:

1. Administrative law judges who handle only medical malpractice disputes, with written opinions on standards of care;

2. Neutral experts, drawn from approved lists, would advise the court;

3. Noneconomic damages paid according to a schedule depending on the injury. This achieves horizontal equity among injuries of the same kind, and also eliminates the incentive to keep litigating in the hopes (or threats) of a windfall award;

4. A liberalized standard of recovery based on whether the injury should have been avoidable. Someone who comes into the hospital with pneumonia and comes out with a staph infection should be able to recover without having to prove how it happened;

5. A requirement of transparency and preliminary procedures designed to resolve claims with a minimum of time and legal cost. Lawyers' fees should be based on the time and investment they commit to the case, not a flat percentage of recovery; and

6. Connection to a regulatory department focused on patient safety and disseminating lessons learned.

Attorney and Common Good founder Philip Howard asserts that:

> The potential advantages of this system are enormous. A court that writes opinions based on accepted medical standards not only holds the promise of overcoming the debilitating distrust, but can provide affirmative guidelines for improving care. The regulatory body can collect and disseminate information to improve care. The incentives for defensive medicine will be sharply reduced. Moreover, affirmative cost containment is only possible when there is a court that will reliably defend the costs contained. Finally, patients will receive settlements much sooner, paying only a fraction of what they now pay in legal fees."[21]

The most interesting and useful aspect of this approach is that it actually promises to *solve* the problems of error, justice, inefficiency, and compensation rather than simply attempting to cover them up with arbitrary caps or insisting that nothing can be done because the right to a jury trial is sacrosanct. The constitutional authority to create this type of dedicated administrative compensation already exists if it is part of a regulatory plan to improve healthcare.[22] Americans seem to agree that this approach makes sense. A Harris Poll found that while 62% of Americans would favor having malpractice cases tried in dedicated medical courts, only 20% opposed the idea, and 18% were undecided.[23] To quote further from Howard's testimony:

> Law is essential to a free society because it provides guidelines for reasonable conduct. Contracts will be enforced by their terms, and people injured by negligence will be compensated for their injuries. But law undermines freedom when it fails to offer predictable guidelines, and when it tolerates claims against reasonable conduct. Because law today offers no guidelines or predictability in healthcare disputes, physicians, nurses, and other dedicated healthcare professionals no longer feel free to act on their best judgment. This

in turn has tragic effects on the quality and affordability of healthcare in our country. By restoring reliability to healthcare disputes, special health courts hold the promise of bringing order and good sense to the vital decisions needed for effective, safe and affordable healthcare in America.

The Financial Impact of "Grit Reduction"

As any mechanic can attest, leaving sand and grit in a complex machine is an expensive proposition. Eventually the whole thing needs to be overhauled and replaced. By relying on healthcare regulations that increase administrative burden without cost or quality data, the government is currently acting as an abrasive. Our approach to medical errors and the medical malpractice system is irrational. How much can we expect to save if these policies are reversed, and the appropriate replacements implemented?

The real cost of healthcare regulation is hard to gauge. Researchers at Duke University and the Cato Institute have used both a "top-down" and a "bottom-up" approach to estimate the net cost (cost incurred less financial benefits derived) of health services regulation in the United States.[24] The bottom-up approach is more useful and detailed, looking at each aspect of healthcare industry regulation and estimating the financial impact on the relevant healthcare activities.

The Cato study grouped the costs and benefits into three separate categories: regulation of health facilities, regulation of health professionals, and regulation of health insurance. We have summarized their estimates of regulatory costs in Table 13.4, after eliminating those that we have already covered in Chapters 11 and 12.

TABLE 13.4   Estimated Source of Annual Cost Savings As a Result of Improvements in Government Regulatory Practices and the Medical Error/Malpractice System

Source	Annual Savings
Health Facilities Regulation	
"Access" regulations that become obsolete with universal healthcare coverage[†].	$7.6 billion
"Quality" regulations[‡]	$1.8 billion
Regulation of Health Professionals & Health Insurance	Covered in previous sections
Reductions in the administrative cost of the medical malpractice system[**]	$6 billion
Clinical Savings	
Reduction in healthcare fraud from simplification of payment rules, research into which interventions are effective, and complete price transparency	$12 billion
Reduction in clinical errors from the multifaceted program proposed	Assume no net savings for the purpose of this analysis
Reduction in defensive medicine with no adverse impact on health status[§]	$8 billion
Total Estimated Annual Savings from These Sources (Based on 2004 or Earlier Spending Levels)	**$35.4 billion**

[*]   Unless otherwise noted, figures are from Cato Institute report "Health Care Regulation—A $169 Billion Hidden Tax," October 2004. Cato numbers based upon 2003 and earlier statistics have NOT been increased to reflect a 41% increase in healthcare spending between 2003 (total U.S. healthcare spending of $1.7 trillion) to 2008 (total U.S. healthcare spending of $2.4 trillion).

[†]   Includes the net cost (after subtracting benefits) of the Emergency Medical Treatment and Active Labor Act (EMTALA), hospital uncompensated care pools, community service requirements, and conversion regulations. Does not include any changes to hospital limited English proficiency requirements.

[‡]   Assumes a 10% reduction in costs attributable to facility accreditation/licensure and other quality-related facilities regulations. These savings will be realized by standardizing all federal, state, and local licensure and credentialing efforts nationwide by the creation and use of standardized web-based documentation applications, and by a dedicated effort to simplify and minimize redundant reporting and reporting of questionable clinical benefit.

[**]   Assumes a net 15% reduction in total medical malpractice administrative cost from current court and attorney fees, as well as faster processing of claims in specialized health courts.

[§]   Assumes a 10% reduction in defensive medicine costs based upon the range of 6.2% to nearly 50% as discussed in the Conover/Cato Institute report. In turn, their analysis relies upon work by Kessler-McClellan.[25]

14

Lubricating Points of Friction

"Complexity kills. It sucks the life out of developers, it makes products difficult to plan, build and test, it introduces security challenges, and it causes end-user and administrator frustration."

—*Ray Ozzie*

Because of the co-dependencies inherent in crafting solutions to other problems, we have already discussed proposed fixes for universal patient identification and government regulatory efforts. One result is that our discussion of "lubricating" points of friction within healthcare has been reduced to the sole topic of optimizing medical recordkeeping and transaction processing. They are important enough to merit their own chapter. In many respects, these two tasks make up the bulk of what clinicians and their supporting organizations actually do in the course of a 24-hour day.

The good thing about friction is that it often responds to simple, inexpensive, and rapidly deployable solutions. The bad thing about friction is that it's ubiquitous, and poor decisions can easily make it worse.

Understanding the Role of Transactions and Information in the Healthcare Industry

No matter how much technology and "progress" might suggest otherwise, every industry—including healthcare—is based on a few simple underlying principles. Its basic stock in trade is to gather information about people, process it in some way, and then use the results to prescribe and execute a management plan of some type, whether that plan happens to be a prescription, an operation, physical therapy, or counseling.

The net result is that healthcare is an industry based upon the generation and dissemination of enormous amounts of data. In 2007, there were 3.8 billion prescriptions filled, 600 million outpatient visits, and 3.5 million hospitalizations in the United States. Each of these represents multiple transactions—from the writing and filling of a prescription, to scheduling patients for outpatient visits, to the hundreds of tests, examinations, prescriptions, and visits performed in the course of a typical hospitalization.

With so many transactions, anything that slows down the process of obtaining, processing, and relaying accurate information is the source of friction in the healthcare world. It does not matter where in the process the delay occurs—delays in extracting the correct referral and insurance information from a patient can be just as disruptive as the time taken to pull a chart or losing a prescription. This is a key point, and explains in large part why it is that the newest, fanciest, and most expensive technologies do not always improve the speed and accuracy of healthcare transactions. If a computer program speeds up one part of the process (for example, data retrieval) but slows down another essential transaction (for example, having to record information by forcing a provider to type and click with a keyboard and mouse or having to navigate a cluttered and poorly designed computer screen), no net benefit is derived.

Primary Sources of Friction in Healthcare Transaction Processing

There are many different types of healthcare transactions, and therefore many potential sources of friction. However, as in many other industries, the vast majority of healthcare transactions are repetitive. This means that a relatively few simple tasks consume an inordinate amount of the time and effort required of healthcare personnel. The most important are

- **Gathering information.** Medical information comes from many sources: patients, families, existing medical records (either in-office or in the clinics and offices of others), in-person observations such as physical examinations, imaging centers, laboratories, and insurance and billing companies.

- **Recording information.** Nearly every healthcare transaction involves recording information. The results of patient histories and physical exams are recorded as baselines for later reference, for legal purposes, and as a way of justifying charges. Clinicians write prescriptions and order tests by recording their requests. Laboratories and imaging centers record their results for reference, comparison, and transmission to the providers who ordered them. Patients are asked to record data at home to bring back to the office, and billers have to record procedure information in a specific desired format for it to be acceptable to insurers.

- **Storing information.** Data generated and recorded internally or externally generally has to be stored in case it's needed again.

- **Retrieving information.** Some, but not all, of the information recorded in the course of healthcare transactions ends up being retrieved. Some of this information is retrieved quite often. Examples include insurance information, patient identifiers, prescription information, and test results. Some of the information might never be seen again after it is recorded. Examples of these include most provider progress notes, vital signs, records of medications and treatments provided, and correspondence. Not all healthcare information is equal in importance, quality, or value over time.

- **Transmitting information.** Decisions made and results obtained are of little or no value unless they are passed on to others for the appropriate action.

Although the amount of time required for each of these functions might only take from a few seconds (in the case of pulling a chart close at hand) to many minutes (in the case of trying to secure copies of records held far away), the sheer number of such transactions is staggering. Every minute of effort spent in data entry, retrieval, or transmission is a minute of effort that is not spent in patient care or making better decisions.

Because friction is common, expensive, and hazardous to our health, the primary criterion for any healthcare information technology needs to be that it reduces friction rather than increases it. How can we know when this is the case? It's simple—the market will tell us. The right health information technologies are those that providers willingly buy and implement on their own, without the need for government subsidies or penalties. Subsidies can speed the deployment of appropriate technologies, but penalties will almost guarantee that inefficient and inappropriate technologies will be deployed. Let's look at how healthcare information technologies (HIT) can serve a positive role in our healthcare system, quickly, cheaply, and efficiently.

Rationally Applying Healthcare Information Technologies

Computers and software systems are simply tools. Their blessing and their curse is that they can be so powerful. It's no exaggeration to say that computers have already revolutionized medicine in a host of ways. They've created whole new fields of medical imaging, ranging from computerized tomography and magnetic resonance imaging to PET scans and telemedicine. The computerization of medical laboratories and pharmacies has produced extraordinary increases in productivity as these functions grew from small operations to an industrial scale. The computerization of healthcare literature and the creation of the World Wide Web have made it possible for researchers, clinicians, and patients to find and disseminate information with a speed and thoroughness that were unheard of just 20 years ago. Computerization of medical information systems over the next decade will undoubtedly make it easier to share and effectively utilize clinical information.

But as we've seen, medical information systems that are poorly designed, implemented, and deployed can be a powerful source of disruption, frustration, clinical error, and deadweight economic loss.

We can do much better than we have at computerizing healthcare information, but we're going to have to approach it in a far more rational and constructive manner than has been the case in the past. We can make this easy, or we can make this hard. We already know how to make it hard. Making it easy is going to require discipline: The discipline to be thoughtful, patient, and most importantly, to keep things simple.

What Are We Trying to Accomplish?

The first step in creating an appropriate solution is to ask two questions: (1) what are we trying to accomplish? and (2) how much are we willing to pay for it? Our most important goal should be to minimize friction in the delivery of healthcare services. This means creating systems that will make it easier, faster, and cheaper to gather, record, store, retrieve, and transmit clinical information securely and on demand. The price that we're willing to pay should be less than the economic benefits we obtain in the process.* If we can accomplish that, any system that we create will sell itself and save money.

Given these goals, some design parameters are self-evident. Although it might be fast and convenient as a means of entering data, paper is bulky and difficult to store, retrieve, and transmit. Medical records have to be computerized if we are to make storage, recall, and transmission easy. A second design parameter is that the system must be easy to learn, use, and maintain—preferably as easy, or easier, than current paper-based systems. Third, whatever we implement must facilitate the secure, rapid, and painless transmission of information. A nationwide HIT system with just these three modest "tier one" capabilities would be a great help.

A "tier two" requirement is that any system we develop ought to be able to store, transmit, and display images of all types—from photographs to video to x-rays.

---

* One could argue that we should be willing to pay as much or more than the current "nontechnological" cost of accomplishing these tasks if we can show an improvement in the quality of care provided, but that will still result in a net increase in the total cost of care. We're looking for ways to reduce total costs, not increase them.

Finally, there is one other capability that would be extremely useful. This is the ability to record, store, retrieve, and transmit *certain types* of data in discrete, quantifiable form. These are specific pieces of information that are routinely referenced, compared, and transmitted on a daily basis for millions of patients nationwide. They include patient demographics, lab values, vital signs, prescription information, diagnoses, and procedures. Each of these pieces of information is routinely generated and used in terms of numbers. Diagnoses and procedures are always assigned codes (ICD and CPT codes) that allow them to be used for billing and record-keeping. Lab values are almost always numerical values that are generated automatically by machine, and immediately stored in computer databases. Prescriptions are also conveniently numeric; each drug can be identified through a universal code number and is associated with a numerical pill or bottle size, dosage, frequency of use, number to dispense, and number of refills. Vital signs are numeric. They can include not only pulse, blood pressure, temperature, and respiration rate, but also machine-generated numbers such as blood sugars and the oxygen saturation of the blood.

Combining these two sets of capabilities (the tier one "have to haves," the ability to handle images, and the ability to capture, store, and transmit naturally quantitative information in a quantitative way) would provide 95% or more of the benefits that our society can expect to receive from *any* widespread healthcare information technology system, no matter how expensive and complex it might be. Although additional bells and whistles might be nice for researchers, IT professionals, historians, and vendors, they are hardly essential.

None of this requires technology that is particularly expensive to deploy, operate, and maintain. More importantly, all these benefits can be obtained without asking providers to change their workflow significantly, undergo long periods of training, or even use a computer when they see patients if they do not wish to do so.

Paying Attention to What's Important

The one thing that we don't want to do is mandate one iota more of cost or functionality than we really need to get the job done. Every additional feature adds complexity, cost, and its own set of adverse side effects. Keeping our HIT efforts as simple as possible will reduce barriers to entry and utilization, therefore giving us the most bang for our bucks.

So what is the lowest common denominator for HIT? Let's start with gathering information.

Basic National HIT Requirements: Gathering and Displaying Information

Information comes into the clinical record from many sources, including conversations, mailed, faxed and emailed correspondence, prescription lists, imaging systems, lab machines that spit out numerical values, and even (occasionally) electronic medical record systems. The lowest common denominator for collecting the data coming from any of these sources is paper. Paper is cheap and ubiquitous, and still accounts for the vast majority of medical record-keeping.

Given this reality, the first requirement of any electronic medical record (EMR) should be able to accommodate paper as a primary data input and output medium. If we simply scanned all our paper medical records and made the images available to authorized users online as PDF files, we would see a huge improvement in healthcare productivity. As low-tech and unsophisticated as this seems, it would allow us to start saving time and money tomorrow.

Still higher productivity could be achieved by making this scanned data searchable. After paper-based medical records (in the form of provider notes, correspondence, test results, and so on) are scanned, they can easily be classified by date, patient, and record type, and placed into a searchable computerized database. (Much of the classification process can be automated.) With this small enhancement, a specific piece of any patient's medical record could be located immediately. From there, a couple of keystrokes could fax or electronically transmit the data to wherever it's needed. Inexpensive systems with these capabilities already exist, and are commonplace in industries such as law, banking, mortgage, trucking, and public schools.

How would such a system fit into the next step in the healthcare process—recording information?

Basic National HIT Requirements: Recording Information

If we're interested in efficiency, providers need to be able to enter data using whatever medium is most effective and convenient for them, including pen and paper, dictation, computer mouse devices, and keyboards, digital cameras, or anything else. A nationwide system that accommodates paper-based input and output allows for this, but is the continued use of pen and paper medically acceptable? After all, poor handwriting has been implicated in a large number of studies and news reports as contributing to medical errors, a loss of productivity, and even deaths.[1,2,3] At least one patient safety organization has called for a complete ban on handwritten prescriptions.[4]

As is often the case in healthcare, the reality is never as simple as the rhetoric. Although there is no question that errors and ambiguity can and do occur with the use of handwriting, there is a good chance that typing, clicking, and computer order entry are not much better. In one of the largest studies of its kind, in 2003 U.S. Pharmacopeia reviewed more than 235,000 error reports submitted by 570 healthcare facilities.[5] The results are shown in Figure 14.1.

As we can see, handwriting accounted for about 2.9% of errors in 2003 and was the 15th leading cause of medication errors. Entering data into computer systems was the 4th leading cause and accounted for 13% of errors. Many of these computer data entry errors were due to mistakes made while transcribing orders from paper into computer software. Presumably what's really needed to reduce errors is to switch completely over to computerized physician order entry (CPOE) systems. If we eliminate the paper and handwriting, surely we'll eliminate the errors?

To test this supposition, the USP study compared the error rates of facilities utilizing CPOE prescribing systems with those that did not utilize CPOE. As shown in Table 14.1, the error rates were almost identical between the two different types of institutions on both an absolute basis and per 100,000 doses prescribed. Although it might appear that there were fewer harmful errors made with CPOE, the difference is not statistically significant.

Another study done in 2009—a meta-analysis of 12 studies looking at prescription errors occurring with and without CPOE in pediatric patients or patients in intensive care units—supports these

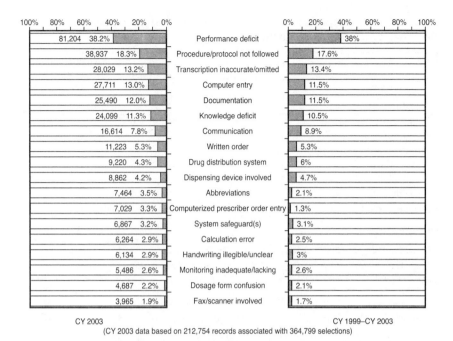

100% 80% 60% 40% 20% 0%		0% 20% 40% 60% 80% 100%
81,204 38.2%	Performance deficit	38%
38,937 18.3%	Procedure/protocol not followed	17.6%
28,029 13.2%	Transcription inaccurate/omitted	13.4%
27,711 13.0%	Computer entry	11.5%
25,490 12.0%	Documentation	11.5%
24,099 11.3%	Knowledge deficit	10.5%
16,614 7.8%	Communication	8.9%
11,223 5.3%	Written order	5.3%
9,220 4.3%	Drug distribution system	6%
8,862 4.2%	Dispensing device involved	4.7%
7,464 3.5%	Abbreviations	2.1%
7,029 3.3%	Computerized prescriber order entry	1.3%
6,867 3.2%	System safeguard(s)	3.1%
6,264 2.9%	Calculation error	2.5%
6,134 2.9%	Handwriting illegible/unclear	3%
5,486 2.6%	Monitoring inadequate/lacking	2.6%
4,687 2.2%	Dosage form confusion	2.1%
3,965 1.9%	Fax/scanner involved	1.7%

CY 2003   CY 1999–CY 2003
(CY 2003 data based on 212,754 records associated with 364,799 selections)

From: U.S. Pharmacopeia. "MEDMARX 5th Anniversary Data Report—A Chartbook of 2003 Findings and Trends 1999-2003," Figure 11.

Figure 14.1 Causes of Medication Errors, Study Year 2003 Compared with 5-Year Data

findings. It found that even though there were fewer reported medication errors when CPOE was used, the use of CPOE produced no significant reduction in adverse drug events or mortality rates.[6]

Ironically, although there are many strategies that could be used to reduce the number of errors associated with the use of pen and paper prescriptions, few ever seem to be implemented.[†] Instead, the emphasis has been on switching over entirely to more expensive and

---

[†] One could, for example, simply ask that the relatively few characters required when writing a prescription be printed rather than written in cursive. Another strategy is to implement relatively inexpensive handwriting/computer software hybrid systems that allow providers to enter data by hand as usual. Their writing is then immediately interpreted by computer (skipping potential human errors in the transcription process) and immediately displayed to the provider, who would verify that the computer got it right. These systems can provide all of the benefits of CPOE with correspondingly fewer errors due to clumsy and complex user interfaces.

TABLE 14.1   Comparison of Reported Medication Errors Between CPOE Facilities and Non-CPOE Facilities

Medication Errors	CPOE Mean (SD)	No CPOE Mean (SD)
Inpatient		
Total Errors	274 (549)	320 (463)
Errors per 100,000 Doses	56 (123)	55 (76)
Harmful Errors	7 (17)	9 (13)
Harmful Errors per 100,000 Doses	1 (1)	2 (4)
Outpatient		
Total Errors	101 (192)	36 (99)
Errors per 100,000 Doses	60 (99)	57 (102)
Harmful Errors	1 (2)	1 (2)
Harmful Errors per 100,000 Doses	1 (3)	1 (4)

From: U.S. Pharmacopeia. "MEDMARX 5th Anniversary Data Report—A Chartbook of 2003 Findings and Trends 1999-2003," Figure 14.

complex technology-heavy CPOE systems that carry high price tags and introduce their own unique sets of errors and inefficiencies.

A similar situation seems to apply when looking at handwritten chart notes. Although it's obvious that many providers have poor penmanship, there has never been a single published study that looks at whether asking providers to type or point-and-click to create their medical records has any beneficial impact on patient care. Instead, there are many reasons to believe that these systems might be less accurate and informative than the paper records they're replacing.[7] If we can't trust providers to write correctly, can we really trust them to type or use pick-lists properly?[‡] Just because information is neatly typed instead of scrawled doesn't mean that it's more correct or more valuable.

The bottom line is that we're right back to where we began with respect to recording data at the point of care. We should be implementing HIT systems that frankly don't care where or how data is

---

[‡] Two famous quotes by computer technology experts articulate the problem quite well. The first is from Paul Ehrlich: "To err is human, but to really foul things up you need a computer." The second is from Mitch Radcliffe: "A computer lets you make more mistakes faster than any invention in human history—with the possible exceptions of handguns and tequila."

entered—whether by pen and paper, dictation, Palm Pilot, or computer mouse and keyboard. The decision of which medium to use should be left up to healthcare providers based upon their own practice, their own finances, and what works best for them. In the meantime, both government and private industry should develop strategies and technologies that make *all* forms of healthcare data entry faster, safer, and more reliable.

Basic National HIT Requirements: Storing, Retrieving, and Transmitting Information

Storing, retrieving, and transmitting information is where computers really demonstrate unequivocal value, and the reason that we desperately need a basic, nationwide healthcare information technology infrastructure. Computers can handle images, documents, text, sound, and video equally well; a big advantage in a diverse and complex medical environment. Given the unparalleled supremacy of computing for these functions, what type of functional infrastructure makes the most sense?

Here as elsewhere, there is no one-size-fits-all solution. Large and technologically sophisticated medical centers and health systems such as Kaiser, the Mayo Clinic, and the Veterans Administration will have their own business reasons for deploying expensive, complex integrated systems. Because they own their own labs, pharmacies, providers, and facilities, they have powerful business reasons to force everyone to use the same systems and the same centralized and wholly owned data centers. As large institutions, they are in a position to bear the high cost of training and maintenance.

Smaller providers are in a completely different position. Already strapped with expenses, staff shortages, and administrative overhead, they are in a poor position to take on the additional expense of buying and maintaining computer and software systems that require constant attention, upgrades, and maintenance. Moreover, the systems that they do buy are unlikely to be the same as systems owned by other providers and healthcare facilities in the community. The integration of proprietary medical software systems is one of the most difficult and expensive challenges in HIT today. For them, it makes far more sense to outsource their HIT needs to Internet and web-enabled applications service providers (ASPs). By leasing the software and storage as a service (in fact, much like a utility), these clinics can concentrate on providing care instead of supporting IT departments.

With all the different pieces of proprietary software in use nationwide, what's needed most is for all HIT systems be able to seamlessly communicate on the most basic level—that of at least being able to transmit, receive, and handle PDF-based healthcare data without the need for any special software integration whatever. In this respect, each piece of medical record software should behave something like a fax machine. When one piece of software requests another distant system, something like a "handshake" should occur in which the systems describe each other's capabilities. If they are integrated to the extent that they are custom-integrated and can share formatted quantitative data such as text-based notes, lab results, vital signs, prescriptions, and so on, information is transferred as discrete, formatted computer-readable data. If, on the other hand, the two systems are either not integrated or one system only reads and writes to image-based documents, the clinical information is written to a common format such as PDF, and sent as a set of labeled documents to the receiving healthcare facility.

What has largely prevented the implementation of such a simple solution to sharing records is the attitude of HIT advocates and the HIT industry that such a simple, inexpensive, and rudimentary solution is somehow insufficiently "technologically advanced," "state-of-the-art," and "clinically sophisticated." It is as if solving the problem of medical data transparency and portability must somehow be solved perfectly and in favor of high-tech, or it should not be solved at all.

The irony is that if had we chosen to support and deploy this basic healthcare data storage and transfer technologies 10 or 15 years ago, every practice in America would already be connected. Technology adequate to the task existed then, as it does now. Even these basic capabilities would have saved thousands of lives and billions of dollars in the interim—from results that were available faster and more completely, tests that did not need to be repeated because their results were available, and emergency services that could have been delivered after referencing the history, physical, allergy, medication, and lab information that resides even in the most basic paper health record. With every provider connected and functioning at a higher level of clinical efficiency, we would now be talking about incremental increases in capability rather than wallowing in the mire of trying to get more than 10% of providers to use an expensive "certified" system.

To quote Voltaire: "the perfect is the enemy of the good."[8]

Basic National HIT Requirements: Dealing with Quantitative Data

Simply being able to exchange images of medical data in the form of PDFs and image files meets our tier one basic criteria, but does not address our tier two desire to capture and maintain inherently quantitative information as discrete digital data. A great deal of this information is currently recorded in handwritten form—as vital signs, lab results, medication lists, allergies, patient demographics, and prescription information. Turning these values into discrete data (or keeping them as discrete values when imported from other medical information systems) would greatly expand the degree to which automation could be used to enhance healthcare services. Indeed, combining tier one and tier two data would give us the potential to have at least 95% of the functionality of the most expensive and sophisticated electronic health records (EHRs) in existence. How can we provide this capability quickly and cheaply?

There are at least three ways to make this happen. All of them use relatively inexpensive computer technologies that have already been proven in medical practice.

Tablet computers use a pen-type stylus to record information on-screen using a number of different tools, including handwriting recognition, radio buttons, check boxes, and even built-in cameras for capturing images. They are extremely useful for entering relatively small amounts of discrete data, and many manufacturers are now specifically building them with clinical use in mind. There are many obvious advantages of using a tablet configuration with pen-based input rather than typing, including greater portability, the ability to interact with patients rather than type, and the ability to take advantage of computing power to convert handwriting to text in real time as the data is being entered. Although heavier and far more expensive than paper in most situations, one can easily see how using a tablet for quantitative data such as prescriptions, vital signs, checklists, and emergency room and home health care examinations would be an excellent alternative to both paper and conventional EHRs.

Tablets are already in everyday use in a wide variety of clinical applications. These include home-based eye exams, pharmaceutical trials, CPOE, oncology, sports medicine, nursing home care, and many more.

Digital pens use a special pattern of dots printed on a page of paper to "read" and record pen strokes with respect to size, shape, and location. Once the position and shape of these strokes is interpreted by computer, they can be converted into machine-readable text, interpreted as check marks and saved as image data depending upon the type of data they represent and the desired application. Digital pen technology allows providers to use paper for virtually any data capture purpose; it has already been tested successfully in a number of different clinical applications. Implementations include the creation of medical records on cruise ships, traumatic brain injury screening for the Department of Defense, data collection in pharmaceutical studies and other clinical trials, long-term care, and the recording of vital signs in acute care facilities.

A recent public health drill tested this technology as a very quick way to enter clinic registration data in the event of flu pandemic. It was extremely successful, allowing for vaccination rates of up to 350 patients per hour. This rate would have been difficult or impossible to achieve in a timely fashion, and at a reasonable cost, with ordinary paper records or conventional EHRs.[9] Even in situations where digital pen implementation has been troubled with programming errors, defective printers, and substantial system downtime, user satisfaction is high and the technology was found to be very workflow-friendly.[10]

Paper scanning with handwriting recognition is a third, inexpensive, and very reliable technology for capturing handwritten data in digital form. It has the added advantages of being able to scan any type of document into a digital record and not requiring the use of a special pen. High-quality scanners are now inexpensive and able to scan both sides of a page simultaneously. Multifunctional peripheral devices (MFPs) produced by companies such as Canon and Xerox give clinics the ability to scan, print, fax, and copy in a single high-speed digital machine. Properly designed, scanning-based clinical software can essentially duplicate the capabilities of digital pen-based applications, handle all types of medical paperwork, and yet minimize the need for specialized hardware.

The author has personal experience with one such system that was developed specifically for the purpose of improving the speed and efficiency of data capture and office workflow. Tested and found to be extremely effective in clinical practice, the system allowed providers and their staff to enter vital signs, lab results, prescriptions, and billing information on paper forms specifically customized for each individual patient, provider, visit, and clinic for which they are being used. These individually identifiable pages can be mixed up or even scanned upside down without affecting the results.

Quantitative data is automatically converted to digital form and verified, while other information such as progress notes and correspondence is saved in image form. All the information is uploaded to a simple searchable electronic medical record. Once the data is safely stored, a password-protected website specifically customized for each patient is automatically created and populated with listings of the patient's providers, medical conditions, procedures, medications and links to medical consent forms and educational materials on each one. All this—along with processing the data needed for medical billing—happens within minutes of scanning.

Simple but effective systems like this provide the vast majority of benefit that anyone would want from an electronic health record. This includes instant 24-hour accessibility, the ability to search for specific quantitative data, and the ability to add considerable numbers of quality and safety features. Perhaps the most extraordinary thing about this system is its cost. At less than $200 per provider per month, it would take 20 years of use before equaling the per-provider purchase price of a "conventional" EHR.

Basic National HIT Requirements: Sharing Information

With widespread provider deployment of a basic computer-accessible medical record, the final step is to share this clinical information quickly, safely, and securely.

There is certainly no shortage of proposals with respect to how medical records might be distributed. The most commonly cited suggestions include community health information networks (CHINs), medical record "health banks," and peer-to-peer file sharing that takes place directly from one provider's computer to another. Recently some of the largest technology companies in the world got into the act when Google and Microsoft launched their respective medical record archives.

From the perspective of healing, it makes no difference how the information gets from Point A to Point B. However, exactly who has control over our medical records and how that data can be accessed or released makes a great deal of difference. According to public polls, Americans are extremely concerned about the privacy of their medical information and wary of the willingness or ability of the government to protect it. Sixty-two percent of adults are concerned that the existing federal health privacy rules protecting patient information will be reduced in the name of efficiency, and 68% feel that the trend toward EMRs threatens their privacy.[11] An overwhelming 92% oppose allowing government agencies to see their medical records without their permission. This suggests that, at least in the eyes of voters, centralized government-sponsored medical data repositories might not be the best way of distributing medical information.§

To the extent that we want to improve the efficiency of healthcare, we really need two distinct methods of storing and sharing

---

§ In fact, medical information can be so sensitive that its large-scale aggregation by *any* entity could signal a broad erosion of personal privacy. An individual's medical and demographic information contains such a large amount of personal information that it might as well be the starting point for their dossier. Medical files routinely include information about age, sex, race, occupation, address, phone, spouses and children, medications, smoking, drug, and alcohol histories, illnesses of family members, and a host of other details. Combined with financial information from the Internal Revenue Service, they can paint quite a detailed portrait of any private citizen or political opponent. Moreover, information does not always have to be leaked to exercise untoward influence. Simply the threat of release can have a chilling effect on careers and behavior. A single centralized medical record under the control of government officials would represent a profound change in the social status quo.

medical data. The first is the point-to-point transfer of data from the records of one provider to another. Because this data is created by providers and must be maintained by them anyway, it requires no action on the part of patients to create or maintain. It is the only "mandatory" system because providers with this capability can get along just fine without "health data banks." A second optional system would be largely under the control of patients, who could then choose to aggregate, update, and share whatever specific medical information they want in their own time and in their own way—or even choose not to have their data centralized at all. These records would be stored in health banks, via online services, on hard disks or smart cards, or in any other way that makes sense to patients and the businesses that offer these services. While nice to have, it has to be assumed that patient participation in health banks and similar efforts cannot be relied on 100% of the time. This means that we need to concentrate on an economical and efficient way to transmit medical data to and from point-to-point storehouses. In this model, health banks simply become an additional point on a diffused Internet-like medical network.

Putting It All Together

There is no doubt that the widespread computerization of medical information can increase the speed, economy, and efficiency of providing healthcare services. The important take-home message is that we can achieve these goals much faster, more efficiently and with less expense than we've been led to believe. The key lies in understanding that we don't need to start with the fanciest, most expensive, and feature-laden capabilities for the vast majority of our healthcare information needs. The notion of forcing doctors to buy expensive, elaborate, centralized, and feature-laden "certified" systems as the only way to promote health is a false one, and the sooner we abandon it, the better. If the government is going to provide money to stimulate adoption of HIT, it should be awarded for purchases that meet the lowest common denominator for rapid storage recall and transmission. As shown in Figure 14.2, this consists of scanned paper documents residing in a database that can be sorted by patient, date, and provider. Higher levels of functionality are a bonus, but not nearly as important. As in so many other areas of healthcare, simplicity, ease of

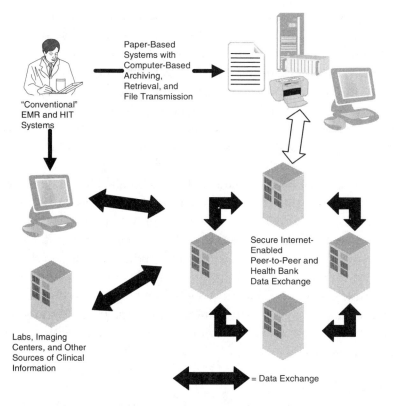

Figure 14.2   Key Components of a Basic, Inexpensive, and Rapidly Deployable National HIT Infrastructure

use, and universality are the real sources of lubrication, and the solution to what ails us.

Government can help in this process by helping establish and promulgate minimal, secure, healthcare file and data-sharing standards that can be rapidly adopted by vendors of even the most rudimentary HIT systems.

The Financial Impact of Realistic HIT Deployment

The best known study of the financial benefits of widespread HIT deployment in the United States was published by Hillestad et al in the September/October 2005 edition of *Health Affairs*.[12] This analysis was part of a 2003–2005 RAND Health survey titled "Extrapolating Evidence of Health Information Technology Savings and Costs."[**,13] Based on the RAND survey data, Hillestad and colleagues concluded that:

> "...effective EMR implementation and networking could eventually save more than $81 billion annually—by improving health care efficiency and safety—and that HIT-enabled prevention and management of chronic disease could eventually double those savings while increasing health and other social benefits. However, this is unlikely to be realized without related changes to the healthcare system."

To roughly $77 billion in efficiency gains, Hillestad adds additional financial benefits of $4 billion dollars from preventive services and improvements in the care of chronic diseases.[††]

The fact is that it's extremely difficult to calculate the benefits of HIT with any degree of confidence. There are too many assumptions involved. For example, this study calculated that CPOE could eliminate 200,000 adverse drug events and save about $1 billion annually if installed in all hospitals. It predicts that even larger savings would accrue in outpatient practice—about 2 million adverse drug events and annual savings of $3.5 billion yearly. But as we've seen previously, it's not clear that CPOE (at least as currently implemented), actually has any significant impact on medication errors or adverse drug events. Unless CPOE technology and operational effectiveness increases substantially, it is difficult to know what the true savings (if any) would actually be.

Other assumptions are equally tenuous. The analysis assumes that the information technology will cause preventive medicine interventions to reach 100% of people not currently complying with the

---

[**] This study was funded by Cerner Corporation, General Electric, Hewlett-Packard, Johnson & Johnson, and Xerox. These companies all have substantial HIT business interests and happen to be potential beneficiaries of the results.

[††] Many of these economic gains may be questionable. As we've seen, studies have shown that at least the use of EMRs does not have a measureable impact on diabetes care.

U.S. Preventive Task Force's recommendations regarding vaccinations and screening for preventable cancers. But as the study's authors correctly point out, it's impossible to imagine how those savings might be achieved without a wholesale overhaul of the healthcare machine. Other questionable assumptions include: (1) the period of time over which providers lose productivity after installing conventional EMRs (this was only three months in the analysis); (2) intentionally disregarding evidence of HIT having negative or no beneficial effect on efficiency; and (3) that HIT can potentially produce "lifestyle changes" that will prevent chronic disease.

It is possible that a basic, inexpensive, and rapidly achievable nationwide HIT infrastructure based upon simple record imaging and transmission could produce even more savings than Hillestad and his colleagues project. A simpler approach could be implemented far faster, at a lower cost, and with fewer cost and productivity losses than the vast majority of "conventional" HIT systems—even as it achieves virtually all the projected benefits. But it seems more realistic to question many of the health and productivity gains (such as those from CPOE) for which there is hope and anticipation, but little or no objective evidence.

Rather than attempting a wholesale revision of assumptions and assaulting on the evidence (or lack of it) for various aspects of HIT productivity, for our purposes it seems most rational to be grimly optimistic, but more conservative.

As a result of all this uncertainty, we can somewhat arbitrarily take Hillestad's figures and uniformly reduce the projected economic benefits attributed to HIT by 50%. The results are shown in Table 14.2. While possibly high in some areas and low in others, this probably represents a more realistic overall estimate of the *likely* financial impact (as opposed to the *potential* impact) of HIT than the original report.

TABLE 14.2 Estimated Source of Annual Cost Savings As a Result of Widespread Implementation of a Basic System for Gathering and Sharing Healthcare Information

Source	Annual Savings*
Efficiency Savings	
Assorted "improvements in healthcare efficiency and safety"	$38.7 billion
Estimated savings based upon increasing five preventive services (influenza and pneumococcal vaccination, and screening for breast, cervical, and colon cancer).	$1.46 billion
Savings from disease management programs	$14.3 billion
Total Estimated Annual Savings	**$54.5 billion**

* Estimate generated by simply reducing all HIT savings projected by Hillestad et al by 50%, without making any adjustments in assumptions or factoring in savings caused by use of less expensive HIT systems. Numbers are at 15 years, and assume 90% deployment.

15

Where Does the Money Come From?

"A billion here, a billion there, pretty soon it adds up to real money."

—*Everett Dirksen*

Based upon the financial estimates made in previous chapters, the proposed overhaul of the healthcare machine that we have described can be expected to generate total annual savings of just over $572 billion. These are summarized in Table 15.1. We have not balanced these savings with some additional costs that we know will be incurred by the newly revised system—partly because estimates of those costs are best done by organizations with enough resources to make them meaningful (for example, the Congressional Budget Office), and partly because many of those costs represent investments rather than consumption. Examples of these investments include a nationwide network for posting and comparing healthcare prices and services, research into the comparative benefit of competing tests and therapies with respect to QALYs, and a nationwide network for storing and recalling a standard set of information to be used for credentialing providers nationwide. However, even the most extravagant funding of these investments will be only a small fraction of the estimated savings. Many other changes, such as replacing single-state licensure of providers with reciprocal licensure, are probably budget-neutral. Finally, some increases in expenditures will occur simply because all Americans will finally receive at least a basic level healthcare coverage. In this case, the true comparison that needs to be made is the comparative cost of universal coverage in the overhauled system proposed when compared to providing the same level of coverage in the current dysfunctional environment.

TABLE 15.1   Total Projected Financial Savings from All Healthcare System Overhaul Measures Described in Previous Chapters

Source	Annual Savings*
Described changes to the U.S. healthcare financing and payment system (Chapter 12)	$478 billion
Eliminating redundancy in medical licensure and credentialing and instituting a universal patient identifier system (Chapter 13)	$4.3 billion
Improvements in government regulatory practices and the medical error/malpractice system (Chapter 14)	$35.4 billion
Widespread implementation of a basic HIT system for gathering and sharing healthcare information (Chapter 15)	$54.5 billion
Total Estimated Annual Savings	**$572.2 billion**

* Estimate generated by simply reducing all HIT savings projected by Hillestad, et al. by 50%, without making any adjustments in assumptions or factoring in savings caused by use of less expensive HIT systems. Numbers are at 15 years and assume 90% deployment.

But let's not kid ourselves—there is no such thing as free money. These savings came from somewhere. Every dollar "saved" represents a loss of revenue to someone in the existing healthcare system. Like any major change, this one is going to create winners and losers. Who are those most affected in the overhaul that we've proposed?

Healthcare Providers

One of the largest blocks of savings will come from a substantial reduction in total payments to healthcare providers. Paradoxically, most of those same healthcare providers will probably see their net income remain stable or even increase.

Price transparency will create competitive price pressure on all providers—something that simply doesn't exist within the current system. At the same time, switching from procedure-based compensation to hourly compensation for physicians and other healthcare providers will almost certainly reduce the number of procedures performed as a result of the revenue bias built in to the current system.

Reducing the number of procedures has a much greater cost impact than reducing provider charges alone. Nearly all procedures incur considerable non-provider expense such as anesthesia, equipment, and material costs, and (most importantly) the risk of complications. When combined, all these factors tend to reduce provider charge inflation, reduce the number of procedures performed, and direct patients and their families toward lower-cost providers. Gross provider charges will fall accordingly.

On the flip side, the accompanying reduction in administrative overhead for all providers will reduce provider expenses further and faster than their reduction in gross income. By way of example, the average incurred billing expense for a medical internist is about 7% of gross collections. For an internist who operates her business with a 50% overhead rate, reducing the cost of billing from 7% of collections to 2% of collections would increase her net take-home pay by 10%. If we further reduce the practice overhead rate by eliminating the need for referrals, state-based licensure and redundant credentialing, lowering medical malpractice premiums, and implementing inexpensive and nondisruptive HIT systems, provider profitability will increase still further. The net result is a win-win for providers, patients, and payers alike. Reduced costs make it possible for providers to lower their rates to attract patients while still retaining the profit margins they need to stay in business. These economics apply more or less equally to all providers, ranging from physicians to hospitals to pharmacies and medical laboratories.

The one caveat in all this is that we must take considerable care to guard against "administrative creep." New regulatory efforts will be described as initiatives designed to "improve quality," "prevent fraud and abuse," and "contain costs." In fact, they will really be an attempt to add covert rationing back into a system already constrained by overt rationing. The only antidote is eternal vigilance—a conscious effort to "regulate the regulators" to keep healthcare costs down. We'll need a new bureaucracy just to fight the old bureaucracy.

Private Health Insurers

The financial contribution of private insurers within the healthcare overhaul depends entirely upon the rules and regulation placed upon them during the conversion from covert to overt rationing. Depending upon the rates they are allowed to charge for the UBHP (which should be uniform for all people regardless of location or pre-existing conditions), and the coverage limits established on a cost/QALY basis, it is possible to craft a plan that is more profitable, less profitable, or revenue-neutral when compared to the status quo. Insurers will be able to supplement the income derived from the UBHP with Tier 3 coverage in a fashion similar to the way they provide elective coverage now, but with strict adherence to cost/QALY-based coverage and continued standardization of forms and processes.

Ironically, the change from covert to overt healthcare rationing should reduce the administrative expenses of insurers as well as providers. Standardized forms and software obviates the need to re-invent administrative processes at each insurer. Eliminating custom formularies, provider panels, referrals, pre-authorizations, and screening for pre-existing conditions will render thousands of administrative positions obsolete, reducing insurer overhead accordingly. It is the duty of agencies regulating the insurance industry to see that some or all of these administrative savings are passed on to rate-payers in the form of lower premiums. There is no reason why insurers—public or private—should not use their fair share of efficiencies gained to reduce the cost of insurance to the general public.

Pharmaceutical Manufacturers

Like insurers and providers, drugmakers in the overhauled system will have the opportunity to expand their overall profitability, but will have to change their sales model to do so. The current system essentially has two different types of drugs in two different price tiers: drugs priced at the highest level the market will bear, and generic medications with low profit margins. The new system will replace this with an approach that is based upon the marginal value that each drug provides when compared with a reference medication in the same class. This is good news for many drugmakers. Under the existing formulary system, a manufacturer's options are extremely limited. If your drug is not selected for a specific health plan formulary, there might be no way to sell it to health plan patients, regardless of positive features that might differentiate it. These might include producing superior results in a specific patient population, slightly better clinical performance at a slightly higher price, or a superior side effect profile. Using a market-based approach with reference pricing, patients and their providers become the final arbiters of what elements of value they will choose to pay extra for, and how much. Pricing is ultimately based upon a drug's value to each individual patient, rather than its "average" value as determined by a formulary committee.

For new drugs with no competitive equivalent, the process is slightly different. Here the decisions about insurance coverage and pricing revolve around the comparative benefits of the medication in cost/QALY terms, and on the cost/QALY of whatever alternatives might exist. If a manufacturer wants access to the general UBHP market, the cost of the medication simply cannot exceed the cost/QALY limit and still receive coverage.

The ultimate result is that many drugmakers will have to give up "whatever the market will bear" pricing in favor of what it makes sense for the market to pay, based on the treatment of individual patients. In some cases, this will mean that more expensive drugs will be used first, because they produce more clinical benefit early in the course of an illness. This differs dramatically from the current approach of starting with the least expensive medication and only moving to more expensive drugs as the patient's condition worsens.[*]

---

[*] One example is the way health plans treat new Type 2 diabetes (so-called "adult onset" diabetes) in America today. The current approach is almost always to mandate the cheapest class of drugs available. These medicines, called "sulfonylureas," force pancreatic islet cells to produce more insulin, thereby reducing blood sugar. In many patients, flogging islet cells with these drugs causes them to "burn out" and die. Patients must then inject man-made insulin. Only after islet cells die and the sulfonylureas cease to be effective will health plans permit the use of more expensive "islet sparing" agents that reduce sugar uptake and production and increase the body's sensitivity to insulin. They tend to preserve islet cell function. From a long-term medical and economic perspective, it is more rational to begin new Type 2 diabetics on islet-cell sparing drugs as the first line of treatment, even if they are more expensive. Combined with a other measures, this strategy gives new Type 2 diabetics the best possible chance of reversing their disease and leading a normal life without the need for any medication. Sometimes spending a little more for the better therapy up front leads to the best (and cheapest) long-term result.

By pricing and marketing based upon effectiveness and education, many drugmakers will see drug sales increase substantially as providers and patients weigh the true costs and benefits of competing therapies. In other cases, it means that drugmakers will need to cut prices on treatments that might be new and still on patent, but not effective enough to justify a substantially higher cost than alternatives. On balance, price transparency and allowing patients and providers to tailor therapies to specific medical conditions and pocketbooks will produce a more rational and sustainable pharmaceutical market.

Administrative Staff and Intermediaries

By far the biggest financial contributors to the healthcare savings we've identified are those who currently make their living doing all the pointless busywork created by the existing system. These include legions of medical coders and billers, administrative personnel at hospitals, medical practices, health insurance companies, Medicare, and hosts of other businesses. For most of these businesses and employees, there will be little or no financial benefit—only losses of the work and opportunities that redundancy, red tape, and bureaucratic obstacles provide. There is no avoiding the fact that this means the loss of hundreds of thousands of jobs. There are an estimated 50,000 Americans employed by independent medical billing companies alone. These are good people, but their efforts need to be redirected into more productive areas of healthcare. All these jobs are currently supported by our taxes and insurance premiums, but contribute little or nothing to the health of the population.

HIT Vendors

As an industry, HIT will grow and expand considerably as a result of the changes we've identified, but that growth will be distributed over a much broader range of companies and technologies than is currently the case. Sales of all types of systems will grow over time, but cost and efficiency considerations will redirect a substantial amount of investment into companies that can implement simple, intuitive, and inexpensive solutions quickly. Makers of "conventional" EHRs, elaborate CPOE software, and medical billing systems will lose much of the market that they are currently seeking to secure through government mandates and regulations. The net effect will be a larger and more sustainable HIT industry, but one less dependent upon proprietary systems, government subsidies, and the oligopoly power of a few large vendors.

Government

It is difficult to say whether more or fewer federal dollars will flow into the healthcare system as a result of implementing more rational regulation and incentives. For one thing, it depends upon how one does the accounting. If a national tax system is used to collect premiums and place them into UBHP patient accounts, do those become "federal dollars"? Does using these patient accounts to purchase health insurance constitute federal expenditures? We will not argue these points here. What is certain is that the nature of the government's healthcare expenditures will change. There will be far more investment, and far less unproductive consumption of resources. Our goal should be to replace all government-run healthcare programs (including Medicare and Medicaid) with the UBHP.

As in the private sector, state and federal expenditures for paperwork and administrative services will fall dramatically. The cost of insurance processing, patient identification, HIT subsidies, "quality of care" programs, and a host of other functions will plummet. There is also every reason to believe that true market competition, lower provider overhead, and realigned payment incentives will reduce the cost of healthcare services that the government purchases either directly or indirectly. On the other hand, the UBHP will result in health insurance reaching a larger portion of the population, including many of the poor who are currently not receiving care. A comprehensive economic analysis will be needed to "score" these changes with respect to the net effect on federal healthcare spending on administration and healthcare services. However, one thing is certain: Overhauling the healthcare system should have a profoundly beneficial effect on the rate of medical inflation and deficit spending.

From an investment perspective, far more federal dollars will need to be invested in cost-effectiveness research and a comparison of different treatments for the same condition in terms of cost per QALY. Federal investment should also be used to make this data readily available to patients and providers in real time via the Internet, and for continuously gathering and posting comparative pricing information from all providers and for all healthcare products and services. These data are fundamental to the success of a value-based free market healthcare system, and it is appropriate that the federal government invest in their creation and maintenance over time.

16

The End of an Era

"A designer knows he has achieved perfection not when there is nothing left to add, but when there is nothing left to take away."

—*Antoine de Saint-Exupery*

All machines with moving parts wear over time. Generally speaking, the useful life of any machine is inversely related to the machine's complexity and the number of moving parts. Engines are a marvelous example. The famous Rolls-Royce Merlin engine that powered the Spitfire and Mustang fighters of World War II was composed of 14,000 parts, and needed to be overhauled after only 800 hours of use. A modern jet engine might have only 4,000 parts, but is far more powerful and can run for at least 3,500 hours between overhauls. When it comes to complex systems with lots of parts that are continually interacting, less really can be more.

From a functional perspective, our current healthcare system is a machine that has reached a level of complexity, wear, and abuse that can simply no longer be sustained. Like an old, inefficient, and worn-out engine, it has finally reached a point where trying to replace the oil, stop the leaks, and make incremental repairs around the edges is more expensive than replacing the whole thing. It's time that we replaced the existing monstrosity with something that is smaller, more efficient, more understandable, more powerful, and cheaper to operate.

Americans have now been discussing "healthcare reform" for nearly 100 years. In 1915, social activists proposed a system of compulsory health insurance to protect workers against both medical costs and wage loss due to sickness.[1] In the 1920s, the Committee on the Costs of Medical Care proposed modest steps toward group medicine and voluntary health insurance (measures that were, by the way, immediately denounced by the American Medical Association as representing "socialized medicine").

Since that time, every change that has been made to the healthcare system has been made by *adding* something. Workplace insurance was added in the 1940s. Government-run health insurance (Medicare and Medicaid) was added in the 1960s. Escalating healthcare inflation in the 1970s and 1980s saw the addition of "managed care": the concept that central bureaucracies and nonmedical administrators could do a better job of controlling costs and making decisions about the care of individual patients than market forces, patients, and providers combined. The RBRVS and prospective payment systems of provider compensation were then layered on top of a multipayer insurance system. Most recently Medicare drug reimbursement, Medicare Choice, and a host of "pay-for-performance" and "quality" initiatives have been stacked on top of everything else. The Obama administration and Congress have now added guaranteed and unlimited coverage for millions of Americans, along with an unaccountable Independent Payment Advisory Board and Department of Health and Human Services. Together, they will have nearly unlimited power to artificially manipulate payments, issue new regulations and ignore the most basic laws of medical economics.

All this change has been arbitrary and piecemeal. Virtually no thought has been given to how we might craft a solution that balances the interests of healthcare as a business, as a science, and as a way of satisfying medical needs that are completely unique to each individual.

Real reform doesn't mean simply adding more parts and more complexity to a system that is already overwhelmed by them. Universal healthcare coverage without comprehensive administrative simplification just dumps more patients into a system in which every new patient means more forms and paperwork, more statistical searches to identify them, more CPT and ICD codes, more billing, more paper-based data transfer, and more typing into expensive, complex computer systems whose benefits are questionable at best.

Adding new federal, state, or regional insurance programs without standardizing benefits and simplifying payment simply adds more insurers into a system that already has thousands of them.

Adding new "quality" guidelines and regulations to a system in which exceptions are nearly as common as the rules produces less productivity and higher costs.

It is no accident that no one has been able to come up with a way of paying for all these added "benefits" without increasing taxes and reducing the income of healthcare providers. You can't add more seats, wheels, weight, and a bigger engine to a car and expect it to get better mileage. After 50 years of adding, the healthcare system that we've created has reached the point of diminishing returns.

What we've learned through our research is that *real* reform consists of making American healthcare simpler rather than more complex. The irony is that simplification is actually easier, cheaper, and less fraught with political hazard than the more expensive and less desirable alternatives currently being added. It's easier to eliminate artificially created expenses than to pay for new ones. It's cheaper to regulate supply and demand through the invisible hand of the marketplace than with regulatory commissions. And it's politically safer to have a combination of market forces and education make a patient say "I don't think that I really want that medical service given the costs and alternatives that have been presented to me," than to mindlessly deny care covertly or overtly.

So how does one begin a new, simpler era in American healthcare? For better or worse, the answer is both "all at once," and "on the national level."

Only a national effort can overhaul the existing RBRVS payment system and mandate uniform universal payment provisions, benefit levels, and premiums for the UBHP. Only a national approach can defragment nonreciprocal state-based licensure, professional credentialing, and certification requirements. And only the federal government can correct its own flawed approach to improving "quality"; one that promotes assembly-line treatment of intrinsically different patients and promises little or no benefit while incurring steadily increasing amounts of administrative overhead.

The need for national leadership is something of a "good news-bad news" story. On one hand, it is far easier to coordinate the actions of Congress and the executive branch in Washington than it is to try to coordinate the separate and individual actions of hundreds of different federal, state, and local legislatures and agencies. (In fact, it is the only plausible way to bring order and efficiency to healthcare delivery nationwide.) On the other hand, patients, providers, and taxpayers are rightly suspicious of any universal healthcare plan coming out of Washington.

To understand why, we need look no further than Medicare and Medicaid. To save money, Congress and the executive branch have long set Medicare payments to providers at levels far lower than those offered by most private insurers, and often below the cost of providing the goods or services rendered. (Medicaid is even worse—almost universally paying less than the cost of actually *providing* the services.) At the same time, Medicare requires providers to deliver some services free of charge, to refrain from billing patients for reasonable balances, and demands enormous amounts of documentation to comply with its cumbersome RBRVS-mediated payment methodology. The net result is that private insurance is actively and continuously subsidizing Medicare and Medicaid. The current healthcare system would fall apart almost overnight if these private subsidies of the public healthcare system were to disappear. If Medicare and Medicaid are good examples of government leadership in healthcare, the world has reason to worry.

A second rational concern about federal leadership is that whenever governments change, our federal healthcare policies change with them. Left to their own means, it would be relatively easy for a new Congress and/or administration to undo the components of a simplified and rational market-based system with little or no warning, logic, or societal recourse. Healthcare is far too large of a personal and industrial concern to have its operations and underlying business assumptions whiplashed every few years when power changes hands. Patients, families, businesses, and providers have too much at stake to risk having their worlds thrown into turmoil by a few bad politically motivated decisions.

A third concern about establishing universal health insurance (regardless of whether this insurance is administered through a network of private insurance carriers, a government-sponsored insurance plan, or both) is that reducing government regulation and control over the marketplace is antithetical to what regulators and bureaucracies typically do. This calls into question the long-term viability of any healthcare system that is based upon achieving efficiency and cost controls by use of market forces. Regulatory control is addictive, particularly when it is possible to use public health and welfare as a justification for intervening in the marketplace. This raises the question of whether it's humanly possible for a bureaucracy to control its natural tendency to create more rules, requirements, and obligations for those that it regulates. Increasing the efficiency of healthcare is critically dependent on employing *just enough* regulation to allow the market to function, while actively battling initiatives that increase administrative overhead at every level (federal, state, local, and corporate). It is not clear whether there is a successful precedent for this behavior in the entire history of U.S. healthcare.

The best way to address these concerns is to adopt the equivalent of a dedicated "constitution" for our new simplified and overhauled healthcare system. The purpose of a healthcare constitution is to formally lay out the purpose, goals, and design of a market and medical science-based system that is sufficiently affordable, fair, and flexible enough to carry us through the next 250 years without the need for substantial revision. Future government administrations, Congress, and the public itself would be able to measure proposed legislation, regulation, and other actions against the stated terms of this constitution. If sufficiently simple, clear, and articulate, this type of document could be very helpful to future generations.

More than anything, adopting and abiding by a good healthcare constitution would be tangible evidence that we have come to the end of an era in American healthcare: an era in which we spent our wealth and resources without regard to how much might be wasted by the system. A Wild West era, in which insurers and federal, state, and local governments could make their own rules about providing care without concern for the harmful physical or financial side effects they might cause. A time in which mass confusion was itself confused with a market system and freedom of choice. And an era in which patients and providers were routinely abused and driven apart by policies that paid lip service to quality while actually rationing care in the most arbitrary ways possible. There are many reasons to be glad that we can make the transition with a minimum of cost and disruption. The power to begin a new era is within our political capabilities, our creative capacity, and our budget.

All we need is the will.

A

"Brief Strategy B" from the Federal Guidelines Regarding Smokers Who Report That They Are Unwilling to Quit

Strategy B1. Motivational Interviewing Strategies

Express empathy	• Use open-ended questions to explore:
	    The importance of addressing smoking or other tobacco use (e.g., "How important do you think it is for you to quit smoking?")
	    Concerns and benefits of quitting (e.g., "What might happen if you quit?")
	• Use reflective listening to seek shared understanding:
	    Reflect words or meaning (e.g., "So you think smoking helps you to maintain your weight.").
	    Summarize (e.g.,"What I have heard so far is that smoking is something you enjoy. On the other hand, your boyfriend hates your smoking, and you are worried you might develop a serious disease.").
	• Normalize feelings and concerns (e.g., "Many people worry about managing without cigarettes.").
	• Support the patient s autonomy and right to choose or reject change (e.g., "I hear you saying you are not ready to quit smoking right now. I m here to help you when you are ready.").

Develop discrepancy	• Highlight the discrepancy between the patient s present behavior and expressed priorities, values, and goals (e.g., "It sounds like you are very devoted to your family. How do you think your smoking is affecting your children?").
	• Reinforce and support "change talk" and "commitment" language:
	    "So, you realize how smoking is affecting your breathing and making it hard to keep up with your kids."
	    "It s great that you are going to quit when you get through this busy time at work."
	• Build and deepen commitment to change:
	    "There are effective treatments that will ease the pain of quitting, including counseling and many medication options."
	    "We would like to help you avoid a stroke like the one your father had."

Roll with resistance	• Back off and use reflection when the patient expresses resistance:
	    "Sounds like you are feeling pressured about your smoking."
	• Express empathy:
	    "You are worried about how you would manage withdrawal symptoms."
	• Ask permission to provide information:
	    "Would you like to hear about some strategies that can help you address that concern when you quit?"

Support self-efficacy	• Help the patient to identify and build on past successes:
	    "So you were fairly successful the last time you tried to quit."
	• Offer options for achievable small steps toward change:
	    Call the quitline (1-800-QUIT-NOW) for advice and information.
	    Read about quitting benefits and strategies.
	    Change smoking patterns (e.g., no smoking in the home).
	    Ask the patient to share his or her ideas about quitting strategies.

Strategy B2. Enhancing Motivation to Quit Tobacco—the "5 R's"

Relevance	Encourage the patient to indicate why quitting is personally relev ant, being as specific as possible. Motivational information has the greatest impact if it is relevant to a patient s disease status or risk, family or social situation (e.g., having children in the home), health concerns, age, gender, and other important patient characteristics (e.g., prior quitting experience, personal barriers to cessation).
Risks	The clinician should ask the patient to identify potential negative consequences of tobacco use. The clinician may suggest and highlight those that seem most relevant to the patient. The clinician should emphasize that smoking low-tar/low-nicotine cigarettes or use of other forms of tobacco (e.g., smokeless tobacco, cigars, and pipes) will not eliminate these risks. Examples of risks are: • *Acute risks:*Shortness of breath, exacerbation of asthma, increased risk of respiratory infections, harm to pregnancy, impotence, infertility. • *Long-term risks:* Heart attacks and strokes, lung and other cancers (e.g., larynx, oral cavity, pharynx, esophagus, pancreas, stomach, kidney, bladder, cervix, and acute myelocytic leukemia), chronic obstructive pulmonary diseases (chronic bronchitis and emphysema), osteoporosis, long-term disability, and need for extended care. • *Environmental risks:* Increased risk of lung cancer and heart disease in spouses; increased risk for low birth-weight, sudden infant death syndrome (SIDS), asthma, middle ear disease, and respiratory infections in children of smokers.
Rewards	The clinician should ask the patient to identify potential benefits of stopping tobacco use. The clinician may suggest and highlight those that seem most relevant to the patient. Examples of rewards follow: • Improved health • Food will taste better • Improved sense of smell • Saving money • Feeling better about oneself • Home, car, clothing, breath will smell better • Setting a good example for children and decreasing the likelihood that they will smoke • Having healthier babies and children • Feeling better physically • Performing better in physical activities • Improved appearance, including reduced wrinkling/aging of skin and whiter teeth
Roadblocks	The clinician should ask the patient to identify barriers or impediments to quitting and provide treatment (problemsolving counseling, medication) that could address barriers. Typical barriers might include: • Withdrawal symptoms • Fear of failure • Weight gain • Lack of support • Depression • Enjoyment of tobacco • Being around other tobacco users • Limited knowledge of effective treatment options
Repetition	The motivational intervention should be repeated every time an unmotivated patient visits the clinic setting. Tobacco users who have failed in previous quit attempts should be told that most people make repeated quit attempts before they are successful.

References

Chapter 1

1. Energy Information Administration. Annual Energy Outlook 2008. Report #DOE/EIA-0383(2008).

Chapter 2

1. The 30 countries in the Organization for Economic Cooperation and Development are: Australia, Austria, Belgium, Canada, Czech Republic, Denmark, Finland, France, Germany, Greece, Hungary, Iceland, Ireland, Italy, Japan, Sought Korea, Luxembourg, Mexico, Netherlands, New Zealand, Norway, Poland, Portugal, Slovak Republic, Spain, Sweden, Switzerland, Turkey, the United Kingdom, and the United States.

2. http://ucatlas.ucsc.edu/spend.php.

3. Ellen Nolte and C. Martin McKee, "Measuring The Health Of Nations: Updating An Earlier Analysis." *Health Affairs*, 27, no. 1 (2008): 58-71.

4. Amenable mortality data from Cathy Schoen, Robin Osborn, Phuong Trang Huynh, et al., "Primary Care And Health System Performance: Adults' Experiences in Five Countries." *Health Affairs*, Web exclusive, October 28, 2004, pp. W4-487-W4-503, available at [http://content.healthaffairs.org/cgi/reprint/hlthaff.w4.487v1.pdf].

Chapter 3

1. Glabman, Maureen. "Lobbyists That the Founders Just Never Dreamed Of." *Managed Care*, August 2002.

2. California Healthcare Foundation. "Health Care Costs 101." Data from Centers for Medicare & Medicaid Services (CMS), Office of the Actuary (http://www.chcf.org/~/media/Files/PDF/H/HealthCareCosts10.pdf).

3. Anderson GF, Frogner BK, Reinhardt UE. "Health Spending in OECD Countries in 2004: An Update." *Health Affairs* (2007); 26(4): 1481-1489.

4. Redelmeier DA, Fuchs VR. "Hospital Expenditures in the United States and Canada." *New England Journal of Medicine* (1993); 328: 772-778.

5. Ibid.

6. Antoniou J, Martineau PA, Filion KB, et al. "In-Hospital Cost of Total Hip Arthroplasty in Canada and the United States." *J Bone Joint Surg Am.* (2004); 86-A(11): 2435-9.

7. Brox AC, Filion KB, Zhang X, et al. "In-Hospital Cost of Abdominal Aortic Aneurysm Repair in Canada and the United States." *Archives of Internal Medicine* (2003); 163: 2500-2504.

8. Frech HE, Miller RD. "The Productivity of Health Care and Pharmaceuticals: An International Comparison." UCLA Research Program in Pharmaceutical Economics and Policy (1996); Paper 97-1. Posted at http://repositories.cdlib.org/pep/97-1.

9. Dickson M, Jacobzone S. "Pharmaceutical Use and Expenditures for Cardiovascular Disease and Stroke: A Study of 12 OECD Countries." OECD Health Working Papers No. 1, 2003.

10. Ibid. Figure 42.

11. "Prescription Drug Prices in Canada and the United States—Part 3. Retail Price Distribution." The Fraser Institute, Public Policy Sources No. 50, 2001.

12. Danzon PM, Furukawa MF. "Prices and Availability of Pharmaceuticals: Evidence from Nine Countries." *Health Affairs* (2004); Web Exclusive W3, 29 October 2003: 521-536.

13. Ibid. Exhibit 2.

14. Data taken from Danzon and Furukawa (Ibid.) and Peterson and Burton (CRS Report for Congress, U.S. Health Care Spending: Comparison with Other OECD Countries).

15. Anderson GF, Frogner BK, Reinhardt UE. "Health Spending in OECD Countries in 2004: An Update." *Health Affairs* (2007); 26(5): 1481-1489.

16. "U.S. Healthcare Spending: Comparison with Other OECD Countries." OECD.

17. Ibid.

18. Buske L. "MD Fees Much Higher in U.S." *Can Med Assoc J* (1997); 156(6): 960.

19. Tu HT, Ginsburg PB. Center for Studying Health System Change Tracking Report. Results from the Community Tracking Study No. 15. June 2006.

20. Peterson CL and Burton R. "U.S. Health Care Spending: Comparison with Other OECD Countries." Congressional Research Service Report to Congress, September 17, 2007. Table 2.

Chapter 4

1. Kaiser Family Foundation, Fast Facts. http://facts.kff.org/chart.aspx?ch=179. This information was reprinted with permission from the Henry J. Kaiser Family Foundation. The Kaiser Family Foundation is a nonprofit private operating foundation, based in Menlo Park, California, dedicated to producing and communicating the best possible analysis and information on health issues.

2. Himmelstein DU, Lewontin JP, Woolhandler S. "Who Administers? Who Cares? Medical Administrative and Clinical Employment in the United States and Canada." *American Journal of Public Health* (1996); 86: 172-78.

3. Ibid.

4. http://www.bls.gov/oco/cg/cgs035.htm.

5. Ibid.

6. Woolhandler S, Campbell T, Himmelstein DU. "Costs of Healthcare Administration in the United States and Canada." *New England Journal of Medicine* (2003); 349: 768-775.

7. Congressional Budget Office Director's blog. "Effects of the Patient Protection and Affordable Care Act on the Federal Budget and the Balance in the Hospital Insurance Trust Fund." http://cboblog.cbo.gov/?p=448.

8. Fortune on CNNmoney.com: http://money.cnn.com/2008/03/03/news/economy/104239768.fortune/index.htm.

9. Committee for a Responsible Federal Budget. "The 2010 Medicare Trustees Report." August 9, 2010. http://crfb.org/sites/default/files/The_2010_Medicare_Trustees_Report.pdf.

10. Fortune on CNNmoney.com: http://money.cnn.com/2008/03/03/news/economy/104239768.fortune/index.htm.

11. Fortune on CNNmoney.com: http://money.cnn.com/2008/03/03/news/economy/104239768.fortune/index.htm.

Chapter 5

1. Johnston, David Clay. "Tax Cheats Called Out of Control." *The New York Times*, August 1, 2006.

2. Chadwick, Stephen Howard. "Defense Acquisition: Overview, Issues and Options for Congress." Congressional Research Service. CRS Report for Congress, Updated June 20, 2007.

3. www.iii.org/media/facts/statsbyissue/industry.

4. Kaiser Family Foundation. http://www.statehealthfacts.org/profileind. jsp?sub=66&rgn=1&cat=5.

Chapter 6

1. California Healthcare Foundation. "Snapshot—Health Care Costs 101," 2008.

2. Tu HT, Ginsberg PB. "Losing Ground: Physician Income, 1995-2003." Center for Studying Health System Change, Tracking Report No. 15, June 2006.

3. Dolan PM. MGMA: "Doctors On 'Unsustainable Course.'" amednews.com. Nov 6, 2006. http://www.amaassn.org/amednews/2006/11/06/bisd1106.htm.

4. GAO Report GAO-08-472T, "Primary Care Professionals—Recent Supply Trends, Projections, and Valuation of Services." Statement of A. Bruce Steinwald, Director of Health Care, Feb. 12, 1008.

5. Barry P. "Where Have All the Doctors Gone?" *AARP Bulletin* (2008); 49(7): 12-14.

6. Sack K. "In Massachusetts, Universal Coverage Strains Care." *The New York Times*, April 5, 2008.

7. Korn P. "Lack of Primary Care Physicians Boosting Health Costs, Hassles." *The Portland Physician Scribe* (2008); 26(17): 5.

8. U.S. Department of Health and Human Services. Health, United States, 2007.

9. Kahn JG, Kronick R, Kreger M, Gans DN. "The Cost of Health Insurance Administration in California: Estimates for Insurers, Physicians, and Hospitals." *Health Affairs* (2005); 24(6): 1629-1639.

10. California Medical Associaton. "15th Annual Knox-Keene Health Plan Expenditures Report." June 2008.

11. Kipp R, Cookson JP, Lattie LL. "Health Insurance Underwriting Cycle Effect on Health Plan Premiums and Profitability." Milliman USA Report. April 10, 2003.

12. Ibid.

13. Ibid.

14. Girion L, Rau J. ""Blue Cross Halts Letters Amid Furor." *The Los Angeles Times*, February 13, 2008.

15. "Insurer Fined $9M for Dropping Cancer Patient." *USA Today*, Feb. 23, 2008. http://www.usatoday.com/money/industries/insurance/2008-02-23-healthnet_N. htm.

16. http://www.aaos.org/news/bulletin/sep07/reimbursement4.asp.

17. Fuhrmans V. "Billing Battle—Fights Over Health Claims Spawn a New Arms Race." *The Wall Street Journal*, February 14, 2007. Page A1.

18. Fogoros RN. "Fixing American Healthcare: Wonkonians, Gekkonians, and the Grand Unification Theory of Healthcare." (2007) Publish or Perish DBS, Pittsburg, PA. 28. http://covertrationingblog.com/guidelines-abuse-of/ is-guideline-tyranny-causing-guideline-anarchy-part-i.

19. Grumbach K, Osmond D, Vranizan K, Jaffe D, Bindman AB. "Primary Care Physicians' Experience of Financial Incentives in Managed-Care Systems." *New England Journal of Medicine* (1998 Nov 19);339(21):1516-21.

20. Gaynor M, Rebitzer JB, Taylor LJ. "Incentives in HMOs." National Bureau of Economic Research (2002); Working Paper 8522. (http://www..nber.org/papers/ w8522).

21. http://covertrationingblog.com/general-rationing-issues/physician-report-cards-and-the-designated-driver.

22. Apolito RA, Greenberg MA, Menegus MA, Lowe AM, Sleeper LA, Goldberger MH, Remick J, Radford MJ, Hochman JS. "Impact of the New York State Cardiac Surgery and Percutaneous Coronary Intervention Reporting System on the Management of Patients with Acute Myocardial Infarction Complicated by Cardiogenic Shock." *Am Heart J*. (2008 Feb);155(2):267-73. Epub 2007 Dec 19.

23. The Henry J. Kaiser Family Foundation. "Medicare Fact Sheet—Medicare Spending and Financing." September 2008. http://www.kff.org/medicare/ upload/7305_03.pdf. This information was reprinted with permission from the Henry J. Kaiser Family Foundation. The Kaiser Family Foundation is a nonprofit private operating foundation, based in Menlo Park, California, dedicated to producing and communicating the best possible analysis and information on health issues.

24. Much of this discussion is simply a restatement of observations made by Dr. Fogoros in his weblog and book *Fixing American Healthcare* (2007) Publish or Perish DBS, Pittsburg, PA.

25. Fogoros RN. "Fixing American Healthcare: Wonkonians, Gekkonians, and the Grand Unification Theory of Healthcare." (2007) Publish or Perish DBS, Pittsburg, PA. 28. http://covertrationingblog.com/guidelines-abuse-of/ is-guideline-tyranny-causing-guideline-anarchy-part-i.

26. Albert T. "Medical Interpreter Rule Faces Review, Legislative Challenge." amednews.com, May 21, 2001.

27. Fogoros RN. "Fixing American Healthcare: Wonkonians, Gekkonians, and the Grand Unification Theory of Healthcare." (2007) Publish or Perish DBS, Pittsburg, PA.

28. http://covertrationingblog.com/guidelines-abuse-of/is-guideline-tyranny-causing-guideline-anarchy-part-i.

29. Pear R. "Senate Bars Medicare Talks for Lower Drug Prices." *The New York Times*, April 18, 2007.

30. Glabman M. "Lobbyists That the Founders Just Never Dreamed Of." *Managed Care*, August 2002. http://www.managedcaremag.com/archives/0208/0208.lobbying.html.

31. Anderson G, Black C, Dunn E, et al. "Willingness to Pay to Shorten Waiting Time for Cataract Surgery." *Health Affairs* (1997): 16(5); 181-190.

32. http://www.pollingreport.com/health3.htm.

33. Miller TP. "What Do We Know About the Uninsured?" *The American*, July/August 2008. http://www.american.com/archive/2008/july-august-magazine-contents/what-do-we-know-about-the-uninsured.

34. Gruber J. "The Role of Consumer Copayments for Health Care: Lessons from the RAND Health Insurance Experiment and Beyond." Report for the Henry J. Kaiser Family Foundation, October 2006. http://www.kff.org/insurance/upload/7566.pdf.

35. Piette JD, Wagner TH, Potter MB, Schillinger D. "Health Insurance Status, Cost-Related Medication Undersue, and Outcomes Among Diabetes Patients in Three Systems of Care." *Medical Care* (February 2004); 42(2): 102-109.

36. Keeler EB, Brook RH, Goldberg GA, Kamberg CJ, Newhouse JP. "How Free Care Reduced Hypertension in the Health Insurance Experiment." *JAMA* (1985); 254(14): 1926-1931.

37. Otto R, Valdez B. "The Effects of Cost Sharing on the Health of Children." RAND Corporation Report R-3270-HHS, March 1986.

38. "My Unhealthy Lifestyle is Your Problem!" *Business Wire*. FindArticles.com. 01 Dec. 2008. http://findarticles.com/p/articles/mi_m0EIN/is_2008_July_23/ai_n27933814.

39. http://www.harrisinteractive.com/news/newsletters/wsjhealthnews/WSJOnline_HI_Health-CarePoll2003vol2_iss11.pdf.

40. Volpp K, Gurmankin A, Asch D, Murphy J, Sox H, Lerman C. "The Effect of Financial Incentives on Smoking Cessation Program Attendance and Completion." *Abstr AcademyHealth Meet*. 2004; 21: abstract no. 1556.

41. Jacobs LR. "1994 All Over Again? Public Opinion and Health Care." *New England Journal of Medicine* (2008 May 1);358(18):1881-3.

42. Quinnipiac University Poll, Nov. 6-10, 2008.

43. Gallup Poll, surveys done each November, 2001-2007.

44. Jacobs LR. "1994 All Over Again? Public Opinion and Health Care." *New England Journal of Medicine* (2008 May 1);358(18):1881-3.

45. Kaiser Health Tracking Poll Election 2008. Issue 11, October 2008. The Henry J. Kaiser Family Foundation. http://www.kff.org/kaiserpolls/upload/7832.pdf. This information was reprinted with permission from the Henry J. Kaiser Family Foundation. The Kaiser Family Foundation is a nonprofit private operating foundation, based in Menlo Park, California, dedicated to producing and communicating the best possible analysis and information on health issues.

Chapter 7

1. http://www.encyclopedia.com/doc/1G2-3468301638.html.

2. http://www.trumanlibrary.org/anniversaries/healthprogram.htm.

3. www.iii.org/media/facts/statsbyissue/industry.

4. Saul S. "Geography Has Role in Medicare Cancer Coverage." *The New York Times*, December 17, 2008.

5. *Medical Regulatory Authorities and the Quality of Medical Services in Canada and the United States*. Milbank Memorial Fund, 2008. ISBN 978-1-887748-69-8.

6. Davis D. "Does CME Work? An Analysis of the Effect of Educational Activities on Physician Performance or Health Care Outcomes." *Int J Psychiatry Med* (1998); 28(1): 21-39.

7. Tanne JH. "Requiring Doctors to Take Part in Continuing Medical Education Doesn't Improve Heart Attack Care." *BMJ* (2004); 328:664.

8. Bloon BS. "Effects of Continuing Medical Education on Improving Physician Clinical Care and Patient Health: A Review of Systematic Reviews." *Int J Technol Assess Health Care* (2005); 21(3): 380-385.

9. http://abms.org/News_and_Events/Media_Newsroom/pdf/ABMS_EditorialBackground.pdf.

Chapter 8

1. Relman AS. *A Second Opinion: Rescuing America's Health Care: A Plan for Universal Coverage Serving Patients Over Profit*. Public Affairs, 2007. ISBN 9781586484811.

2. American Medical Association. Medicare RBRVS: *The Physician's Guide* 2006.

3. MacKinney AC, Mueller KJ, McBride TD. "Medical Physician Payment Policy and the Rural Perspective—Final Report for the Project." RUPRI Center for Health Policy Analysis, November 2008. http://www.unmc.edu/ruprihealth/ Pubs/Medicare%20Physician%20Payment%20Policy%20and%20the%20Rural %20Perspective%20Final%20Report.pdf.

4. AMA website: http://www.ama-assn.org/go/rbrvs-ruc.

5. http://thehappyhospitalist.blogspot.com/2007/11/in-eyes-of-medicare-you-are-99223.html.

6. http://www.aapsonline.org/fraud/fraud.htm.

7. "Bringing Common Sense to Health Care Regulation." Report of the Secretary's Advisory Committee on Regulatory Reform, 2002.

8. Information drawn from National Quality Measures Clearinghouse, Agency for Healthcare Research and Quality (AHRQ). http://www.qualitymeasures.ahrq. gov/content.aspx?id=4077.

9. Mottur-Pilson C, Snow V, Bartlett K. "Physician Explanations for Failing To Comply with 'Best Practices'". *Effective Clinical Practice*, September/October 2001.

10. Meunch J, Blenning C. "Angiotensin Blockade for Diabetes: Monitor Microalbuminuria?" *J Fam Pract* (2007); 56(2): 145-146.

11. Federal Clinical Practice Guideline, Treating Tobacco Use and Dependence: 2008 Update. U.S. Department of Health and Human Services, Public Health Service. May 2008.

12. http://covertrationingblog.com/general-rationing-issues/more-guidelines-what-are-they-smoking.

13. Wald HL, Kramer AM. "Nonpayment for Harms Resulting from Medical Care: Catheter-Associated Urinary Tract Infections." *JAMA* (2007); 298(23): 2782-2784.

14. Rosenthal MB, Landon BE, Normand ST, Frank RG, Epstein AM. "Pay for Performance in Commercial HMOs." *New England Journal of Medicine* (2006); 355 (18): 1895-1902.

15. Centers for Medicare and Medicaid Services (CMS) / Premier Hospital Quality Incentive Demonstration Project. "Project Overview and Findings from Year One." April 13, 2006. http://www.allhealth.org/BriefingMaterials/Centerform edicareandMedicaidsercives(CMS)PremierHospitalQualityandincentive DemonstrationProject-Premier-515.pdf.

16. Sackett DL. "Evidence-Based Medicine." *Spine* (15 May 1998); 23(10): 1085-1086.

17. Sackett DL, Rosenberg WMC, Gray JAM, Haynes RB, Richardson WS. "Evidence-Based Medicine: What It Is and What It Isn't." *BMJ* (1996); 312:71-72.

18. Dolinar R, Leininger SL. "Par for Performance or Compliance? A Second Opinion on Medicare Reimbursement." *Backgrounder* (October 5, 2005); No. 1882. The Heritage Foundation.

19. Pearson SD, Schneider EC, Kleinman KP, Coltin KL, Singer JA. "The Impact of Pay-for-Performance on Health Care Quality in Massachusetts, 2001-2003." *Health Affairs* (2008); 27(4): 1167-1176.

20. Rosenthal MB, Frank RG, Li Z, Epstein AM. "Early Experience with Pay-for-Performance." *JAMA* (2005); 294: 1788-1793.

21. http://thehappyhospitalist.blogspot.com/2008/11/pushing-paper-from-one-cubicle-to.html.

22. Halladay JR, Stearns SC, Wroth T, et al. "Cost to Primary Care Practices of Responding to Payer Requests for Quality and Performance Data." *Ann Fam Med* 2009; 7: 495-503.

23. Task Force on Contingency Fees. "Report on Contingency Fees in Medical Malpractice Litigation." American Bar Association, Tort Trial & Insurance Practice Section, Draft of September 20, 2004. http://www.abanet.org/tips/contingent/MedMalReport092004DCW2.pdf.

24. Studdert DM, Mello MM, Gawande AA, et al. "Claims, Errors, and Compensation Payments in Medical Malpractice Litigation." *New England Journal of Medicine* (2006); 354: 19: 2024-2033.

25. Harvard Medical Practice Study, Patients, Doctors, and Lawyers: Medical Injury, Malpractice Litigation, and Patient Compensation in New York, Cambridge, Mass.: The President and Fellows of Harvard College, 1990; P.C. Weiler et al., "A Measure of Malpractice: Medical Injury, Malpractice Litigation, and Patient Compensation," p. 139. Cambridge, Mass.: Harvard University Press, 1993.

26. Sloan FA, Githerns PB, Clayton EW, Hickson GB, Gentile DA, and Partlett DF. "Suing for Medical Malpractice," Table 2.4. Chicago: University of Chicago Press, 1993.

27. Mello MM, Studdert DM, DesRoches CM, et al. "Caring For Patients In A Malpractice Crisis: Physician Satisfaction and Quality of Care." *Health Affairs* (2004): 21(4): 42-53.

28. "Hype Outraces Facts in Malpractice Debate," *USA Today*, March 5, 2003.

29. Kolodkin C, Greve P. "Medical Malpractice: The High Cost of Meritless Claims." (January 2007) http://www.irmi.com/Expert/Articles/2007/Kolodkin01.aspx.

30. Klein E. "The Medical Malpractice Myth." Slate.com, July 11, 2006. http://www.slate.com/id/2145400/.

31. Congressional Budget Office. "Limiting Tort Liability fr Medical Malpractice." Economic and Budget Issue Brief. January 8, 2004.

32. *Business Wire*, December 12, 2007. "U.S. Tort Costs Down in 2006, According to Towers Perrin Study." http://www.reuters.com/article/pressRelease/idUS191518+12-Dec-2007+BW20071212.

33. Tillinghast Towers Perrin. "U.S. Tort Costs: 2004 Update. Trends and Findings on the Cost of the U.S. Tort System."

34. Studdert DM, Mello MM, Sage WM, et al. "Defensive Medicine Among High-Risk Specialist Physicians in a Volatile Malpractice Environment." *JAMA* (2005); 293(21): 2609-2617.

35. Office of Technology Assessment. "Defensive Medicine and Medical Malpractice." OTA-H-602, (July 1994).

36. Studdert DM, Mello MM, Sage WM, et al. "Defensive Medicine Among High-Risk Specialist Physicians in a Volatile Malpractice Environment." *JAMA* (2005); 293(21): 2609-2617.

37. Massachusetts Medical Society. "Investigation of Defensive Medicine in Massachusetts." November 2008.

38. http://scalpelorsword.blogspot.com/2009/01/coo-coo-or-contra-coup.html#links.

39. Congressional Budget Office. "Medical Malpractice Tort Limits and Health Care Spending." April 2006.

40. Hellinger FJ, Encinosa WE. "The Impact of State Laws Limiting Malpractice Damage Awards on Health Care Expenditures." *American Journal of Public Health* 2006 Aug;96(8):1375-81. Epub 2006 Jun 29.

41. Kessler DP, McClellan MB. "Do Doctors Practice Defensive Medicine?" *Quarterly Review Economics Finance* (1996). http://ssrn.com/abstract=5060.

42. PricewaterhouseCoopers' Health Research Institute. "The Price of Excess—Identifying Waste in Healthcare Spending." http://www.pwc.com/extweb/pwcpublications.nsf/docid/73272CB152086C6385257425006BA2FC.

Chapter 9

1. Hillestad R, Bigelow JH, Chaudhry B. "Identity Crisis: An Examination of the Costs and Benefits of a Unique Patient Identifier for the U.S. Health Care System." Copyright © RAND Corporation (2008). http://www.rand.org/pubs/monographs/MG753/. Used with permission.

2. Ibid.

3. Remarks of President-Elect Barack Obama As Prepared for Delivery American Recovery and Reinvestment, Thursday, January 8, 2009. http://change.gov/newsroom/entry/dramatic_action/.

4. http://www.acpinternist.org/archives/2008/09/erx.htm.

5. DuBosar R. "E-Prescribing Order Hits Unprepared Internists." *ACP Internist*, September, 2008.

6. DesRoches CM, Campbell EG, Rao SR. "Electronic Health Records in Ambulatory Care—A National Survey of Physicians." *New England Journal of Medicine* ((2008); 359(1): 50-60.

7. http://www.healthbeatblog.com/2008/09/ahlta-textbook.html.

8. Costello D. "Kaiser Has Aches, Pains Going Digital." *Los Angeles Times*, February 15, 2007, Page A1.

9. Makoul G, Curry RH, Tang PC. "The Use of Electronic Medical Records—Communication Patterns in Outpatient Encounters." *J Am Inform Assoc* (2001): 8(6): 610-615.

10. Poissant L, Jennifer Pereira J, Tamblyn R, Kawasumi Y. "The Impact of Electronic Health Records on Time Efficiency of Physicians and Nurses: A Systematic Review." *J Am Med Inform Assoc* 12: 505-516.

11. Pizzi R. "Beware of the EMR 'Ponzi Scheme,' Warns Physician Leader." *Healthcare IT News*, September 19, 2008.

12. Tipimeni K. "The Problem With EMRs." http://imaging.stryker.com/imaging2006/media/OrthoPad_ProblemWithEMRs.pdf.

13. Laerum H, Ellingsen G, Faxvaag A. "Doctors' Use of Electronic Medical Records Systems in Hospitals: Cross Sectional Study." *BMJ* (2001); 323: 1344-1348.

14. Dreaper J. "NHS Boss Attacks E-Records System." *BC News*, February 13, 2009.

15. Rosencrance L. "Problems Abound for Kaiser E-Health Records Management System." *Computerworld*, November 13, 2006.

16. http://www.health.mil/AHLTAWebhall.aspx. AHLTA Webhall of June 20, 2008.

17. Silverman SM. "Sociotechnologic Issues in Clinical Computing: Common Examples of Healthcare IT Difficulties." http://www.ischool.drexel.edu/faculty/ssilverstein/failurecases/?loc=home.

18. Quote from Joan Ash, PhD., as cited in OHSU press release of November 24, 2003. http://www.eurekalert.org/pub_releases/2003-11/ohs-mhd112403.php.

19. Weiner JP, Kfuri T, Chan K, Fowles JB. "e-Iatrogenesis": The Most Critical Unintended Consequence of CPOE and Other HIT." *J Am Med Inform Assoc* 2007 May-June; 14(3): 387-388.

20. Koppel R, Metlay JP, Cohen A, et al. "Role of Computerized Physician Order Entry Systems in Facilitating Medication Errors." *JAMA* (2003); 293(10): 1197-1203.

21. Campbell EM, Sittic DF, Ash JS, Guappone KP, Dykstra RH. "In Reply to: "e-Iatrogenesis: The Most Critical Consequence of CPOE and Other HIT." *J Am Med Inform Assoc* 2007 May-June; 14(3): 389.

22. Isaac T, Weissman JS, Davis RB, Massagli M, Cyrulik A, Sands DZ, Weingart SN. "Overrides of Medication Alerts in Ambulatory Care." *Archives of Internal Medicine* (2009); 169(3): 305-311.

23. O'Reilly KB. "Doctors Override Most e-Rx Safety Alerts." *American Medical News* (ammednews.com), March 9, 2009.

24. Conn J. "Failure, De-Installation of EHRs Abound: Study." *Modern Healthcare*, October 30, 2007.

25. Chin T. "Avoiding EMR Meltdown: How to Get Your Money's Worth." *American Medical News* (amnews.com), December 11, 2006.

26. Kleinke JD. "Dot-Gov: Market Failure and the Creation of a National Health Information Technology System." *Health Affairs* (2005); 27(5): 1246-1262.

27. Taken from Rippen H. "Summary of the Findings Assessing the Economics of EMR Adoption and Successful Implementation in Physician Small Office Settings." Powerpoint presentation, October 13, 2006. www.hhs.gov/healthit/ahic/materials/meeting10/ehr/Rippen.ppt.

28. Ibid.

29. Hansen D. "EMR Deadline Does Not Compute: Falling Short of 2104 Goals." *American Medical News* (amednews.com), May 19, 2008.

30. Dolan PL. "Insurer Finds EMRs Won't Pay Off for Doctors." *American Medical News* (amednews.com), March 10, 2008.

31. Congressional Budget Office. "Evidence on the Costs and Benefits of Health Information Technology." May 2008.

32. Wang SJ, Middleton B, Prosser LA, et al. "A Cost-Benefit Analysis of Electronic Medical Records in Primary Care." *Am J Med* (2003); 114: 397-403.

33. Thompson DI, Fleming NS. "Finding the ROI in EMRs: Financial Data in Clinical Studies that Document the Value of Electronic Medical Records Must be Adjusted for Use in ROI Calculations to Provide Credible Estimates of EMR Benefits." *Healthcare Financial Management*, July, 2008.

34. http://www.os.dhhs.gov/healthit/barrierAdpt.html.

35. Walsh MN, Fonarow G, Yancy CW, et al. "The Influence of Electronic Health Records on Quality of Care for Heart Failure." *Circulation* (2008); 118: S_714.

36. Meigs JB, Cagliero E, Bubey A, et al. "A Controlled Trial of Web-Based Diabetes Management: The MGH Diabetes Primary Care Improvement Project." *Diabetes Care* (2003); 26: 750-757.

37. Montori VM, Dinneen SF, Gorman CA, et al. "The Impact of Planned Care and a Diabetes Electronic Management System on Community-Based Diabetes Care: The Mayo Health System Diabetes Translation Project." *Diabetes Care* (2002); 25: 1952-1957.

38. O'Connor PJ, Crain AL, Rush WA, Sperl-Hillen JM, Gutenkauf JJ, Duncan JE. "Impact of an Electronic Medical Record on Diabetes Quality of Care." *Ann Fam Med* (2005); 3: 300-306.

39. Jones D. Curry W. "Impact of a PDA-Based Diabetes Electronic Management System in a Primary Care Office." *Am J Med Qual* (2006); 21(6): 401-407.

40. Orzano AJ, Strickland PO, Tallia AF, Hudson S, Balasubramanian B, Nuttig PA, Crabtree BF. "Improving Outcomes for High-Risk Diabetics Using Information Systems." *J Am Board Fam Med* (2007); 20(3): 245-251.

41. Crosson JC, Ohman-Strickland PA, Hahn KA, DiCicco-Bloom B, Shaw E, Orzano AJ, Crabtree BF. "Electronic Medical Records and Diabetes Quality of Care: Results from a Sample of Family Medicine Practices." *Ann Fam Med* (2007); 5: 209-215.

42. O'Connor PJ, Asche SE, Crain AL, Solberg LI, Rush WA, Whitebird RR. "EMR Use Is Not Associated With Better Diabetes Care." http://www.hmoresearchnetwork.org/archives/2007/concurrent/2007_A1-2.pdf.

43. Amarasingham R, Platinga L, Diener-West M, Gaskin DJ, Powe NR. "Clinical Information Technologies and Inpatient Outcomes." *Archives of Internal Medicine* (2009); 169(2): 108-114.

44. http://healthit.hhs.gov/portal/server.pt?open=512&objID=1473&&PageID=17117&mode=2&in_hi_userid=11673&cached=true.

45. http://hcrenewal.blogspot.com/2010/02/fda-on-health-it-adverse-consequences.html.

46. Federal Register: August 19, 2005 (Volume 70, Number 160): pages 48718–48720. http://edocket.access.gpo.gov/2005/05-16446.htm.

47. HHS Press Office news release, December 3, 2007. http://www.os.dhhs.gov/news/press/2007pres/12/pr20071203a.html.

48. Jones KC. "Obama Wants E-Health Records In Five Years." *InformationWeek*, January 12, 2009. http://www.informationweek.com/news/industry/health-care/showArticle.jhtml?articleID=212800199.

49. http://www.ischool.drexel.edu/faculty/ssilverstein/failurecases/.

50. http://www.ischool.drexel.edu/faculty/ssilverstein/failurecases/?loc=cases&sloc=granger_speaks_out.

51. http://www.ischool.drexel.edu/faculty/ssilverstein/failurecases/?loccases&sloc=australia.

52. http://iig.umit.at/efmi/badinformatics.htm.

53. Stead WW, Lin HS, editors; Committee on Engaging the Computer Science Research Community in Health Care Informatics; National Research Council. *Computational Technology for Effective Health Care: Immediate Steps and Strategic Directions.* The National Academies Press (2009); ISBN-10: 0-309-13050-6.

Chapter 11

1. Reinhardt U. "An 'All-American' Health Reform Proposal." *J Amer Health Policy* (May/June 1993): 11-17.

2. Fogoros RN. "Fixing American Healthcare: Wonkonians, Gekkonians, and the Grand Unification Theory of Healthcare." (2007) Publish or Perish DBS, Pittsburg, PA. 28. http://covertrationingblog.com/guidelines-abuse-of/is-guideline-tyranny-causing-guideline-anarchy-part-i.

3. The Physicians' Working Group for Single-Payer Health Insurance. "Proposal of the Physicians' Working Group for Single-Payer Health Insurance." *JAMA* (2003); 290(6); 798-805.

4. Casalino LP, Nicholson S, Gans DN et al. "What Does It Cost Physician Practices To Interact With Health Insurance Plans?" *Health Affairs*, 28, no. 4 (2009): w533-w543.

5. McKinsey Global Institute. "Accounting for the Cost of U.S. Health Care: A New Look at Why Americans Spend More." December 2008.

6. Tierney WM, Miller ME, McDonald CJ. "The Effect On Test Ordering of Informing Physicians of the Charges for Outpatient Diagnostic Tests." *New England Journal of Medicine* (1990 May 24);322(21):1499-504.

7. "Lessons from a Frugal Innovator." *The Economist*, April 16, 2009.

8. Ibid.

9. Zhang B, Alexi A. Wright AA, Huskamp HA, et al. "Health Care Costs in the Last Week of Life Associations With End-of-Life Conversations." *Archives of Internal Medicine* 2009;169(5):480-488.

10. Ibid.

Chapter 12

1. Conover CJ. "Health Care Regulation, A $169 Billion Hidden Tax." Cato Institute Policy Analysis No. 52, October 4, 2004.

2. Hillestad R, Bigelow JH, Chaudhry B. "Identity Crisis: An Examination of the Costs and Benefits of a Unique Patient Identifier for the U.S. Health Care System." RAND Corporation (2008). http://www.rand.org/pubs/monographs/MG753/.

Chapter 13

1. http://esciencenews.com/articles/2009/01/21/uc.davis.study.links.smoking.with.most.male.cancer.deaths.

2. http://www.sciencedaily.com/releases/2009/05/090508045321.htm.

3. Damberg CL, Raube K, Teleki SS, dela Cruz E. "Taking Stock of Pay-for-Performance: A Candid Assessment From the Front Lines." *Health Affairs* (2009); 28(2): 517-525.

4. McDonald R, Roland M. "Pay-for-Performance in Primary Care in England and California: Comparison of Unintended Consequences." *Ann Fam Med* (2009); 7:121-127.

5. Petersen LA, Woodard LD, Urech T, Daw C, Sookanan S. "Does Pay-for-Performance Improve the Quality of Health Care?" *Ann Intern Med* (2006); 145: 265-272.

6. Testimony of Daniel R. Levinson, Inspector General, before the Senate Special Committee on Aging, May 6, 2009.

7. Elder NC, Pallerla H, Regan S. "What Do Family Physicians Consider an Error? A Comparison of Definitions and Physician Perception." *BMC Family Medicine* (2006); 7: 73.

8. Kohn LT, Corrigon JM, Donaldson MS, editors. *To Err Is Human: Building a Safer Health System.* Institute of Medicine, 2000. ISBN-13: 978-0-309-06837-6.

9. Phillips RL, Dovey SM, Graham D, Elder NC, Hickner JM. "Learning From Different Lenses: Reports of Medical Errors in Primary Care by Clinicians, Staff, and Patients." *Journal of Patient Safety* (2006); 2: 140-146.

10. Rosser W, Dovey S, Bordman R, White D, Crighton E, Drummond N. "Medical Errors in Primary Care." *Canadian Family Physician* (2005); 51: 386-387.

11. Ibid.

12. Elder NC, McEwen TR, Flach JM, Gallimore JJ. "Creating Safety in the Testing Process in Primary Care Offices." http://www.ahrq.gov/downloads/pub/advances2/vol2/Advances-Elder_18.pdf.

13. Ibid.

14. Bhasale AL, Miller GC, Reid SE, Britt HC. "Analysing Potential Harm in Australian General Practice: An Incident-Monitoring Study." *Med J Austr* (1998); 169: 73-76.

15. Bedell SE, Jabbour S, Goldberg R, et al. "Discrepancies in the Use of Medications." *Archives of Internal Medicine* (2000); 160: 2129-2134.

16. Petrilla AA, Benner JS, Battleman DS, Tierce JC, Hazard EH. "Evidence-Based Interventions to Improve Patient Compliance with Antihypertensive and Lipid-Lowering Medications." *Int J Clin Pract* 2005 Dec;59(12): 1441-51.

17. Mager DR. "Medications Errors and the Home Patient." *Home Healthcare Nurse* (2007); 25(3): 151-155.

18. Van Horst RF, Araya-Guerra R, Felzien M, et al. "Rural Community Members' Perceptions of Harm From Medical Mistakes: A High Plains Research Network (HPRN) Study." *J Am Board Fam Med* (2007); 20: 135-143.

19. http://www.legalethicsandreform.com/hm_pg39.html.

20. http://www.legalaffairs.org/webexclusive/debateclub_medmal0305.msp.

21. Testimony of Philip K. Howard before the Senate Committee on Health, Education, Labor, and Pensions Hearing on Medical Liability. June 22, 2006. http://frwebgate.access.gpo.gov/cgi-bin/getdoc.cgi?dbname=109_senate_hearings&docid=f:28417.pdf.

22. Ibid.

23. http://commongood.org/assets/attachments/74.pdf.

24. Conover CJ. "Health Care Regulation, A $169 Billion Hidden Tax." Cato Institute Policy Analysis No. 52, October 4, 2004.

25. Kessler DP, McClellan MB. "How Medical Liability Laws Affect Medical Productivity." *NBER* Working Paper no. W7533, National Bureau of Economic Research, February 2000.

Chapter 14

1. http://www.time.com/time/health/article/0,8599,1578074,00.html.

2. Bruner A. Kasdan ML. "Handwriting Errors: Harmful, Wasteful, and Preventable." http://www.kyma.org/uploads/file/Patient_Safety/Physicians/Harmful_wasteful_and_preventable.pdf.

3. Phillips J, Beam S, Brinker A, Holquist C, Honig P, Lee LY, Pamer C. "Retrospective Analysis of Mortalities Associated With Medication Errors." *American Journal of Health-System Pharmacy* October 1, 2001. http://www.medscape.com/viewarticle/407005.

4. http://www.ismp.org/newsletters/acutecare/articles/whitepaper.asp.

5. U.S. Pharmacopeia. "MEDMARX 5th Anniversary Data Report—A Chartbook of 2003 Findings and Trends 1999-2003."

6. Van Rosse F, Maat B, Rademaker CMA, van Vught AJ, Egberts ACG, Bollen CW. "The Effect of Computerized Physician Order Entry on Medication Prescription Errors and Clinical Outcome in Pediatric and Intensive Care: A Systematic Review." *Pediatrics* (2009); 123 (4): 1184-1190.

7. Wilkes M. "Inside Medicine: So Far, Electronic Records Don't Help Patients Much." *Sacramento Bee*, January 20, 2007. http://www.sacbee.com/107/v-print/story/110007.html.

8. http://www.famous-quotes.net/Quote.aspx?The_perfect_is_the_enemy_of_the_good.

9. http://www.bjhcim.co.uk/features/2009/905002.htm.

10. Dykes PC, BComm AB, Chang F, Gallagher J, et al. "The Feasibility of Digital Pen and Paper Technology for Vital Sign Data Capture in Acute Care Settings." AMIA 2006 Symposium Proceedings: 229-233.

11. http://epic.org/privacy/medical/polls.html.

12. Hillestad R, Bigelow J, Bower A, Girosi F, Meili R, Scoville R, Taylor R. "Can Electronic Medical Record Systems Transform Health Care? Potential Health Benefits, Savings, and Costs." *Health Affairs* (2005); 24(5): 1103-1117.

13. Girosi F, Meili R, Scoville R. "Extrapolating Evidence of Health Information Technology Savings and Costs." *RAND Health* (2005), Pub. No. MG-410 (Santa Monica, Calif.)

Chapter 16

1. Hoffman B. "Health Care Reform and Social Movements in the United States." *American Journal of Public Health* (2003); 93(1): 75-85.

INDEX

Number

2010 healthcare reform law, 6

A

ABMS (American Board of Medical
Specialties), 131
ABMS Maintenance of Certification
(ABMS MOC), 133
abuse, forestalling through
regulation, 280-282
ACOs (Accountable Care
Organizations), 84
administrative overhead, 43-46, 239
health insurers, 73
savings from healthcare
overhaul, 328
United States versus Canada, 46
AHLTA, 198-199
AMA (American Medical
Association), CPT codes, 143
AMA/Specialty Society Relative Value
Scale Update Committee (RUC),
143-144
amenable mortality rates, United
States compared with other
developed countries, 12-13
American Board of Medical
Specialties (ABMS), 131
American Medical Association
(AMA), CPT codes, 143
Apollo Hospitals, 254

applying HIT, 304-305
gathering and displaying
information, 307
what are we trying to accomplish,
305-306
aspirin, 166
automated medication dispenser, 293

B

Banzhaf, John, 159
Barry, Dave, 9
benefits
minimizing to patients, 79-86
quantifying, 276-280
Blue Cross/Blue Shield, 124
preventing high-risk individuals
from entering the insurance
pool, 78
underwriting gains and losses from
1965-2001, 74
board certified, 131
bonus pools, covert rationing, 84
"Brief Strategy B," 337
"Bringing Common Sense to Health
Care Regulation," 151
Buddha, 1
bundling, 68
bureaucracy, 98
Bush, George W., 210
business models, private insurers, 71

C

Canada
    life expectancy in, 10
    pricing healthcare services, 43
    versus United States
        administrative overhead, 46
        comparison of procedure
            charges for outpatient
            services, 34
        hospital procedure cost
            comparision, 21
capitation, 84
cash, paying for healthcare
    services, 41
certification, 130-132
CF (conversion factor), 140
changing healthcare, 48-51
CHINs (community health
    information networks), 316
Churchill, Winston, 3, 217
civil servants, healthcare priorities,
    104-105
claims
    denying, 82
    reducing, 283
    resolving, 294-298
    unwarranted malpractice claims,
        reducing, 294
clean claims, 81, 151
clinicians, how they get paid, 136-141
CME (continuing medical education),
    131-134
co-insurance, 111-112
co-payments, 111-113
    raising, 79
collapsed lungs, 161
Columbia Asia, 254
Colvin, Geoff, 50
Common Good, 297
communication between providers
    and patients, 291
community health information
    networks (CHINs), 316
comparing treatments, 235-237
compensation, malpractice, 171
complexity, 54
    EMRs, 195-201
    excessive complexity, 53

computerized physician order entry
    (CPOE), 194, 199, 308-310
computers versus paper for
    recordkeeping, 205-209
connectivity, EMRs, 201-204
continuing medical education (CME),
    131-134
controlling resource utilization
    through patient economic behavior,
    110-113
conversion factor (CF), 140
cost
    defensive medicine, 180
    EMRs, 201-204
    healthcare, 17-19
        hospital care, 19-21
        outpatient care, 31-36
        pharmaceuticals, 24-30
    malpractice insurance, 173-174
    medical errors, 290
    over-the-counter drugs, 28
    overhead costs, malpractice, 181
    quantifying, 276-280
cost sharing, 248
covert rationing, 79, 83-84
    public insurers, 92-101
CPOE (computerized physician order
    entry), 194, 199, 308-310
CPR (customary, prevailing, and
    reasonable charges), 136-137
CPT codes, 136, 143, 146, 149
crank-'em out option, 69
credentialing, 129-130, 265-267
critical pathways, 96, 159
CT scans, 176
CyberKnife, 126

D

data
    collection, role of government,
        273-274
    quantitative data, HIT, 313-315
DDD (defined daily dose), 26
deductibles, raising, 79
defensive medicine, 175-181,
    282-283, 295
    cost of, 180
    defined, 175

medical errors, reducing, 283-291
patient-mediated errors, reducing, 291-294
defined daily dose (DDD), 26
delaying payments, private insurers, 80
denying claims, 82
diagnosis related group (DRG), 138
digital pens, 314
discounts, insurance companies, 41
doctors, 64, 67
    capitation, 84
    economics and motivation, 67-70
    income levels, 65
    limiting access to, 80
    payment contracts, 85
    payment for procedures, 68
    report cards, 86
    shortage of, 65-66
    time, 68
    versus attorneys, payment comparisons, 69
documentation, CPT codes, 149
DRG (diagnosis related group), 138
drug formularies, 80
drugs
    early adopters (U.S.), 26
    over-the-counter, 25, 28

E

e-iatrogenesis, 200
E&M codes (Evaluation and Management), 146-150
economics
    doctors, 67-70
    patients, 108-110
        controlling resource utilization, 110-113
    private insurers, 74
        investment income, 77
        minimizing benefits provided to patients, 79-80, 83-86
        premiums, 74-77
        preventing high-risk individuals from entering the insurance, 78-79
efficiency of pharmaceuticals, outpatient, and hospital care services, 260

efficient, 220
EHRs (electronic health records). *See* EMRs (electronic medical records)
Elder, Nancy, 285
elective surgery, waiting times for, 14
electronic healthcare information systems, 191-193
    complexity, 195-201
    high cost, poor connectivity, 201-204
    provider timeand workflow, 193-194
electronic medical records. *See* EMRs (electronic medical records)
elements of a universal healthcare plan, 230-233
    QALL, 233
    QALY, 234-237
Employee Retirement Income Security Act (ERISA), 81
Employment Cost Index for Health Insurance Premiums versus Health Cost Index, 76
EMRs (electronic medical records), 187-189, 192
    benefits of, 205-208
    complexity, 195-201
    good or bad, 210-215
    high cost, poor connectivity, 201-204
    provider time and workflow, 193-194
Equal Opportunity Standard (EOS), 234
ERISA (Employee Retirement Income Security Act), 81
errors, primary care, 285
estimated spending according to wealth (ESAW), 258
Evaluation and Management (E&M) codes, 146-150
evidence-based medicine, 162-163
executive branch, healthcare, 104-105
expeditures, minimizing, 91

F

failure of RBRVS, 141-151
fairness, 220
fear, 93, 119
Federation of State Medical Boards (FSMB), 130
fees, 40-41

financial impact of HIT deployment,
318-320
financial unsustainability of U.S.
healthcare system, 3-7
financing UBHP (Universal Basic
Health Plan), 238-241
Fogoros, Richard, 79, 83, 95
forestalling fraud and abuse, 280-282
fraud
forestalling through regulation,
280-282
Medicare fraud, 150
friction, 183
processing transactions, 304
systemic, 60
FSMB (Federation of State Medical
Boards), 130

G

gag clauses, payment contracts, 85
garnering revenue, public
insurers, 89
Gates, Bill, 210
Geographic Practice Cost Index
(GPCI), 140
goals for healthcare, 220
overt rationing, 224-226
pricing services freely, 222
retention of a private market,
221-222
transparent, disclosed and available
pricing, 223
universal healthcare, 220-221
goods, underpaying for, 81
government, 101
as a growth industry within
healthcare system, 107
healthcare and
executive branch priorities,
104-105
legislative branch priorities,
102-104
regulators and providers, 105-106
role in healthcare, 271-272
collection of data, 273-274
do not harm, 272
never mandate the use of
healthcare technology, 273
savings from healthcare overhaul,
329-330

government regulation, 275-276, 299
forestalling fraud and abuse,
280-282
quantifying cost and benefit,
276-280
government-run healthcare, 332
GPCIs (Geographic Practice Cost
Index), 140
Granger, Richard, 214
guidelines, 100
of care, 154-160
for smokers who are unwilling to
quit, 337

H

HAC (hospital-acquired
conditions), 160
Happy Hospitalist
E&M codes, 147-149
pay-for-performance, 164-167
health behavior, patients, 108,
113-115
Health Cost Index versus
Employment Cost Index for Health
Insurance Premiums, 76
health insurance
administrative overhead, 239
history of, 124-125
need for, 123-124
underwriting cycle, 74-75
variability in plans, 126-127
health insurers
administrative overhead, 73
private insurers. *See* private insurers
public insurers, 88-89
covert rationing, 92-101
ganering revenue, 89-91
minimizing expenditures, 91
minimizing provider outlays, 92
savings from healthcare overhaul,
325-326
self-insured businesses, 87-88
Health Quality Incentive (HQI), 161
health standards commission, 235
healthcare
changing, 48-51
costs of, 17-19
hospital care, 19-21
outpatient care, 31-36
pharmaceuticals, 24-30

goals, 220
  overt rationing, 224-226
  pricing services freely, 222
  retention of a private market, 221-222
  transparent, disclosed and available pricing, 223
  universal healthcare, 220-221
political lobbying, 18
role of government, 271-272
  collection of data, 273-274
  do not harm, 272
  never mandate the use of healthcare technology, 273
healthcare constitution, 335
healthcare funding, sources of, 228-230
healthcare information technology (HIT), 195
healthcare providers, 64, 67-70
healthcare reform, 331-335
healthcare spending per capita, 4-5
healthcare system
  jamming, 60
  specific elements with direct effect on, 60
healthcare transactions, 55-60
Hennesy, Katherine, 179
HIE (Health Insurance Experiment), 111
high-risk individuals, preventing from entering the insurance pool, 78-79
history of health insurance, 124-125
HIT (healthcare information technology), 195, 209, 215
  applying rationally, 304-305
    gathering and displaying information, 307
    what are we trying to accomplish, 305-306
  financial impact of deployment, 318-320
  requirements
    dealing with quantitative data, 313-315
    gathering and displaying information, 307
    recording information, 308-311

sharing information, 315-317
  storing, retrieving, and transmitting information, 311-313
HIT vendors, savings from healthcare overhaul, 328
hospital-acquired conditions (HAC), 160
hospital care, cost of, 19, 21, 253
hospital procedure cost comparions, United States versus Canada, 21
hospitals, medical errors, 284
Howard, Philip, 298
HQI (Health Quality Incentive), 161
HSA (health savings account), 248
  universal healthcare, 232

I

iatrogenic lpneumothorax, 160
incentives
  defensive medicine, 177
  physician incentives, manipulating, 83
income of doctors, 65
India, free-market, 254-255
inefficiency of U.S. healthcare system, 5
infant mortality rate, U.S. compared with other developed countries, 11
information
  recording, 308-311
  role of, 301-302
  sharing, HIT, 315-317
  storing, retrieving, and transmitting, 311-313
inpatient records, 188
insurance companies, discounts, 41. See also private insurers; public insurers
insurance overhead, minimizing, 251-257
interactions, 55-60
investment income, private insurers, 77

J–K

jamming healthcare systems, 60
Japan, life expectancy in, 10
Johnson, Lyndon B., 137

JPTA (Joint Patient Tracking
    Application), 189

Kaiser Permanente, electronic record
    systems, 192

L

leadership, healthcare reform, 334
Leavitt, Mike, 211
legislation, 2010 healthcare reform
    law, 6
legislative branch, healthcare,
    102-104
licensure, 127-129, 263-264, 267
life expectancy, United States
    compared with other developed
    countries, 10-11
LifeSpring Hospitals, 255
limiting access to doctors, 80

M

malpractice, 282-283
    claims, resolving, 294-298
    comparison of claims with and
        without clinician errors, 171
    medical errors, reducing, 283-291
    overhead costs, 181
    patient-mediated errors, reducing,
        291-294
    reducing errors versus reducing
        harm versus reducing claims, 283
    unwarranted claims, reducing, 294
malpractice insurance, cost of,
    173-174
malpractice liability, 167-168
    compensation, 171
    current system, 168-175
mandates, standards, 100
manipulating physician incentives, 83
market principles
    minimizing overhead, 252-257
    simplifying payments, 243-250
Medicaid, 88, 125, 332
    covert rationing, 92-101
    fraud, 281
    future of, 51
    garnering revenue, 89-91
    minimizing expenditures, 91
    minimizing provider outlays, 92

paying for less than the actual cost of
    procedures, 41
medical billing, 259
medical errors, reducing, 283-291
medical interventions, percentage
    undertaken with liability concerns
    as a priority, 177
medical licensure, 127-129,
    263-264, 267
medical loss ratio (MLR), 73
medical losses, 73
medical malpractice. *See* malpractice
medical practices, production
    process, 67
medical recordkeeping, 186-189
    electronic healthcare information
        systems, 191-193
    EMRs (electronic medical records)
        complexity, 195-201
        high cost, poor connectivity,
            201-204
        provider time and workflow,
            193-194
    paper-based healthcare information
        systems, 190-191
    paper versus computers, 205-209
medical services
    pricing and billing, 135
        failure of RBRVS, 141-151
        how clinicians get paid,
            136-141
    simplifying payment for, 241-242
        based on market principles,
            243-250
medical testing, problems with,
    286-287
Medicare, 88, 125, 332
    administrative overhead, 239
    covert rationing, 92-101
    CPT codes, 143
    fraud, 281
    garnering revenue, 89-91
    how clinicians get paid, 136-141
    lack of funding for, 50
    minimizing expenditures, 91-92
    paying for less than the actual cost of
        procedures, 41
    pricing and billing, 136
    RBRVS, 139
Medicare Advantage, 89, 125
Medicare Choice, 125, 332

Medicare fraud, 150
Medicare Part A, 89
Medicare Part B, 89
Medicare Part C, 89
Medicare Part D, 90, 103
medication compliance, 292-293
medication errors, 292
Merkle, Ralph, 121
MFPs (multifunctional peripheral
   devices), 314
microalbuminuria, 155
minimizing
   benefits provided to patients, private
      insurers, 79-86
   expenditures, public insurers, 91
   provider outlays, public insurers, 92
   regulatory overhead, 251-252
      market principles, 252-257
MLR (medical loss ratio), 73
moral hazard, 72
mortality rates, United States
   compared with other developed
   countries, 11
Mossberg, Walter, 195
motivation
   doctors, 67-70
   private insurers, 74
      investment income, 77
      minimizing benefits provided to
         patients, 79-86
      premiums, 74-77
      preventing high-risk
         individuals from entering the
         insurance, 78-79
multifunctional peripheral devices
   (MFPs), 314

N

National Board of Medical
   Examiners, 130
National Health Care Anti-Fraud
   Association, 282
national health insurance
   programs, 124
need for health insurance, 123-124
never events, 160-161
No-fault, 296

O

Obama, Barack, 211, 214
OECD (Organization for Economic
   Cooperation and Development)
   countries
   amenable mortality rates, 12-13
   life expectancy, 10-11
   mortality rates, 11
   waiting times for elective surgery, 14
OHITA (Office of Health Information
   Technology Adoption), 210
ONCHIT (Office of the National
   Coordinator for Health Information
   Technology), 210
outpatient care, cost of, 31-36
outpatient records, 187
outpatient services, comparison of
   charges in United States versus
   Canada, 34
over-the-counter drugs, 25, 28
overhead, 43-46
   health insurers, 73
   malpractice, 181
   minimizing, 251-252
      through market principles,
         252-257
overt rationing, 224-226

P

P4P (pay-for-performance), 154-156,
   161-167
paper-based healthcare information
   systems, 190-191
paper scanning with handwriting
   recognition, 314
paper versus computers,
   recordkeeping, 205-209
patient-mediated errors, reducing,
   291-294
Patient Protection and Affordable
   Care Act (PPACA), 79, 125
patients, 108
   economic behavior, 108-110
      controlling resource utilization,
         110-113
   health behavior, 108, 113-115
   political behavior, 108, 115-118

pay-for-performance (P4P), 154-156, 161-167
payment
    with cash, 41
    delaying by private insurers, 80
    for medical services
        simplifying, 241-242
        simplifying based on market principles, 243-250
payment comparisons, doctors versus attorneys, 69
payment contracts, 85
peer pressure, covert rationing, 85
Pennsylvania, satisfaction of physicians, 172
pharmaceutical manufacturers
    negotiating prices, 103
    savings from healthcare overhaul, 326-328
pharmaceuticals, cost of, 24-30
physician incentives, manipulating, 83
Physician Insurers Association of America (PIAA), 174
physicians
    uniformity of training in developed countries, 10
    wounded physicians, 172
PIAA (Physician Insurers Association of America), 174
political behavior, patients, 108, 115-118
political interests, 49
political lobbying, healthcare, 18
politics
    mandated standards, 99
    public insurers, 89
POMR (problem-oriented medical record), 191
positive sum games, 48
PPACA (Patient Protection and Affordable Care Act), 79, 125
premiums, private insurers, 74-77
preventing high-risk individuals from entering the insurance pool, 78-79
pricing, 39-43, 135
    how clinicians get paid, 136-141
    rational pricing, 39
    RBRVS, failure of, 141-151
    transparent, disclosed and available pricing, 223

pricing services freely, 222
primary care errors, 285
primary care providers, healthcare transactions, 58
prior authorization, 56
privacy, unique patient identifiers, 265
private insurers, 70-74
    business models, 71
    economics and motivation, 74
        investment income, 77
        minimizing benefits provided to patients, 79-80, 83-86
        premiums, 74-77
        preventing high-risk individuals from entering, 78-79
    payment contracts, 85
private markets, retention of, 221-222
problem-oriented medical records (POMR), 191
problems with medical testing, 286-287
procedures, 68, 139
processes of medical practices, 67
processing transactions, 302-304
productivity, EMRs, 193-194
profits, 71
prompt payment laws, 81
provider compensation under universal healthcare, 250
provider outlays, minimizing, 92
provider time, EMRs, 193-194
providers
    government, 105-106
    pricing services freely, 222
    savings from healthcare overhaul, 324-325
public insurers, 88-89
    covert rationing, 92-101
    garnering revenue, 89-91
    minimizing expenditures, 91
    minimizing provider outlays, 92

Q

QALY (quality-adjusted life year), 233-237, 260
    quantifying cost and benefit, 276-280

quality, regulation, 275-276
  forestalling fraud and abuse,
    280-282
  quantifying cost and benefit,
    276-280
quality-adjusted life year (QALY),
  233-237, 260
  quantifying cost and benefit,
    276-280
quality of care, 153-154
  guidelines of care, 154-160
  never events, 160-161
  pay-for-performance, 161-167
quality of life scales, 235
quality of U.S. healthcare system,
  9-10
  administration and delivery
    system, 14
  amenable mortality rates, 12-13
  life expectancy, 10-11
  mortality rates, 11
  politics of claims about U.S. health
    care quality, 14-16
  waiting times for doctor visits, 14
  waiting times for elective surgery, 14
quantitative data, HIT, 313-315

R

rational pricing, 39
rationing
  covert rationing, 79, 83-84
    public insurers, 92-101
  minimizing overhead, 252
  overt rationing, 224-226
RBRVS (resource-based relative
  value scale), 139-141, 333
  failure of, 141-151
recording information, 308-311
reducing
  medical errors, 283-291
  patient-mediated errors, 291-294
  unwarranted medical malpractice
    claims, 294
redundancy
  credentialing, 266
  medical licensure, 263-264

savings from eliminating, 266
  medical licensure and
    credentialing, 267
  unique patient identifiers,
    267-268
reference pricing, 252
regulation, 107, 275-276, 299
  forestalling fraud and abuse,
    280-282
  minimizing overhead, 251-257
  quantifying cost and benefit,
    276-280
regulators, 105-106
regulatory complexity, 93
regulatory speed trap, 94
Reinhardt, Uwe, 227
relative value scale (RVS), 139
report cards, physicians, 86
requirements, HIT
  dealing with quantitative data,
    313-315
  gathering and displaying
    information, 307
  recording information, 308-311
  sharing information, 315-317
  storing, retrieving, and transmitting
    information, 311-313
resolving medical malpractice claims,
  294-298
resource-based relative value scale
  (RBRVS), 139-141, 333
  failure of, 141-151
resource utilization, controlling
  through patient economic behavior,
  110-113
retrieving information, 311-313
revenue, garnering, 89
role
  of information, 301-302
  of transactions, 301-302
routine medical encounters,
  interactions, 55-56
RUC (AMA/Specialty Society
  Relative Value Scale Update
  Committee), 143-144
RVS (relative value scale), 139
RVU, 140, 145

S

satisfaction of physicians in
Pennsylvania, 172
savings
from eliminating redundancy, 266
*medical licensure and
credentialing,* 267
unique patient identifiers,
267-268
from healthcare overhaul, 324
*administrative staff and
intermediaries,* 328
government, 329-330
healthcare providers, 324-325
HIT vendors, 328
pharmaceutical manufacturers,
326-328
private health insurers, 325-326
from universal healthcare, 257-261
self-insured businesses, 87-88
services, underpaying for, 81
sharing information, HIT, 315-317
shortage of doctors, 65-66
Silverstein, Scot, 199, 209
simplifying payment for medical
services, 241-242
based on market principles, 243-250
smoking, 157
socialized medicine, 124
sources of healthcare funding,
228-230
Sowell, Thomas, 48
specialty boards, 131
spending. *See* healthcare spending
standardization, 93-99
state licensure, 127-129
statistical identification system, 185
statistical mapping, 184
storing information, 311-313
streamlined healthcare financing and
payment, 257-261
sustainability, 220
systems failures, 284

T

tablet computers, 313
telemedicine, 129
testing medical errors, 286, 289

third-party benefits administrators
(TPAs), 87
Thompson, Tommy, 151
Tier 3 insurance, 240
time of doctors, 68
Tipimeni, Kishore, 195
tort reform, 179, 296
tort system, 168
TPAs (third-party benefits
administrators), 87
training, E&M codes, 150
transaction processing, 186-189
electronic healthcare information
systems, 191-193
EMRs (electronic medical records)
complexity, 195-201
high cost, poor connectivity,
201-204
provider time andworkflow,
193-194
paper-based healthcare information
systems, 190-191
transactions
processing, 302-304
role of, 301-302
transmitting information, 311-313
treatments, comparing, 235-237
Truman, Harry, 124
2010 healthcare reform law, 6
Type 2 diabetes, 327

U–V

United States versus Canada
administrative overhead, 46
hospital procedure cost
comparison, 21
outpatient services cost
comparison, 34
UBHP (Universal Basic Health
Plan), 233
efficiencies in financing, 238-241
regulation, 276
underpaying for goods and
services, 81
underwriting cycle, 74-75
unfunded mandates, 93-95
unique patient identifiers,
183-186, 265
savings from eliminating
redundancy, 267-268

Universal Basic Health Plan
  (UBHP), 233
universal healthcare, 220-221
    elements of, 230-237
    funding, 229-230
    HSA (health savings account), 232
    provider compensation, 250
    savings from, 257-261
    waiting times, 249
universal healthcare identifiers, 264
UPI. *See* unique patient identifiers

voters, what they want in
  healthcare, 115

W–Z

waiting times
    for doctor visits, 14
    for elective surgery, 14
    universal healthcare, 249
willingness to pay (WTP), 109
workflow, EMRs, 193-194
wounded physicians, 172
WTP (willingness to pay), 109

zero sum game, 48

FT Press

FINANCIAL TIMES

In an increasingly competitive world, it is quality of thinking that gives an edge—an idea that opens new doors, a technique that solves a problem, or an insight that simply helps make sense of it all.

We work with leading authors in the various arenas of business and finance to bring cutting-edge thinking and best-learning practices to a global market.

It is our goal to create world-class print publications and electronic products that give readers knowledge and understanding that can then be applied, whether studying or at work.

To find out more about our business products, you can visit us at www.ftpress.com.